FRANKS FOR THE MEMORY

A Lifetime of Memories

Robert J Franks

Pen Press

First published in Great Britain by Pen Press

All paper used in the printing of this book has been made from wood grown in managed, sustainable forests.

ISBN 978-1-78003-628-1

Printed and bound in the UK
Pen Press is an imprint of
Indepenpress Publishing Limited
25 Eastern Place
Brighton
BN2 1GJ

A catalogue record of this book is available from the British Library

The author is grateful to the copyright holders
for permission to reproduce the London Fire Brigade
photographs numbers 1, 2 and 3.
All efforts were made to trace the copyright holders of numbers
4, 5 and 6.
Any other errors of omissions were inadvertent and will be
corrected in any future printing.

Cover design by Jacqueline Abromeit

FRANKS FOR THE MEMORY

A Lifetime of Memories

Chapter 1

Historic events of 1936 included the death of King George V; George VI becoming King following the abdication of Edward VIII. Jesse Owens won four Gold Medals at the Berlin Olympic Games. The Crystal Palace was destroyed by fire, and the most important event of all that year was the birth of Robert James Franks. By no means headline news but personally very important, because that was the beginning of my existence. What follows is a tour through my lifelong memories from a very early age and maybe with any luck right up to a very old age, but who knows? Anyway, you are about to embark on a journey of recollections and descriptions within my memoirs – some funny, some exciting and some tragic. But that's life isn't it?

I could only have been between three or four years old but I remember quite clearly, sitting at the kitchen table having something to eat when I was suddenly hit on the head by something very hard, making a noise that made me believe that my head had exploded. I screamed at the top of my voice and called for my mother who dashed in from the scullery when she heard the noise of the ceiling crashing down. Covered in dust, I was whisked out of my chair into my mother's arms and out of the house. As she lifted me I looked up and saw, through my tears, a patch of bare wooden laths where the ceiling had been and a large thick cloud of dust floating around the kitchen.

Once outside, my mother inspected my head where the large lump of ceiling plaster had landed. I don't remember being cut or badly hurt but I began crying very loud when I realised that my hand-knitted penguin doll was still on the table in the kitchen. I treasured that penguin and wouldn't go anywhere without it and I didn't stop crying until it was retrieved from the dust and debris. I believe that bump on my head, which was indelibly printed in my memory, to be my earliest recollection of my childhood.

We were a family of four – mother, father and two boys. Herbert, named after our father and known as Berty, is my elder

1

brother born in April 1934, and I Robert, known as Bobby, born on 28th August 1936.

We moved house after the ceiling came crashing down, to a rented ground-floor flat just across the road at number fourteen Blenheim Road, Penge, South East London. It was a two-up two-down house consisting of two small flats with common front door and a shared outside toilet. A family named Weaver lived in the upstairs flat. I understood some time later that Mrs Weaver's little girl had died of diphtheria just before we moved in.

Eventually we took over the upstairs flat. Mrs Weaver moved out so we had the run of the whole house. Bert and I shared a double bed in the upstairs back bedroom. The bed was the only piece of furniture in the room, standing on a square of old cold brown linoleum. The cast iron Victorian fireplace, which was never used, incorporated a mantelpiece where a solitary candle stood in a cracked saucer, used as a candle holder, surrounded by spent matchsticks and half-burned tapers made from folded strips of newspaper. Above and to the left of the mantelshelf was a gas light. I don't ever remember it being used; in fact I don't remember it ever having a mantle. Bert and I slept in that dull cold room for years. The bedcovers consisted of a couple of old blankets and some old overcoats. In the winter I remember being fascinated by the fern-shaped patterns formed by the frozen condensation on the glass of the old wooden sash windows which I don't recall ever being opened; on reflection they didn't need to be opened because we got all the fresh air that we needed through the gaps as they rattled in the wind.

The house did not have electricity. Coal gas, paid for through a penny slot meter, was the only means of light other than candles. Often the mantle would be broken by accidentally poking the matchstick through it when trying to light it. The dull light would become even more dull and constantly flicker, accompanied by a soft popping sound as the gas burned outside of the mantle. I spent hours watching the coloured flames jumping in and out of the side of broken mantles. The only means used to heat the house was the fire in the black-leaded kitchen stove. The exception to that was during a couple of days over Christmas, when as a treat a coal fire was lit in the front room. My mother always made a point of regularly black-leading the kitchen stove and whitening the front doorstep. Those two jobs around the house seemed to be a priority. Bert was often sent to the shop to buy a lump of whitening for the front step. I suppose a nice clean white step at the entrance to the house was meant as a message to passers-by that this was a well-kept nice, clean, tidy house. Unfortunately if that was the case, then the white step was a white lie.

The kitchen stove was about one yard wide, positioned within an alcove at the base of the chimney stack which protruded into the room forming two more alcoves on either side. The left-hand side of the stove consisted of an oven with the fire grate on the right. Disappearing into the brickwork of the chimney stack was a straight metal flue, about half a yard long, incorporating a sliding damper. Placed to the left of and facing the stove, was a single reclining armchair with a well-worn flattened artificial leather Rexene seat and back rest. It had wooden arms that had to be raised to allow the back rest to be adjusted for comfort.

That chair was one of a pair, the other one was in the front room which was out of bounds to me and Bert. The bare wooden kitchen table was placed against the wall beneath the kitchen window surrounded by four chairs. Under the table was an assortment of shoes, it was the practice to remove our shoes and kick them under the table out of the way.

My father when he was at home used to sit in the kitchen armchair, lift the wooden arms and adjust the chair back. He would pull out the damper in the chimney to make the fire roar until the metal flue began to glow red hot. The kitchen used to get lovely and warm as a result.

My father would sit in that chair after having his meal, always a lovely meal, different from what we had. It used to smell wonderful. I remember standing near the kitchen table, hardly tall enough to see over it watching him eat, while he struggled to read his newspaper by the flickering gas light. I didn't know then that he was reading, I didn't know what reading was, he just seemed to put some food into his mouth begin to chew and stare at the newspaper. When I had learned to read a little bit I was told off for copying him by trying to read a newspaper while I was eating. That stuck in my mind because I couldn't understand what I was doing wrong, or what I was reading.

We had mice living under the timber floorboards, they used to run out of a hole that they made in the skirting board at the side of the fireplace. My father placed baited traps around the house and often during the evening we could hear them snap shut. He would pick up the trap with the mouse still wriggling; when it died he would release it and put it in the dustbin, he would then bait the trap again after scorching it with a candle. He said that scorching the trap would prevent the other mice from smelling the blood which would stop them from entering the trap. I have no idea if that worked or not but he caught lots of mice.

As a young child I cannot remember my father not being in the army. He was away for long periods and my mother was the boss of the house. She ruled with an iron fist – well, it felt like iron sometimes. I was a great teaser or aggravator as my aunt Else used to call me. I often aggravated Bert until he lost his temper and hit me, then I would scream and get him into trouble. My aunt Else was my mother's sister. She gave a great deal of support to my mother, especially during the 1939–1945 war years and later to me as I grew up.

Christmas 1939, then there were three. The twenty-second of December to be exact, Christopher Peter was born. He was named Christopher because he was born so near to Christmas Day; for some reason he was to be known thereafter by his second name Peter. A later memory is when Peter was old enough to sit up unaided. Mother was going to wash him so she sat him on the kitchen table with his legs dangling over the side. I was sitting on the floor in the kitchen, probably dismantling a toy because that is what I loved to do and was always in trouble for doing it. Mother had to go into the scullery to get a bowl of warm water from the kettle (all the water had to be heated either in a kettle or in saucepans), so she told me to keep my eye on him. I thought that to be a peculiar request but I did just as she said. When she returned to the kitchen she burst out laughing because I was standing with my eye pressed against Peter's knee as he sat on the edge of the table.

The war had begun and with three young children to care for Aunt Else became a great help to my mother, like an unpaid nanny.

My father only came home on leave some weekends and I didn't really know him but gradually as I got older I began to understand. There were always a lot of army men and sailors in uniform about and lots of fathers were away from home because of the war. Times were hard for my mum because we, as I now know, were living in poverty. As I got a little older and badly wanted something and my mother wouldn't let me have it (or more than likely couldn't afford it because we were a very poor family) I would go and scrounge from Aunt Else and invariably she would give in to my persistent demands. Aunt Else lived with my grandparents in the same road as us, at number sixty-one, and next door at number sixty-three another of my mother's sisters lived with seven of my cousins. Aunt Else was a spinster and remained so for all of her eighty-six years. The memories and pictures in my mind of my maternal grandparents and their house at number sixty-one, are that they were very old. My grandfather walked with the aid of two walking sticks. He was a big man and spent most of the time when I knew him, sitting in his ground floor back bedroom in the dark, with only the light from the flickering fire in the grate dimly illuminating the room. I used to be frightened to go in there and hated its smell of stale tobacco. I recall that he sat in his chair facing the fire grate, leaning slightly forward – I presume that was the position which was most comfortable. He would support himself by placing one of his walking sticks on the floor between his legs and with both hands clasping the top of the stick he would stare into the fire and make a quiet whistling sound and gently rock forward and back on his stick. He would interrupt that habit by involuntary cries of pain as his legs went into sudden spasms. He only struggled out of the room to visit the outside toilet and that usually sparked off a swearing match between him and my grandmother. I recall that they used to argue a lot but they must have got on with each other at some point, or should I say several points, because they produced ten children. The eight surviving children retained the tradition – they all argued and didn't see each other for sometimes years and in some cases not at all – with the exception of Aunt Else, she was the go-between, she visited them all and passed on any gossip.

When the air raids began and the howl of the air-raid warning sirens filled the air, my mother seemed to go frantic. If I was playing in the street she would call me in, of course I used to protest because I didn't understand what all the fuss was about. As far as I was concerned it was a nuisance because it interfered with my play time and I couldn't see the aeroplanes fly over from indoors. When we heard the sound of bombs exploding in the distance Bert and I were made to sit and sometimes sleep under the back stairs during an air raid in case our house was bombed; I discovered the reason later that under the stairs was the safest part of the house because of its load-bearing structure. That wasn't very nice because the coal for the kitchen stove was stored there. I can recall sitting under the stairs on the lumpy coal with my knees right up under my chin and getting told off for stretching my woollen jersey over my legs to keep warm. We had a corrugated iron Anderson Air Raid Shelter in the back garden but we couldn't use it because it was always very wet inside. Whenever there was an air raid at night, I always wanted to go to the toilet. I refused to use a bucket so that I could go out to the back garden and watch the searchlights looking for German aeroplanes in the sky.

Poor Bert, he didn't have it so good being the eldest, he was always the one who had to go to the shops. He had to look after me and Peter and had to put up with me deliberately aggravating him until he threatened me then I would scream blue murder. Sometimes it would go wrong though because every now and then when we were in bed I would keep fidgeting or make noises through my nose just to make him mad. He would put up with it for a while, then lose his temper and dig me with his elbow. I would cry out and Mother would come storming into our bedroom and beat us both. I have probably still got some dents in the back of my head, caused by her thick gold wedding ring. I must have been a horrible child.

Between the gaps in my memory I can recall hot dusty summer days, when I used to get into trouble for getting tar on my hands and clothes. The road outside of our house was my playground and in the summer the hot sun would soften and bubble the tar on the road. I could never resist popping the bubbles with my finger. Even in the heavy summer rainstorms I found a way of occupying my time. I used to take some garden peas from the kitchen, open them up and eat the raw peas. Then I would take some used matchsticks from our bedroom or from around the gas stove in the scullery and by sticking them into the centre of the pea pods to look like masts, I would make a couple of boats. I had great fun racing the boats in the streams of rainwater rushing along the gutter in the roadway and eventually losing them down a drain.

Melvin Road Infants School, I remember it well. My mother took me right into the classroom, there were some small chairs with other new infants sitting in them, one or two were crying. The teacher took me by the hand and led me to a chair where I was told to sit down. Sitting in the next chair was a boy named Billy Harrison, we became friends which lasted throughout our school days.

Most of my memories as a young boy are about the war, carrying a gas mask around in a small square cardboard box, the sound of aeroplanes and heavy gunfire, air-raid sirens and exploding bombs, puffs of black smoke high up in the sky as shells exploded, the sight of searchlights criss-crossing in the sky at night, searching for and fixing on German aeroplanes.

Children were being evacuated from London, they had labels tied on to their clothing and were put on trains and sent to live in the countryside away from the bombing. My mother wouldn't allow us to be taken away so I enjoyed myself collecting shrapnel after the air raids. I had a big box full – all shapes and sizes, pieces of aeroplanes, bombs and shells.

The windows of our house had strips of pale brown sticky paper stuck on them to prevent them from shattering if they were blown in. Talking of windows, Bert was sent to the shops one day to buy a piece of cheese and when he returned with a piece hardly large enough to make a sandwich because of the rationing, Mother flew into a rage and slammed it on to the kitchen table. Bert took a defensive step backwards and I looked up from where I was sitting on the floor, probably dismantling another toy (most likely a clockwork one because the workings fascinated me) just as the cheese bounced off the kitchen table and smashed its way through a window pane landing outside in the garden. Mother's face was a picture, turning to Bert she snapped:

"Now go and pick it up!"

Bert returned with a terrified look on his face holding the cheese in his outstretched hand, offering it to our mother. We both wondered what she was going to do with it next; after a period of dead silence with Mother and I just staring at Bert, all three of us burst into laughter. It wasn't long before all of the windows were blown in anyway and the glass replaced with a kind of white fabric. You couldn't see through it but it allowed some light to penetrate into the room. All the windows had to have some means of stopping the light shining out at night, usually by way of a black-out curtain, in case the German planes could see where to drop their bombs, but I don't believe our flickering gas light would have given them much of a clue.

Every Sunday lunch time we all had to go across the road to my grandparents' house at number sixty-one for lunch. On reflection it was for dinner, because it was never ready until late afternoon and every Sunday without fail we had rice pudding for sweet or afters as we called it. Sixty-one was a very dark and depressing house, made worse for me by a clock that ticked loud and slow, and to this day I detest ticking clocks and dark depressing decor.

As the air raids began to get more frequent and houses were being bombed in the area, my mother decided that sitting under the stairs in the coal cupboard was not safe enough. So we then had to run down the road to sixty-one and get into the shelter in my grandparents' back garden which was a lot dryer than ours at number fourteen. That was alright in the day time but I have vivid memories of sometimes sleeping in the same bed as my aunt Else, quite often during the war she would sleep in our house. She would wake up at the sound of the air raid siren and drag me half asleep down the road to number sixty-one in the middle of the night, night after night, to get into the shelter. Bert would be close by and mother, bringing up the rear, would be scurrying along carrying Peter and her handbag, she didn't go anywhere without her big black handbag. Always at bedtime Bert and I were made to say our prayers, it was in the form of a little hymn which began "Lord keep us safe this night secure from all our fears, may angels guard us while we sleep till morning light appears." I can't remember any more than that but it worked, he did keep us safe.

My grandfather would never come out of his room even during an air raid. He would just sit and lean on one of his sticks whistling softly through his teeth and, I am told, he would swear his head off every time the house was shaken by a nearby bomb. Bombs landed at each end of Blenheim Road, which was only about one hundred yards or so long. The first one took down a few houses in Franklin Road at the junction with Blenheim Road; my aunt Flo's house, another one of my mother's sisters, was bombed. She had a little black and white dog named Chub, it was never found and I was told that it ran away. I always expected it to come home one day and used to think about it a lot. At the other end of Blenheim Road, about fifty yards from our house, a bomb made a direct hit on an air raid shelter in a back garden and killed the entire family, my school friend Brenda Slater was killed there.

My mother suffered badly with her nerves because of the bombing; I understood when I grew up, but at the time I couldn't understand why she would suddenly cry. It all seemed normal to me, that was how it was, I knew no different and being so young I obviously didn't realise the gravity of it all.

They took away our railings. Men came and cut the ornamental steel railings from the copings on the little walls outside of the houses along the whole length of the road; they were taken away to be melted down to make weapons. The only good thing about that was that I could then sit comfortably on the coping outside of our house.

One particular air raid began just as school finished. I was nonchalantly strolling home, I could hear the sound of gunfire and aircraft engines and could see people running about but it didn't mean anything to me. As I turned the corner from Maple Road into Franklin Road I saw my mother running towards me shouting my name, even that didn't encourage me to move myself. She screamed at me to hurry then took me by the hand. I seemed to sail through the air, my feet only touching the ground about every three yards as she ran with me for cover across the previously bombed open ground on the corner of Blenheim Road and Franklin Road, where my aunt's house used to be. As we ran I saw a very low flying plane coming towards us, firing its guns apparently at anything that moved – mostly school children at that time of day. It was so low I could see the pilot as it flew past. Bert, having more common sense than me, had run for cover in a church in Maple Road known locally as the Tabernacle.

Although it made no sense to me I used to listen to the comments of the grown-ups about the progress of the war. I could tell by their reactions and gestures whether it was good news or bad. There seemed to be a lot of men in uniform about. If my friends and I saw what we thought was an American soldier, some of us would shout:

"Got any gum chum?"

And sometimes we were given some chocolate or chewing gum.

Men would come home on embarkation leave. I didn't have a clue what that meant but I would hear the grown-ups talking about someone who had been on embarkation leave a few weeks ago and had been killed in a battle somewhere. If a telegram boy appeared cycling along the street everyone would watch with grim expressions on their faces, to see whose house he was delivering to – it was mostly bad news.

It used to make me wonder what a dead person looked like. Then I would hear them talking about men being taken prisoner and being tortured. The worst stories were about the Japanese. I heard someone say that they used to throw babies up in the air and catch them on their bayonets. When I asked questions I was told to go away and that little children should be seen and not heard.

Sir Winston Churchill came to Penge, not to stay of course; he was just driven through in his open car along Maple Road and crowds of people gathered to cheer him. I stood in the front and was given a small Union Jack flag on a stick and was told to wave it and cheer. I didn't know what it was all about really and I was even more confused when someone asked me if I saw his cigar.

Somehow I acquired a grey-coloured Air Raid Warden's steel helmet, I used to put it on every time the air raid sirens sounded, it was too big and used to wobble about on my head but it made me feel safe. It made me feel indestructible, so I always wanted to go out to the street and walk about wearing it when the siren sounded but was never allowed to, can't think why?

Bombed buildings became the playgrounds of the youngsters. I once followed some big boys and climbed out of a window and on to the roof of a bomb-damaged house at the end of our road. On all fours I crawled up to the ridge and looked over the top, it was frightening. It took me a long time to make my way down again and the most scaring part was hanging from an old piece of rusty cast-iron guttering, stretching my leg out to reach the window sill so that I could get back in the house. I was terrified that my mother would find out because she forbade me to even enter the bombed houses, never mind climb on to a roof.

On the bomb site at the end of Blenheim Road, where my aunt used to live, a large emergency water tank had been erected; it contained thousands of gallons of water for putting out fires in the event of the water mains being fractured in the bombing. By the end of the war it contained more old bicycles, prams and old beds than a junk yard. On warm days some of the big boys used to swim in it.

In our kitchen we had an old valve-type wireless. Having no electricity we had to run it by a battery or an accumulator as it was called. The accumulator was made of glass and the acid and cells were visible. It always seemed to work when the grown-ups were listening to the news of the war but whenever 'Just William' came on, the sound would fade. Someone would fiddle with the aerial which was in the form of a long length of wire stretching right along the garden like a washing line with the end wound around a nail hammered into the fence. When it was realised that the accumulator had run down, poor Bert had to trudge all the way to Avenue Road to exchange it at the cost of sixpence (two and a half new pence) for a fully charged one. Sometimes I had to go with him and I didn't think that was very fair, so I would trail behind him, moaning all the way, refusing to have a turn at carrying the accumulator because it was too heavy. Anyway I couldn't see anything wrong with it, the new one looked exactly the same.

We didn't have holidays away, couldn't afford it. Summers seemed to be longer then and it appeared to rain harder; sudden downpours flooded the gutters in the road, I didn't mind that because I could then race my pea-pod yachts. As a treat I used to take a jam sandwich and a bottle of water to the park and have a picnic. Sometimes the big boys were there, they used to find cigarette ends, break them open to get the tobacco then roll a new cigarette and share it.

Aunt Else used to take me to the cinema to see *Tarzan*, *Robin Hood*, Roy Rogers and other Cowboys and Indians films. I wasn't keen on cartoons, they used to frighten me. Saturday morning cinema for children used to be good, especially the serials; *The Man in the Iron Mask*, *The Lone Ranger*, Kit Carson and many others that slip my memory. I was always starving hungry when I got home from those Saturday morning shows. Because my mother would take advantage of not having any kids around she used to get on with the housework and to see the kitchen chairs on the table and nothing ready to eat used to really upset me and then to be sent to buy a loaf of bread while she finished the housework really got me going.

"Why can't Bert go?" I used to mumble through my tears.

On the way home the temptation was always too great to resist so I would nibble the corners of the loaf of bread to satisfy my hunger, then deny it emphatically saying that it was like it when the lady gave it to me – what a liar. One day my mother sent me to the shop to buy a jar of jam.

After mumbling, "Why can't Berty go, I'm fed up with having to do everything?" I sauntered off to the shops, head hanging low, staring at the ground in absolute misery. On the way home with the jar of jam a terrible thing happened, I dropped it. I will always remember the dull explosive thud as that jar hit the pavement. I stood and stared at the sticky mess for a while then went home leaving it on the pavement. As I walked indoors, looking and feeling terrified, my mother looked at me for a moment and then asked me where the jam was.

"I dropped it," I whispered looking guiltily at the floor.

"What?" she snapped in a very loud voice.

My response to that was to turn and run but as I did so I ran into the door. The door latch was eye height to me and the protruding latch buried itself in my eyebrow.

Panic stations. I stood and screamed; my mother grabbed a towel and wrapped it around my head. I was put in a pushchair and rushed to the local fire station still screaming. The fire station was in Croydon Road, Penge, adjoining the rear of the local district council yard, we called it the Board Yard. The yard's main gate was at the top end of Blenheim Road opposite the emergency water tank. Just inside were neat stacks of paving slabs and piles of sand and ballast which made the yard a wonderful place for young kids to play. We were always being chased out of the yard and would run away laughing at the old workman as he shouted at us to clear off. Now that I was being taken there that workman will surely get me, I thought, so I screamed louder. A fireman took the towel from around my head and when I saw all the blood soaked into it I raised the volume of my screams once more.

As the fireman bent down and looked at my wound he muttered something about stitches and hospitals. Absolutely terrified I was taken to Beckenham Hospital where I again demonstrated the power of my lungs. I remember struggling and being held down on a bed while my eyebrow was stitched. Then I heard someone tell my mother that I should stay in for the rest of the day under observation. Another prolonged demonstration of lung power gained my freedom. I was taken home with a large pad tied over my eye which I was truly proud of and couldn't wait to show it off to my friends. I carry the scar to this day, on my eyebrow and in my mind. I have hated hospitals ever since.

Poor Bert had a bit of a rough deal being the eldest. He had to do the weekly shopping for groceries at the local Co-op store, it must have been at least a one and a half miles round trip to the Co-op and Bert had to carry two big bags of shopping all the way home. I was made to go with him sometimes and I always made a fuss. I used to think the lady in the Co-op was very clever because she used to write all the prices on the back of a packet of sugar and quickly add them up. She would then take the money and put it in a small cylinder and screw it into a holder suspended above her head by some cables. Then she would pull on a handle and catapult the cylinder along a wire into the cashier's office surrounded by glass. The cashier in the office would unscrew the cylinder, take out the money and replace it with the appropriate change and then catapult it back to the lady serving us. I was truly fascinated by the mechanics of the system. Then I would stroll home a couple of paces behind Bert who was struggling with two heavy bags.

Bath time was normally on a Sunday morning which I considered to be a bit of an ordeal. We had occupied the upstairs flat since Mrs Weaver had moved out of number fourteen so we used her kitchen as a bathroom. Our tin bath had to be filled with hot water, which was carried upstairs in buckets and saucepans. Because of that great inconvenience we had to use the same bath water and the last one had to bail the dirty water out of the bath and pour it down the sink – what a chore, good job it was only once a week. I used to moan and groan about it and make a mess, in the end Aunt Else would do it for me. I couldn't see the sense in having a bath anyway because I only got dirty again. It was a ritual though, along with having to put on our best clothes and go to Sunday school at the Salvation Army Hall, the rear of which was in Blenheim Road adjacent to our house.

Bert and I used to attend band practice; we both learned to play the tenor horn and used to play in the Salvation Army Junior Band. Being a lazy boy I couldn't be bothered to really try hard therefore I couldn't play very well, probably because I was forced to go to Sunday school and to band practice, while my friends went to the cinema, or pictures as we called it then. I now regret not learning to play well; Bert was very good but even he didn't pursue his talent after he left school to start work. The one thing that I did enjoy about the Salvation Army was the once-a-year Sunday school outings to the seaside, usually to Margate or Brighton on the south coast. I remember the smell of the steam engine and the noise from the wheels running over the joins in the rails. We used to stand by the window in the carriage and wave to people as the train rattled over the level crossings.

Not many people owned cars in those days so the streets were quite safe and empty of traffic, with plenty of room to play. We used to get up to all sorts of tricks – knocking on doors and running away, whip and top, walking on stilts, playing cricket with the wicket drawn in chalk on the Salvation Army wall, playing football with our jackets placed in the road as goal posts, skating and dashing about on bikes. I didn't have my own bike until I was about ten years old when Bert and I had identical bikes for Christmas. They had light blue frames and straight handlebars, how our mother afforded them I will never know, she worked very hard for a pittance cleaning other people's houses and a ladies' hairdresser's shop; if I remember rightly I believe she earned two shillings and sixpence (twelve and a half new pence) an hour.

My two best friends in our road were girls, Muriel Symons and Shirley Kemp. We were friends for years, until we all left school I suppose but sadly Muriel died from leukaemia when she was in her twenties. As I recall, we all had a lot of fun together.

Time marched on, and as the war progressed people learned to identify an aircraft by the sound of its engine, as being either friendly or a German one. Everyone would listen and someone would declare:

"It's OK, it's one of ours."

I remember looking into the sky and seeing squadrons of our bombers groaning their way across the sky like flocks of migrating birds. I also remember the sound of German bombers and the scream of the bombs as they descended, followed by the loud explosions as they hit the ground. One day I was looking in the direction of Croydon Airfield when I saw aeroplanes chasing each other all over the sky. I later found out that I had been watching what was called a 'dog fight'.

When the flying bombs, or doodlebugs, as they became known, began to bombard us, their sound was unique and everyone instantly recognised the drone of the rocket engine. People would turn their faces skywards towards the direction of the sound of the engine and wait for the sudden silence as the engine cut out. Then they would wait in anxious anticipation for the sound of the explosion as it hit the ground and wonder how many victims it had claimed.

Luxuries like sweets and fruit were in short supply during the war, I didn't know what an orange or a banana tasted like. Sweets were rationed so my mother used to cut the occasional chocolate Mars bar into small squares and share it out. My dream was to buy my own Mars bar and bite great big lumps off of it and fill my mouth so full that it would be hard to chew it.

I moved to Oakfield Road School which was a traditional old brick-built school of three floors. For some reason or other, probably because of the shortage of teachers, we spent a lot of time in a church hall just along the road, having stories read to us. I believe I missed out in my education during that period and it showed up in later life. Bert did well though, he passed the necessary examinations which allowed him to attend the local

County Grammar School, something to be proud of because he was the first child from our road to achieve that, I know of only one other and that was a boy named Billy Perks. Bert eventually passed other examinations and won his school certificate. I know our mother was extremely proud of him. My friend Billy Perks, who lived at the opposite end of Blenheim Road, also passed his entrance exam a couple of years later, allowing him to attend the County Grammar School.

Bill and I used to have a lot of fun catching frogs and newts when we were very young. I remember going into his back garden once and being impressed with its neatness. His father, who I believe was a bricklayer by trade, had laid a nice lawn and had surrounded it with bricks, placed on edge at an angle, making a rather spectacular sawtooth design. In general, back gardens in our road were nothing more than tips, with perhaps a patch for some vegetables and a chicken run. Ours was just a bare patch of earth with a chicken run and a sickly looking cherry tree. Billy Perks later became quite famous as bass guitar player with the rock group The Rolling Stones, he was then known as Bill Wyman. Funny though, at school when he sang during a nativity play (he was one of the three kings bearing gifts), I wouldn't have thought then that had an earthly chance of a career in music.

Then there were explosions without the pre-warning of aircraft engines. The V2 rocket had arrived. They just fell from the sky without any warning at all. Apparently that was a very traumatic time for civilians in London, subsequently my mother finally lost her nerve to sit out the war at home.

Blenheim Road under construction

My maternal grandparents, James and Jane Whitehead

My paternal grandparents, Albert and Caroline Franks

My mother and father,
Bert and Daisy Franks,
on their 40th wedding anniversary.

Me and Bert,
I'm on my mother's lap, best clothes
so it must have been a Sunday.

Me and Bert, not so smart,
obviously not on a Sunday.

Me, about eight years old.

Chapter 2

Hurried arrangements were made with relations for my mother and us three children, my father being away in the army, to go to Devonshire to live near a small village named Thorverton. My twin cousins, Dennis and Fred Jones, on my mother's side of the family, had been evacuated to Thorverton for most of the war. With the arrival of the four of us the house was a bit crowded as I remember.

Several memories are lodged in my mind about the short period that we spent living in Devonshire. Today I believe it would be described as a culture shock. Our house in South London was only a small two-up two-down terraced house but it boasted a flush outside toilet, even though the door was no more than that of a shed with splits in the wood and large gaps at the top and bottom, I suppose it could be described as being well ventilated, but it was connected to the sewer. The mod cons in the scullery which also sported a shed door but not as well ventilated as the toilet, consisted of a brass cold-water tap attached to the end of a length of old bent lead pipe, protruding from the scullery wall above a shallow buff-coloured stone sink by the back door. We didn't have the luxury of a bathroom but neither did the house in Devon. It was bewildering for me to discover how the country folk lived. A tin bath I was used to using, but having to wash and clean my teeth in the mornings, standing in the garden while Bert pumped the water up from the well, was a new experience.

I mentioned that we had an outside toilet at home but it wasn't in a small shed some thirty yards down the garden as it was in Devon. We had the luxury of having a flush toilet but the one in Devon only had a timber board with a hole cut in it, not even a bowl, just an open space where everything piled up. The ashes from the fire in the house were emptied into the toilet hole every day and when the apex of the ever growing pyramid got too high, a trap door at the rear of the toilet shed allowed access for the insertion of a rake to level it off.

My mother arranged for me to attend the village school; I was so traumatised that I couldn't stop shaking and the butterflies in my stomach wouldn't go away. On my first day I went into the classroom feeling extremely nervous and self-conscious because it seemed that everyone was looking at me. The other children had obviously been told that a boy from London was joining the class. I was told to sit at an empty desk at the back of the classroom and as I sat down the teacher asked me if I could do the sums that she had chalked on the blackboard. Having spent my early education in a church hall listening to stories, I had no idea what I was looking at and I don't believe I could even read them, but I was too embarrassed to say so because all eyes were upon me. I felt terrified, scared out of my mind and I wanted to cry. I felt hot all over and had a horrible tingling sensation at the back of my neck and I wanted to go to the toilet. After a short time I asked to go to the toilet and went out to the playground where the toilets were situated. I looked at the school gate, dashed through it and ran as fast as I could along the country lane towards where we were living, crying all the way. I stopped a little way before the house, feeling very frightened at what my mother would say. I climbed over the high hedge into a field of almost ripe wheat, where I sat and cried my eyes out.

I felt scared and lonely and I still had not been to the toilet. After relieving myself to get rid of the pain in my stomach, I realised that I didn't have anything that I could use as toilet paper. What I mean is, I didn't have any newspaper with me because that was what was used at home during the war – newspaper torn into small squares. Bert knew that more than anyone because at home there was often a shortage in our outside loo and Bert was always charged with the task of tearing up a newspaper, and after persistent yelling for a piece of paper usually Bert would appear with a bundle. However, the only thing available to me in that field was a leaf which I picked from the hedge. In my ignorance of botany, I learned a painful lesson. Bramble leaves have very sharp prickles on their underside. I drew blood, even more terrified and sorry for myself, I just curled up in a ball at the edge of the cornfield, hidden by the high hedge and sobbed my heart out.

I was there for a long time because I heard children passing by on their way home from school. Later I heard people calling my name. I had obviously been missed and they were out looking for me. After they had passed by I climbed back over the hedge and walked the short distance to the house where we were living. No one really knew what I had been up to that day. All I kept repeating as an answer to the constant questioning was:

"I don't like school."

My mother made me stand in front of a mirror and shouted at me to look at my face and clothes. My face was very dirty with clean white skin around my eyes and clean streaks down my face where my tears had run. Of course my clothes were dirty where I had been lying in the field.

"Where have you been?" she screamed. "We have been looking everywhere for you."

"I don't like school," I mumbled once again.

I was not sent to school again for the duration of our stay in Devon, which was only about six weeks.

That was long enough for me, even at that early age, to notice and enjoy the beauty of the Devonshire countryside and to compare it to Blenheim Road Penge. I watched the harvesting of the ripe golden wheat and joined in the chase when a rabbit bolted from the security of the ever-decreasing protection of the standing wheat stems topped with bent-over ripened seed heads. Lots of people wielding thick sticks would run shouting as the terrified rabbit constantly changed direction in an effort to reach the nearest hedgerow. Unavoidably it would run too close to a pursuer and collapse from a blow from a well-aimed stick and was then finally dispatched by stretching its neck until it snapped. I watched a large pig having a ring put in its nose, it screamed so loud it must have been heard for miles around.

Milk had to be collected from a neighbouring farm, and the first time we saw cows being milked we stood staring in amazement. One day Peter got too close and the dairyman squirted some milk straight from the cow's udder into his face, which made us all laugh. We knew the dairyman as Mr Percy. The milk we got from that farm was so fresh that it was still warm when we carried it home.

It was while we were in Devon that we heard that my school friend Brenda Slater and her family had been killed. I remember seeing my father in his army uniform standing in the lane by the gate to the house. When my mother saw him she started to cry because his visit was unexpected. She looked at him and said, "It's our road again isn't it? I dreamt about it last night."

"Yes," my father replied, "It was at our end, the Slater family were killed." Although my mother was very upset, she was also very relieved to know that my aunt Else and grandparents were safe.

Apparently my mother had a problem getting along with the people whose house we were sharing. Once again she made arrangements for us to go somewhere else. After a long journey we arrived at a Kent Hop Farm, living in one of a terrace of corrugated iron huts, next to my aunt Maf and our cousins from sixty-three Blenheim Road. Apparently my aunt Maf, short for Mafeking, was named after the Siege of Mafeking during the Boar War. Aunt Else was also there but my grandparents, on both my mother and my father's side, remained at home.

The bed in the single-roomed hut was made from bundles of long twigs called faggots, tied together and placed on the floor. Thick layers of straw was spread over the faggots before putting on the blankets and old coats etc. Everyone slept together in the one large makeshift bed.

All cooking was done over a bonfire made from dry twigs or old faggots and the toilets were one up from the Devon design because they had buckets below the hole in the wooden seat.

Hop picking rates amongst the most boring jobs that I have had to do. Even as young kids we all had to contribute to the pile of hops in the bin. Hop vines had to be pulled down and stripped of the hops as quickly as possible in order to collect as many bushels as we could, before the farmer made the next tally round. Payment was made by the bushel and they had to be clean, minimal leaves, otherwise the farmer packed more into the measuring bushel basket and less money was earned. It was a horrible boring job standing by the bin picking all day, it made your hands all black; if you touched your lips or ate a sandwich without washing your hands, which was not possible in the hop field, it tasted foul. The grown-ups could put up with the boredom but most of the kids used to run off and play in the woods. The idea was to collect all the money earned, at the end of the picking period, but people used to ask for a loan during their stay to live on, therefore there was never much left at the end of the picking season.

One day I heard a bit of a commotion and saw people looking skywards and pointing. When I looked up I saw a British Bomber, obviously returning from a raid, flying very low in the sky with an engine on fire; it had come from the direction of the Kent coast and was obviously trying to reach an airfield. All the women stood in silence with tears in their eyes, just staring upwards when one of them whispered, "God bless those poor souls."

I didn't realise the seriousness of the situation and wondered what all the fuss was about. I thought it was great so I stood around looking at the sky for some time, hoping to see another one. I will always remember the image of that aeroplane on fire.

At the end of the picking period we got a lift home to Penge on the back of a lorry. Although we had only been away for a few weeks, everything seemed different. The houses at the end of our road, where the Slater family lived, were not there anymore, just a heap of rubble. Some other nearby houses had walls missing exposing their damaged contents which were spread about in total disarray. The terrace of bombed houses where the Slater family lived backed on to the shops in Penge High Street, opposite the Crooked Billet Pub. Those shops had all of their back walls blown away, leaving the floors looking as though they were suspended in space, the staircases and what was left of the contents of the shops were all exposed. Both ends of the road had suffered bomb damage and there was a dry dusty smell in the air, everything appeared very strange.

The bombed buildings were like a magnet to me and other children. Not realising the dangers lurking in those broken structures, my friends and I used to go inside and search them. It was like an exciting adventure, finding ways to get above the ground floor where the staircase had been blown away was a challenge. Bombed buildings were our forbidden playgrounds and being chased away was all part of the fun, that was until my mother found out.

I was a very athletic youngster and could run swiftly over rough ground and even leap over piles of debris and climb walls with ease. The morning after an air raid I would always seek out the stricken buildings and get as near as I could to watch the rescue services and volunteers searching for victims. I was often told to go away, but of course I didn't. The images of those bombed houses are still vivid in my memory but at the time it just seemed a normal part of life.

School was boring, I didn't feel that I was learning anything and I wasn't at all concerned but I suppose something must have sunk in during the maths and English lessons. Painting pictures and trying to learn poetry seemed to be the major part of the school day, apart from the morning assembly, and the daily singing of the times tables. Sport and physical training was always a great joy, I loved it and became quite good at gymnastics, both somersaulting over vaulting horses and tumbling on the agility mat. School football and cricket matches were played and we constantly practised in the playground during breaks, using a tennis ball with goals and wickets chalked on the school boundary walls.

The war finally came to an end and everyone celebrated with street parties. My father then lived at home and that was something new. The fourth one of the family was born, another brother – he was named Leonard Victor, Leonard because mother liked the name and Victor because we had won the war. My earliest recollection of Leonard was when my aunt Else appeared from my mother's bedroom holding him in her arms. I wanted to see my mother but wasn't allowed into the bedroom. I was very curious because a woman who I had never seen before was in the bedroom with her. Aunt Else told me that she was a nurse and that mummy had a bad leg.

Another later memory was when mother told Bert to go to the shops to buy some Farley's Rusks (a kind of biscuit that is mashed with milk), for Leonard's meal. Bert returned without the Rusks because the shop had sold out. Our mother flew into a rage and told Bert to go and buy some and not to come home until he had found a shop that had some. Poor Bert took her literally, he pushed baby Leonard in his pram, all the way from Penge to Bromley, a journey of about six miles, calling at all the shops that he thought would sell the baby food. Finally managing to get a packet in a shop in Bromley, he pushed Leonard in his pram all the way home again.

At the age of about eleven most of my class moved up to the senior school, situated in the same school building in Oakfield Road but in a separate section. School teachers had returned from the war to take up their civilian occupations once again and the standard of teaching improved. Discipline was much more rigid and the cane was being used quite liberally on us. It was constantly carried by some teachers during class and used as a blackboard pointer, and to whack the desk to wake us up if any of us were daydreaming.

With a proper physical training teacher some of us became very good at gymnastics and could put on quite an impressive display. We were also made to box. I was always a bit of a rough kid so during those boxing matches I discovered that I had a flair for the sport. I had some rough edges but I was good enough to beat everyone in my class of about thirty boys. I took part in and won the school championship at my weight and boxed against other schools. Keen on the sport, my mate Jimmy Buxton, who was also a keen boxer, and I joined the Penge and Beckenham Boxing Club. The physical training teacher for some reason always made me glove-up during physical training lessons. I am sure that he wanted to see me take a beating.

During an English lesson one day I asked to go to the toilet. The teacher told me to hurry and I was lectured by the dragon lady on going before lessons. To get to the toilet I had to pass through the school hall which doubled as a gymnasium where there was a class of senior boys enjoying a boxing match. The Physical Training instructor called me to him rubbing his hands with glee. I was told to pick an opponent and put the gloves on. Protesting that I was supposed to be in an English lesson, I put on a pair of boxing gloves and picked a boy who was older than me but small for his age, about the same size as me. With a sick smile the P.T. instructor pointed to Richard Bird, Dickie for short, and told him to get the gloves on. I knew Dickie Bird, he belonged to the boxing club and was a very good, fast stylish boxer. In the middle of four long wooden forms outlining a square for the boxing ring, lined with shouting boys sitting on them, Dickie and I shaped up. About five minutes later, both of us bruised, red-faced and gasping for breath, were relieved to hear the P.T. instructor blow his whistle to end the match of one long round. I thought it was great even though I was given a boxing lesson and I know that Dickie enjoyed it too.

I returned to the English lesson where I had a bit of a hostile reception. Waving a ruler close to my face, the dragon of an English teacher screamed at me, asking where I had been. When I told her that I had been boxing, she went mad. During her frenzy she waved a ruler too close to my face and poked it in my eye. Already being a bit puffy around the eyes, thanks to Dickie's speed and accurate punching, I couldn't open my eye. It became very painful but because the teacher realised that she had hurt me, she became very sympathetic and nice. Of course I made the most of it and got away with missing a couple of lessons.

Although I detested school at the time, looking back they were enjoyable years. Especially the P.T. and athletics, I was good at the physical stuff and won a school prize for it but on the academic side I was a long way from becoming a scholar.

The walk to the school playing field was about one and a half miles. Each year it was the venue for the school sports day and many hikes to the field for practice were made prior to the big day. I regularly won the hundred yards' sprint and the high jump. I wasn't too keen on the distance races, I found them hard work. There was a 'throwing the cricket ball' competition practice going on one year and while I was training for the high jump in the sand pit (high jump competitors didn't have the luxury of an inflated landing pad in those days), a cricket ball landed near by. I threw the ball back to the ball throwers and because it landed beyond their throwing line, I was roped in on that event for the sports day as well. All that came to an end as I approached school leaving age, fifteen years old in those days. Like most kids I couldn't wait to leave.

I had no idea what kind of job I wanted to do when I left school but I was always interested in how things were made. I frequently got myself in trouble for dismantling things, just to see how they worked, so I thought that something practical was my best bet. I remember saying that I would be happy to get a job where I could earn enough money to buy cigarettes and run a motorbike. Ambition is a wonderful thing.

During our last year at school Jimmy Buxton and I got a part-time job in a drapers-cum-general store. George Smith, another friend a couple of years older than us, worked there full-time. Mr Hewitt, one of the men who ran the Penge and Beckenham Boxing Club, managed the store. George was a very good boxer and could have made a living from it. The shop had a covered frontage where the goods were displayed on stands, which had to be carried outside every morning and back inside at closing time. Jim and I worked there for an hour after school carrying the stands back into the shop and all day Saturdays as shop assistants.

Situated in Maple Road, which was the local open market with fruit and vegetable stalls dominating the scene, the shop always had a lot of passing trade. On Saturdays, our job was to stand outside on the frontage and keep an eye on the stock. When a purchase was made we wrapped it up and took the money inside the shop to Mr Hewitt who was the only one allowed to touch the till. I liked working there and in particular its distinct smell of new clothing and carpets etc. On occasions when I have been walking around large departmental stores and have caught a whiff of that same smell, I seem to be momentarily transported back in my mind, to Mr Hewitt's shop.

By that time my father who had left the army, had begun working in his pre-war job as a lorry driver. Following that he joined the Croydon Airport Fire Service. He used to cycle on a big old roadster bike about ten miles there and home again after his shift. Eventually he was made redundant so other plans had to be made.

Although he was no longer a regular soldier he continued to belong to the Territorial Army, which he joined before the war. Fortunately a vacancy occurred for a caretaker at the local Territorial Army Drill Hall, so after a discussion with mother he applied and got the job. That meant moving from Blenheim Road; I didn't like that very much but it wasn't very far away, just along the Penge High Street.

My mother got me my first real job in a cabinet maker's workshop, in the basement of a furniture showroom near Anerley Railway Station. I had to walk twice as far as when I walked to school, including Saturday mornings, no school dinners, start at 8 a.m. until 5.30 p.m. all for two pounds ten shillings (two pounds fifty) a week. I liked the job but didn't enjoy having three men telling me what to do and always giving me the mundane boring jobs. I soon began to detest the smell of wood and French polish as I entered the workshop every morning. After a few weeks of rebelling I was given a more responsible task to perform. All sawing was done by hand and I was instructed to cut several pieces of plywood for the backs of some wardrobes. Two pieces for each wardrobe, four feet six inches by three feet six inches, I was told.

Delighted with this change of job I borrowed a saw, having no tools of my own, and set to work measuring and sawing. I worked hard and it didn't take very long to cut about six boards. Even the foreman praised me for a change, until he picked one up. I had measured them forty-six inches by thirty-six inches instead of four feet six inches by three feet six inches. He grabbed hold of me and could hardly contain his anger. I thought he was going to hit me so I picked up a piece of wood and took a swipe at him narrowly missing his head but catching him on his arm. That was the end of my cabinet-making career. I ran out of the workshop and went home. When my mother asked me why I was home from work so early, I told her that I didn't like the job after all, so I had left. I won't describe what followed.

That was the beginning of my working life – it didn't take me long to realise that having nothing to offer an employer, only my labour, didn't give me much of a choice of jobs. There were apprenticeships on offer in those days but somehow I didn't fancy signing up for anything long-term, especially as I would be called up for two years' National Service when I was eighteen. I worked for a while for two men that were sub-contractors for a company that installed sanitary ware. Phil Harding and Jim Sharp were skilled wall and floor tilers, I was employed as their labourer.

My job was to prepare the tiles and keep the two of them supplied with cement. In those days wall tiles were fixed with cement and the glazed tiles had to be soaked in water to prevent them from drawing too much water from the cement, causing it to dry too quickly and ending up with the tiles falling off the wall.

Sometimes the tiles were left to soak all night and in the winter the water was often frozen. I had to break the ice and carry the wet freezing tiles to where Phil and Jim were working. My hands were often blue and numb from the effects of putting them in the ice-covered water. Then I would work up a sweat by mixing the cement by hand and carrying it in buckets for the two tilers, who used it up as if it was going out of fashion.

Phil had a Norton motorcycle and side car which he used to transport the three of us to the different jobs. One particular job was in the kitchen of a new school that was being built at White City, Shepherd's Bush, West London. We had not been long on the road after work one day, when, as we drove past White City Underground Station, a car in front of us stopped suddenly at a pedestrian crossing.

Phil was unable to stop. The front of the sidecar that I was riding in was shaped like the front of a speedboat and the rear of the car sloped upwards. The effect of the crash was for the sidecar to ride up the sloping rear of the car. Phil who was holding on to the handle bars was thrown forwards and Jim was tipped off sideways from the pillion seat. I remained in the sidecar which finished up perched in the air with the bike on its side in the roadway.

People rushed to assist us and as I climbed out of the sidecar I saw someone helping Jim. Phil and I seemed all right but Jim was helped on to the pavement where he sat down on a step near the underground station. Phil and I approached him to see how he was. The glazed look in Jim's eyes and the pale colour of his face made him look strange, I wasn't sure what was happening. At sixteen years old I had not experienced anything like that before. He was muttering something about his back.

Phil and I were not aware of what had happened to Jim in the accident but it transpired that he was tipped sideways into the path of a lorry travelling in the opposite direction, which had driven over him. Tragically, Jim Sharp died before he reached hospital.

As a working lad I saved, that's a lie, borrowed from Aunt Else for clothes and shoes, developed a cocky swagger and began to go out with girls, more seriously than when I was at school. It was the era of the drape suit, brogue shoes and gabardine raincoats. Not forgetting the D.A. Haircut. D.A. stands for duck's arse, the hair on the sides of the head was swept around the back to meet in the middle, resembling the wing feathers of a duck. It was a smart fashion though and everyone wore nicely pressed suits.

The main event of the week was the dance at the Regal Ballroom Beckenham, that couldn't be missed. A lot of the girls from a wide area around Beckenham went there and of course a lot of competition in the form of young men also attended. Fortunately for us young up-and-coming lads, there were not a lot of older lads about because most of them, between eighteen and twenty-two years, were in the forces doing their National Service. People came to the dance hall from a wide area and there was often trouble, always over girls of course. A Penge boy would upset a Norwood boy, or a Sydenham boy would upset someone from another mob, gang or group. Whatever the cause, there were always fights.

The cinema was the other major entertainment, not only for the film but because that was the only place you could take a girl. Even with loads of other people around, you felt alone with her in the dark. As always, money was the problem so the cheapest way to take a girl to the pictures was to tell her that you might be late, so it would be better to see her in there. It worked every time.

Maureen Ranger was the name of the girl that I occasionally saw at the Regal Dance Hall and sometimes in the cinema. She fascinated me and she was a pretty girl, so I pursued her and pounced when the time was right. I sat behind her in the pictures and kept making stupid remarks making her laugh, then I swapped seats with her friend and I was home and dry. We became friends and began to see a lot of each other.

When I was sixteen I saved begged and borrowed thirty pounds to buy a motorbike. I had always wanted one, so when a chap that I worked with decided to sell his 350cc Royal Enfield, I had to have it. I didn't know exactly how to drive one but I did have an idea of the basics. Not having to wait around for buses and the convenience of being able to go where I wanted, when I wanted, gave me a feeling of independence. For practice I first drove my bike to all of the places where I used to cycle and then I began to go on longer journeys. Kidding myself that I was a competent driver even though I only had a provisional driving licence, I began to get a bit throttle happy. When waiting at traffic lights, I would rev the engine in short bursts just to hear the note, which made me feel good especially if there were other lads around. Going fast was easy on a straight road but roads tend to have bends in them. I was driving along a country road one day when the slight bend that I was negotiating suddenly turned into a sharp bend. A hedgerow got in my way, causing me to finish up sprawled all over the road. I had learned my first lesson the hard way, never to forget it. Fortunately I only suffered a broken motorcycle.

During the next couple of years I started and left a few mundane jobs. I was very unsettled and frustrated because I couldn't earn enough money to do the things that I wanted. Everyone else seemed to be doing alright in my eyes but I always seemed to be struggling. The age for being called up for National Service was looming. Bert was already serving in a Tank Regiment in Hong Kong and loving it. I was fed up with waiting for things to happen so I contemplated signing on in an effort to get things moving and to stabilise my life. Maureen and I had been seeing a lot of each other and it seemed inevitable that we would eventually marry. We discussed the future and decided that we would get engaged to be married and then I would sign on and not wait for call-up. Living in a Territorial Army Drill Hall and having a father who loved all the bull that went with the army, I had a good idea of what to expect.

Much to the disgust of my mother, Maureen and I became engaged. Like many young people, we thought that we had just invented love. Contrary to all the advice and remarks, we were convinced that we were different from everyone else. We believed we knew what we were doing and no one could persuade us otherwise. All of our friends at the time were just as stupid as us, they thought it was wonderful. On reflection, I more than likely got engaged to stamp a 'reserved' label on Maureen, while I was away in the army. Probably worried that she would get fed up with waiting and being on her own, with nothing to look forward to and would be tempted to find someone else, I admit that to be a really diabolical and selfish attitude.

Around the middle of 1954, before my eighteenth birthday, I boarded a bus and went to an army recruitment centre and joined the army. I was recruited into the Royal Electrical Mechanical Engineers, R.E.M.E. for short. When I told my mother she was very upset, especially as Bert was already away from home. I don't remember what my father said but on reflection he was probably

31

very pleased because he was mad about the army. He joined the Territorial Army as a young man and was still a serving sergeant.

On the 13th July 1954, I reported for duty, along with a mob of other no-hopers, at Blandford Forum Dorset where I got off to a great start. We were taken to a corrugated iron hut, where it was explained to us that we were to live there for the following six weeks whilst on basic training. The hut was dull and depressing with twelve iron beds in it, minus the mattresses, lined up six on each side. The beds were separated by a wooden locker, the gap forming each recruit's individual bed space for which he was responsible. Halfway along the hut was a stove fixed to the floor with a metal flue pipe rising vertically to the apex of the corrugated iron roof.

We were then ordered to the stores to get kitted out. Forming an orderly single file, we slowly made our way past a long counter. Stores personnel working behind the counter asked our sizes and began to issue our kit. I don't know why we were asked our size because everything seemed to come from the same pile. As we progressed towards the end of the counter, we were all laden with everything from mess tins to boots and a steel helmet with camouflage net.

As I came out of the stores I saw in the distance the first lads to be kitted out. They were walking around the perimeter of the parade ground, struggling with their gear. Thanks to Mr Evans, my maths teacher at Oakfield Road School, he drummed Pythagoras's Theorem into my head. I knew that it was a shorter distance to walk diagonally across the hypotenuse, than to walk around the other two sides, so off I went, struggling with my burden. Almost across the parade ground I became conscious of a very loud voice calling:

"Soldier!" in a long drawn-out, almost scream.

Turning to face the direction from which I had just walked, I saw a uniformed figure who I soon discovered to be the Company Sergeant Major. I was made to walk all the way back to the stores balancing two berets and a steel helmet on my head, hugging the rest of my kit and bedding, sweating like the proverbial pig. It was explained to me in a not very nice way, that the parade square was like holy ground and personnel were only allowed on it, when on parade.

After walking around the holy ground to my hut I had to make do with the worst bed space because I was last in. Thank you, Mr Evans, Sir.

The new squad that I was now a attached to was ordered to report to the cook house for fatigues, I and four or five others were put in the bread room and told to cut a great pile of loaves into slices. Having been told to take our knife fork and spoon with us ready for our meal, I decided to put mine on a windowsill just behind where I was working so that I could keep an eye on them. After cutting up all available loaves of bread someone produced some butter. I turned to get my knife to spread some butter on a couple of slices of bread only to find that there was nothing on the windowsill. I shouted in not a very friendly way, asking who had taken my eating irons. There being no response I challenged the nearest chap to me who was using a knife and asked him to give me back my knife. He refused, saying that it was his.

Getting angry I grabbed hold of the blade of the knife and tried to wrench it out of the man's hand. That tussle developed into a bit of a tug of war and, conscious of the possibility that I might cut my hand, I lost my temper and delivered a couple of punches to the guy's face resulting in him releasing his hold on the knife.

As I proceeded to butter my two slices of bread, muttering some very unfriendly remarks about the chap who took my knife, one of the other recruits politely said:

"Is that your knife fork and spoon on that windowsill?"

My jaw dropped as I realised that I was looking for my eating irons on the wrong windowsill. I felt terrible and tried apologise to the chap who was sporting a large lump under his eye but he didn't want to talk to me for some reason.

On parade the next morning the chap's eye was almost closed and when the sergeant asked him how he injured his face I began to feel a bit panicky. Fortunately for me he told the sergeant that he slipped and knocked it on his bed end.

I approached the chap during N.A.A.F.I. break (which stands for Navy Army and Air Force Institute), to apologise again and thank him for not reporting me but he completely ignored me. Can't think why?

Full of anticipation I found the first few days hectic. Even having a father who loved the army and living within the bounds of a Territorial Army Drill Hall, it was still a bit of a shock. I had often watched the T.A. men being drilled so I knew roughly what to expect. I was also aware of some old soldiers' methods of handling all of the bulling up of my boots, brasses and webbing packs. Some of the lads didn't even have a clue how to press their trousers. The main pastime in the evenings was bulling-up equipment and cleaning the hut. Every piece of equipment even the issue underpants, or should I say 'Drawers Cellular' had to be stamped with your army number.

It didn't take long for me to admit that there were times during those first few days that I wished that I could change my mind and go home. I wrote home and telephoned from time to time but the thought of not being allowed leave or to venture out of the camp for any reason during training, was hard to take.

Basic training began in earnest in September, it was tolerable as long as you could switch off your mind and just do as you were told without reacting or questioning some of the ridiculous orders. They called it discipline, I called it bullying and making the little pint-sized corporal feel big and powerful. I suppose he was getting his own back on normal-sized people, probably after being bullied at school. However, contrary to what we were told, after two weeks we were transferred to another training camp at Barton Stacey, Hampshire. There we were introduced to an upgrade in accommodation, we lived in a wooden hut.

The training became harder and the discipline more strict. Kit inspections were regular and we all became victims of the sick humour of the Drill Sergeant and his sidekick, a thick brainless Lance Corporal. In spite of the thoughts of what you would like to do to those people if you ever met them on a dark night outside of the camp, we completed our training. I was awarded a certificate for being the champion recruit, what a load of bull that was.

Being in the R.E.M.E. meant that everyone had to have a trade, so we were all posted to various trade training camps. I was a potential welder so off I went to Gosport for trade training. At least the accommodation at Gosport was brick built and we didn't have to walk about one hundred metres in the open to the toilet and washroom. The trade training was for six months and because we had completed our basic training, we were allowed to go home on leave at weekends.

I was glad to get home on my first leave, it is said that absence makes the heart grow fonder and I am inclined to believe that. Maureen and I discussed marriage so that I could apply for married quarters when I got a permanent posting. Against a good deal of opposition from my mother, a date was set for December 27th 1954.

Typical of a teenager, I couldn't be told. As far as I was concerned the army had me for three years, I had no idea where I would be posted to when I completed my trade training but I banked on getting married and eventually moving into married quarters. In the meantime, the marriage allowance for which I would qualify would accumulate and help with the cost of setting up home. Well, that was the pie in the sky idea, which was all in our imagination and, with hindsight, doomed to failure.

When my squad had almost completed our trade training the rumours began about postings. Most were abroad and I didn't fancy being away for my remaining two and a half years service, so soon after getting married. Finally we were informed that the list of postings would be offered to personnel in the sequence of the highest pass marks gained in their trade test. I had found out that most of the postings were in fact abroad but a few were home postings. I was pleased to be amongst the top scorers in the trade tests so I just kept my fingers crossed that there would be a home posting when it was my turn to select.

Bicester in Oxfordshire, attached to 15 Battalion R.A.O.C. (Royal Army Ordnance Corps) was my choice which turned out to be a mud hole. The R.E.M.E. billets, tin huts again, were positioned quite a long way from the workshops, so every day we had to make the laborious march to a depot known as H.Q.10. There was already a welder attached to the depot and we didn't really hit it off from the start. He was a bit of a wild man and after a drinking session, he was arrested for beating up another soldier and sent to the Army Detention Centre at Colchester, I didn't see him again. I had the welding shop in the H.Q.10 depot to myself after that, which I eventually shared with a sheet metal worker named Derek Chaney.

Derek was from Manchester, we developed a great relationship in our workshop, he was a National Serviceman in for two years as opposed to my three. He completed his apprenticeship before his conscription so was already a qualified sheet metal worker prior to being called up. He was a good tradesman, he knew what he was talking about and I learned a lot from him during the time that we worked together.

I had become aware of the fact that the army did not automatically supply married quarters so the reality was, that unless I managed to find somewhere out of camp to live with Maureen, we were not going to be able to set up home together. I had come to terms with the fact that I was destined to live for the remainder of my service in a tin hut with a dozen blokes, one hundred yards from the ablutions and have to wash and shave in cold water most mornings.

One of the civilian employees in the depot happened to mention that an officer had moved from his accommodation in a farmhouse in a village named Thame a few miles away. He also said that there was a regular bus to the camp from Thame, which the civilian workers who worked in the depot complex use. I discussed the prospect of living out of camp with Maureen and decided to make some enquiries about the rent and employment prospects for her, because my income was limited being the lowest of the low in rank.

We were successful in renting the farmhouse, it was a really nice old oak-beamed place, with a view right across the farmland. I hired a car and we set off with a friend driving it for me, carrying a great pile of belongings on the roof rack. I suppose the journey from Beckenham in Kent to Thame in Oxfordshire was about three hours on ordinary roads, there being no motorways in those days. The farmer and his wife were very nice people, they greeted us on arrival and didn't interfere in any way. We soon settled in and then turned our attention to my daily travel arrangements to my army depot and the prospects of work for Maureen.

The bus service to my depot was a bit long-winded so we decided to buy a motorcycle for me to travel to work and for us to travel home to Beckenham occasionally. I bought a small 150cc B.S.A. Bantam, not a very powerful bike, in fact it really struggled with two of us on it, but it was very cheap to run and that was what mattered to us at that time.

I was a learner rider and I couldn't take a pillion passenger until I had a full licence so I approached the depot motorcycle despatch rider's instructor and asked him for a test. He agreed to test me but said that the test had to be on an army bike and that they were all 350cc bikes, larger than what I was used to riding but the same size as the Royal Enfield that I crashed before I signed on. He said he was too busy at the time but told me to come and see him again in a couple of days. That gave me time to borrow a bike in the pretence of having to do some welding on it, and have a ride around the depot a few times to get used to the larger machine again.

When I felt ready for my motorcycle test I approached the instructor once again. He said he was still too busy to test me so I tried to pin him down to a date and time for a test. Sounding very irritated he asked me if I was a confident rider and a couple of other questions and then he signed a pink form. He gave me the form and told me to send it away and get my licence. I was absolutely amazed, I had become a fully qualified motorcycle rider without even having to sit astride a bike. A bit out of order but I didn't argue, I thanked him, gave him a ten shilling note (fifty-pence) and quickly departed.

I didn't like being in the army but living out of camp made it more tolerable, weekend leave passes were not so important and I didn't have to put up with the disgusting cookhouse food. Maureen got a job and things were not at all bad, we just about made ends meet.

Captain Head was in charge of the R.E.M.E. personnel attached to 15 Battalion R.A.O.C. and like all R.E.M.E. personnel he had a trade. Our captain was a blacksmith. The forge and anvil, plus all of the associated tools were in my welding shop and Captain Head enjoyed nothing more than making the anvil ring whenever he could afford the time. On one of those occasions he was in his shirt sleeves, sweating over the roaring forge when an R.A.O.C. sergeant stormed into the workshop and began to shout at me and Derek, demanding that we work on one of his lorries that had been parked outside of our workshop for more than a day. I tried to explain, by showing him a stack of job cards, that the work was carried out in the order that it came in and that there was still a few jobs to be completed before his lorry. He wouldn't accept that explanation and continued to demand that we did his job, adding that he was ordering us to do it immediately. Meanwhile, Captain Head had stayed in the background listening to the sergeant ranting and raving. He slowly rolled his sleeves down, put on his jacket, removed his cap from the makeshift hook on the wall, made from a length of bent welding wire, put it on and turned to face the sergeant and at the same time coughing loudly.

The irate sergeant was reduced to a quivering jelly before our eyes. I don't believe that I have ever seen anyone salute an officer so many times before managing to make his escape. Captain Head didn't comment to us, he casually removed his jacket and cap, rolled up his sleeves and carried on playing his tune on the anvil. The word got around though because every time that we were visited by a senior rank wanting a job done, they acted very cautiously when they entered the workshop.

On 24th December 1956 Beverly Ann, my first daughter, was born. About one month prior to her birth we vacated our farmhouse accommodation and Maureen went back home to Beckenham Kent to live with her mother. We decided that she and our baby would get better care back home.

It was a very wet day when I moved back into camp. I carried all of my kit and uniforms on the back of my motorbike and consequently, everything got very wet. Spreading all of my kit around the billet to dry, I spent the whole day dressed in pyjamas, sorting everything out and getting shipshape, hoping that I wouldn't be missed at my workshop.

Corporal Frank Coxhead was in charge of the billet and was also based at H.Q.10. He was a vehicle electrician by trade and a good mate. Sergeant Rose had noticed my absence, he ordered Frank to charge me with being absent from my place of duty. The surname Rose didn't mean a lot to me at that stage in my life except for my instant dislike of him because of his refusal to listen to reason, but little did I know then that the surname Rose was to turn up and have some influence over me during the remainder of my working life.

Full of apologies, Frank had to put me on a charge. I was marched into the Company Commander's Office and sentenced to seven days confined to barracks plus the stoppage of three days' pay. I was on jankers and that meant not being allowed out of camp for any reason and parading outside the Guard Room in full battledress and kit, every evening after work. After the parade all the defaulters were detailed off for fatigues, which meant doing mundane and dirty jobs around the camp.

When I reported to the Guardroom for my first defaulter's parade, I was lined up with about nine other men, I was the only R.E.M.E man there. The Colour Sergeant taking the parade looked at me from the end of the line then slowly walked towards me. He stood in front of me with his pacing stick under his arm and his chest out, staring me straight in my eyes. After a few seconds he shouted:

"What's this soldier?"

At the same time he tugged at the fly on my trousers. He had obviously noticed, looking sideways from the end of the line that I had forgotten to fasten my fly buttons, probably due to rushing to get ready for the defaulter's parade, outside of the guard room after work. Consequently I stood rigidly at attention being told what a useless scruffy individual I was and having to shout out loud:

"I am a scruffy individual, Sergeant."

All the time my fly gaped open displaying army issue khaki drawers cellular underpants, daring not to move until I was told.

Jobs were allocated to us after the parade and when it was my turn the sergeant asked me if there was a welder amongst the R.E.M.E lads at the depot. I replied in a questioning tone and an equally questioning expression on my face, that there was and that I was the welder.

"Oh!"

He replied in a much friendlier tone, accompanied by a hint of a smile. Quickly reverting back to his bullying attitude he told me to report to the Sergeants' Mess for fatigues and wait for him there.

"Can you weld cast iron, mate?"

Mate? That made little bells ring in my head, I realised at once that he wanted something from me.

"Of course I can," I replied. "Why is that, Sergeant?"

The sergeant indicated where his bunk room was and told me to wait for him there. After a short time he arrived with two mugs of tea and two hot meat pies. He told me to sit down and gave me one of the teas and a meat pie. I must have looked a bit bewildered because he told me to relax as he wanted to ask me for a favour.

He explained that he couldn't use his car because the manifold was cracked and asked if I could repair it. I explained that cast iron could be difficult because it would require preheating before the weld and slow cooling after to prevent more damage but I would have a look at it. I said that he would have to remove it from the car and get it into the depot to my workshop because I wouldn't be able to get it past the Ministry Of Defence Police at the depot entrance. He told me not to worry about that and that my fatigues were finished for the night so I devoured the delicious meat pie and tea and returned to my billet.

The following afternoon a lorry parked outside of the welding shop and the driver handed me a cardboard box with the manifold inside. He asked when he should return to collect it. I told him that I would let the sergeant know. I had the repair done in a couple of days, taking care not to let Captain Head see it in case he realised that it wasn't an army one. During my fatigues in the Sergeants' Mess, speaking with my mouth full of hot pie and tea, I told the sergeant that the job was done. The next morning it was collected and when I reported for the defaulters' parade at the guard room that evening it had been put back on the car. The sergeant was delighted and showed his pleasure for the remainder of my seven days' jankers.

Living back at the camp in a miserable uncomfortable tin hut made me feel very depressed. At every opportunity, especially at weekends, I either hitchhiked home, which was the cheapest way of travelling, or took the train which was a drain on my pocket, but by far the quickest. My little B.S.A. Bantam motorbike suffered a broken gearbox on the way home on a weekend leave some time ago, so I hadn't any transport of my own any more.

Frank Coxhead and I sometimes got off work early during midweek so we used to make the journey to Beckenham just for the evening. One journey we made was on a borrowed motorcycle, Frank was driving and I was on the pillion during a terrific thunderstorm. How we completed that journey safely I will never know. We arrived back at camp cold, soaking wet and miserable, vowing never to do it again.

Thanks to the efforts of Frank, who was in charge of our billet, we managed to get most weekends off. Every Friday afternoon the billets were inspected and those men in the best kept billet were awarded a forty-eight hour pass starting from Friday evening as opposed to a thirty-six hour pass from Saturday afternoon.

No one was at their best early in the morning so the job was never done very well. Enter Corporal Frank Coxhead. His job was a mobile one, travelling between depots troubleshooting electrical problems on the battalion vehicles, forklift trucks and electric trolleys etc, that were used in the various warehouses. He used to go back to the billet and bull it up until there wasn't a speck of dust to be seen and everything was lined up and set out ready for inspection. It worked most times and no one suspected any foul play.

Frank and I were not very keen on eating in the company cookhouse so most of our money was spent on food in the N.A.A.F.I. Club (National Army Air Force and Naval Institute), which happened to be within the boundary of 15 Battalion Company Lines. We ordered beans on toast one day and was told that the toaster wasn't working. We asked what was wrong with it and got a shrug of the shoulders from the N.A.A.F.I. girl, along with a facial expression indicating that she had no idea. We suggested that we should take a look at it so the girl went behind the scenes to ask the club manager.

A tall blonde woman appeared behind the counter and invited us to go into the kitchen to take a look at the toaster. She was older than us and quite striking in her appearance, her main feature being her long golden hair which had, we were to learn later, earned her the nickname of Sunny. The toaster was made to function once again to the delight of Sunny and as a payment she invited us into her office and insisted that we had a meal on the house. A table was laid for us and a delicious meal of lamb chops was placed in front of us. Fantastic.

From that day we were always welcome behind the scenes at the N.A.A.F.I. Club, where we used to enjoy a good variety of meals and conversation with Sunny. She became quite fond of Frank, who was a single man at the time. She made her feelings known by telling him that she missed him, after we were absent from the club for a few days, but it was all a bit one-sided. Frank was not interested in any relationship with her other than one of cupboard love, friendship for food, and I tagged along as a kind of chaperone, a hungry one at that and I am sure that my presence irritated her at times, if not all of the time.

Time passed and Frank decided that seven years was enough and it was time to leave the army and move on. He made arrangements to buy himself out and after a few more months he had a date to leave. Sunny was disappointed with the news and came on to Frank a bit stronger. He managed by treating it all as a joke to pass it off but during a short embrace, making out that he was a great lover, he tilted Sunny backwards and at the same time grabbed the back of her hair and looked straight into her eyes as if he was about to kiss her.

Shock, horror, fear, panic, terror, all of those things came over us all at once, as her hair came off in Frank's hand – she was wearing a long blonde wig. How we survived the remainder of that evening without bursting into fits of laughter I will never know. As we left the N.A.A.F.I. Club later that evening we looked at each other and just cracked up. We made our way back to our tin hut, tears streaming from our eyes, unable to stop laughing at the evening's previous events.

After that terribly embarrassing moment it dawned on us that we never ever saw Sunny's hair in any other style or length. As we talked and laughed about it back at the billet, the smiles suddenly left our faces as we realised that Sunny could be a man. After a few seconds we erupted once again with raucous laughter.

We continued to visit Sunny but less frequently until Frank was demobbed. He promised Sunny that he would not forget her and that he would visit her after he had sorted himself out with regard to work etc. I on the other hand was still in the army with a few months remaining of my three years. I didn't visit Sunny when I went to the N.A.A.F.I. Club but on some occasions we did see each other and chatted and most times she asked if I had heard from Frank.

At last it was my turn to get out of the army and become a person again. I made a point of visiting Sunny to say goodbye and once again she questioned me about Frank. I admitted that I had his telephone number and she persuaded me to phone him from her office. He was pleased to hear from me and Sunny put her ear close to the telephone to listen to our conversation.

"I'm in the club, Frank, talking to Sunny," I said in a gushing happy tone.

His reply left me speechless and so embarrassed.

"You're not still seeing that silly old cow are you?" he said, laughing down the phone.

I wished that a hole would appear so that I could have disappeared into it. I turned away from her hoping that she had not heard what he had said and at the same time said, "Yes, Frank, have a word with her, she is dying to speak to you."

I passed the phone over to her and prepared to evacuate her office if the need be.

They chatted for a while then I had another quick word with him before I hung up. I felt very awkward and couldn't wait to get out of her office. Despite trying every trick in the book such as checking closely for stubble and looking at her hands and the size of her feet, which were fairly large, we never knew for certain whether she was male or female and no way were we going to try and snatch a hand full of private parts to find out.

After my first daughter Beverly was born, I turned my attention to finding our own accommodation and what I was going to do to earn a living after the army. We lived with Maureen's parents when I was on leave, for convenience and because there was a shortage of houses for rent. I couldn't see any chance of us finding a home of our own even in the distant future.

Eighteen years old. Raw recruit.

Platoon passing out photograph, I'm second from the right top row.

Light-hearted moment at Gosport. I am on the right at the rear.

Another light-hearted moment.

Tin hut at Bicester, just finished bulling-up the stove ready for inspection.
Me and Corporal Frank Coxhead standing each side of the flue pipe.

7th TRAINING BATTALION, R.E.M.E.

This *Proficiency Certificate* is awarded to

No. 23211686 Pte. Franks.R.J.

for being the BEST ALL-ROUND RECRUIT of No. 21 Squad
'C' Company, during his period of Basic Training
from 1st September '54 to 29th September '54

_____ Company Commander _____
O.C. " " Company 7TH TRAINING BATTALION, R.E.M.E.

Gale & Polden Ltd., Aldershot 5894-v

Chapter 3

Soon after Frank left the army Derek Chaney completed his two years' National Service, leaving me to work alone in my welding shop. I found it strange working on my own after nearly two years with Derek, no one to argue or have a laugh with, I didn't like it at all. Captain Head had moved on and our new officer in charge didn't have any particular interest in my workshop. Therefore, I only spoke to those who came into my workshop for a welding job or modification work on their vehicles etc. I still had a couple of months to do and the days couldn't pass quickly enough. I found it hard to imagine life without obeying silly orders from cranky people. In the army you didn't even have the ultimate privilege of being able to put on your coat, walk out and tell them to stuff their job. You were theirs to do what they wanted. I couldn't ever accept that but had to live with it for the duration of my three years. A sergeant described our status when we were on parade one day:

"When the army shouts shit," he shouted, "you all jump on the shovel."

Demob day finally arrived. I reported to the adjutant's office to collect my discharge documents and rail pass. As I walked from the office gazing at my discharge book and other documents, I could hardly believe that it was my turn to leave that prison-like place for good, demobbed from the army and never to return. At last I was going to become just an ordinary citizen once again.

Standing on the timber floorboards of the veranda outside the adjutant's office, wearing a silly grin on my face reflecting my inner feelings, I could hear the familiar sound of marching, Left, left, left right left. My silly grin broadened as around the bend in the road swaggered the R.E.M.E. lads, marching in their own couldn't-be-bothered style, oblivious to the left, left, left right left being shouted by the corporal in charge. They were on their way to work at H.Q.10. About thirty men, consisting of a mixture of regular soldiers and national servicemen, striding nonchalantly along dressed for work in their one-piece brown boiler suit-type overalls.

As they were about to pass the adjutant's office the corporal in charge called them to a halt, it sounded a bit like a machine gun but not too bad for a bunch of tradesmen.

"Right turn!" the corporal shouted.

Surprisingly they all turned together. I didn't think they were capable of that. The squad stood looking at me with envy in their eyes, much as I had done many times before when others had been demobbed.

Putting my suitcase down, I clomped my way off of the wooden veranda on to the tarmac roadway. Standing to attention in front of the squad I bellowed at the top of my voice:

"Open-order-march!"

They all moved as one.

"Amazing," I said, laughing out loud. "Everyone got it together for a change."

I walked between the ranks mimicking an inspecting officer, a big uncontrollable smile on my face.

"Lucky Bastard," muttered someone in a Scottish accent.

"Good luck, Bob mate," said a strong cockney voice.

I adjusted a couple of ill-fitting berets that were perched at a jaunty angle which had been deliberately shrunk by immersing alternately in hot and cold water and then quickly dried, supposedly to give the image of an old soldier. There was nothing worse than advertising that you were a raw recruit, or 'sprog' as new blokes were called, by wearing what resembled a flying saucer on your head.

Returning to the front of the squad I began to give a little speech.

"Cheerio, blokes," I began, still unable to control the big smile on my face. "Nice to have…"

Before I could say any more the friendly atmosphere was abruptly shattered by a long drawn out roar that came from behind me.

"Soldier! Come 'ere, move! Get those men out of here, Corporal, now – at the double! Be outside my office at 1300 hours now move, at the double, move!"

Automatically I turned towards the voice knowing immediately who it belonged to. Standing with his predator-like stare fixed on me, was old gravel guts himself, the regimental sergeant major. A short red-faced stocky man without a neck, the muscles in his cheeks twitching with rage. The only hairs visible below his cap were on his eyebrows; his uniform, as always, was immaculate.

He stood leaning slightly backwards to counterbalance his barrel-shaped forward portion. His rotund torso started from under his little fat chin and ended at his crotch, without a hint of where his chest ended and his stomach began. Clamped under his arm was his pacing stick, it must have been permanently stuck in place as I don't recall ever seeing him without it.

I swallowed hard as a wave of panic flowed through me, breaking into an instant sweat I felt as though I was drowning in hot water.

During the next few minutes, which seemed like hours, I was on the wrong end of the biggest bollocking that I had ever experienced. Standing in front of him with horror written all over my face, thinking of all the dreadful things that he might do to me, my mind was in total confusion.

He was standing so close to me that I could see a small bunch of bristly hair that he had missed with his razor, situated right up under his rubbery looking nose in the middle of his fat face. As he shouted at me I was forced to hold my breath to avoid the smell of yesterday's beer swilling evening in the Sergeants' Mess. He showered me with spittle as he put extra emphasis on words in his determination to frighten the life out of me. His efforts were unnecessary because I was crapping myself anyway.

"If you think you are getting demobbed today, laddie, you had better think again," he growled through clenched teeth.

I gulped as his words registered and quickly took a breath of unpolluted air as he himself paused to breathe.

The panic that flowed through me made me feel sick and weak at the knees. There were five R.A.O.C. men getting out that day and they were about to climb aboard a personnel carrier that had just pulled up in the roadway to take us to Bicester Railway Station.

I heard the driver shout, asking the duty sergeant if there were any more to come.

"No!" replied the sergeant "There's only six today."

The driver shouted back "Only five here, Sarge, where's the other bloke?"

"I've got a feeling he won't be going with you."

I heard the sergeant deliberately shout to add even more pain and confusion to my predicament.

Overwhelmed by my sudden change of fortune I tuned into the sergeant major again, just as he shouted: "Get on that bloody lorry, get out of my sight, move yourself before I throw you in the bloody guardroom, laddie."

I moved all right, like a scared rabbit. I hurled myself into the rear of that personnel carrier as though my life depended upon it, accompanied by raucous laughter from those already on board. The laughter didn't last long when the regimental sergeant major threatened them with the same treatment.

For the time that it took to drive the six miles to the railway station I was the victim of a lot of mickey-taking but that didn't bother me at all, I was out. No more jumping when some little power-crazy bully shouted.

I realised then, that my introduction into the army was by way of a severe telling-off for carrying my kit across the parade square and my three years' service terminated in another but more frightening bollocking.

Civvy Street here I come. I felt good, all I had to do was get a job with decent pay. My mind wandered as I sat alone in a railway carriage on my way home, just me and my thoughts. No uniforms, I didn't want a job with a uniform, I hated uniforms. No more painting the coke bucket and shovel, no more painting the stove in the centre of the hut which we dare not light, even in the winter, before a hut inspection, so that we could win a few more hours' leave at the weekend. No more bullshit or uniforms, ever.

Within a couple of weeks, faced with the reality of having to work for a living and trying to imagine what the future had in store for me, I managed to get a job. The pay was not what I had been hoping for – four shillings and sixpence an hour (twenty-two and a half pence). I started work and soon began to wonder why on earth I had taken a job as a welder in a factory, making tubular steel furniture and ironing boards. Because I was a welder in the army, everyone assumed that I wanted to be a welder in civvy street. The work was simple and extremely boring. Staring at a little flame all day with no variation of the work really got to me, I even began to think that the army wasn't that bad after all.

Thoughts about my past and uncertain future constantly passed through my mind as I worked. I couldn't accept that I would have to stand at a bench and do factory work for the rest of my working life, so after only two weeks I decided that I had to look elsewhere for work. With the responsibility of having a family to support I couldn't afford to be without a job for long, so I had to find an alternative before I quit and I knew that would not be easy. I was looking reality in the face, finding out what being married and having responsibilities was all about. I was at the same time coming to terms with the fact that I would not be able to do the many things that I had missed for the past three years. I was 21 years old and had not really seen anything of life. I felt as though I had just been let out of prison, only to find myself still restricted in my freedom by my circumstances.

I was learning about life very fast and was having to accept the consequences of an immature mind making mature decisions. I was not too happy with the situation that I found myself in but I had made my bed and I had to lie in it. I recalled the advice that people tried to give me when I was 18 years old, which I ignored, I didn't realise that they were words of wisdom. I suppose there is only one way to learn if advice is not accepted and that is from experience.

Several jobs and eighteen months later I was visiting the local job centre when I met a chap that I had known since schooldays. Larry Case was a neighbour of Billy Harrison my school friend, he was reading a job application form that he had been given. We began to talk about the work situation when he showed me his form, it was an application to join the London Fire Brigade.

Larry had generated a spark of interest that nagged me more and more as the days passed. I had to get more information about the fire brigade so I telephoned the recruitment section and requested an application form. The more I thought about it the more attractive it became. When the application form arrived I completed it and sent it back, almost by return of post.

About four weeks later I was invited to attend the London Fire Brigade Headquarters for a selection interview. The letter of invitation indicated that the selection process may take all day and applicants should be prepared for that.

I dressed as smart as I could afford at the time and arrived at the London Fire Brigade Headquarters on the Albert Embankment, Lambeth, with time to spare. I was told to wait in a side room until the recruiting officers arrived. As I entered the room, I was surprised to see about ten other men already there. They were all sat in silence, as I walked in their heads all turned towards the door, reminding me of an 'eyes right' order on the parade ground. They were all looking apprehensive, as though they were waiting for a jury to deliver its verdict. Walking towards an empty chair at the far end of the room I sort of smiled at a couple of them, coughed into my clenched hand, felt a bit self-conscious, sat down and waited along with the rest of the condemned men, who before very long numbered sixteen.

Eventually we were taken to a lecture room and given an outline of the routine for the day. Everyone was measured to make sure that they were at least the minimum size required for the job, and then we had to undergo a strength test. We were taken onto the drill yard, paired off and told to lift our partners on to our shoulders and carry them one hundred yards within one minute. When everyone was ready we were told to begin. We started off at a steady pace and as we progressed the sound of heavy laboured breathing from the carriers became louder, along with some grunts, groans and other cries of pain from those acting as bodies that were being bounced up and down on bony shoulders. Inevitably nobody wanted to be last so it gradually developed into a race with everyone almost running towards the finish line. Then we changed round and the carrier became the body and had a bony shoulder thrust into his groin. That test really broke the ice amongst the applicants because we all finished up laughing about it and from then on we were all much more relaxed.

A written test was next consisting of a simple arithmetic paper followed by a dictation test. Due to the war, my early education suffered somewhat. Groups of children were gathered in a church hall, to have stories read to them by unqualified teachers who were standing in for those who were in the forces That didn't provide much of a foundation on which to build my later education. If I have to thank the army for anything, I suppose it must be for attempting to add to my limited knowledge of the basic three R's. To my surprise, following the educational test three names were called out and the candidates were sent home, so I assumed that I was over the first little hurdle.

After lunch break we were again put into a side room to wait for the face to face interview. Two men who went to a pub for lunch didn't return the remainder of us sat and chatted as one by one we were led to the interview room.

Three officers were sat behind a long highly-polished desk in large high-backed padded chairs. The walk from the door to the lonely looking chair placed a couple of yards from the table in front of the three staring interviewers, made me feel very nervous and self-conscious once again. I stood by the chair until I was invited to sit down, then one by one the officers began to ask me questions. I demonstrated my military training by addressing them as 'Sir' when answering questions and lied through my teeth when asked what I thought about the army and why I decided to leave after only three years. I felt like telling them that I had served my sentence but I learned a long time ago during my army service that 'bullshit baffles brains.'

The sixteen men who had gathered in the waiting room early that morning, had been whittled down to only three – John Davis, Les Whyte and yours truly. We were taken for a medical examination and then sent home to await further instruction.

Faced with the prospect of being back in a uniform again now that I was likely to be accepted for training as a fireman, did not fill me with enthusiasm. Uniforms create images in my mind of power crazy little men wanting to impose their will on others. Added to that was the unappealing thought of working regular night shifts, however, I considered that it must be better than factory work.

Just as I was about to give up hope of hearing from the fire brigade, a letter arrived inviting me to report to the London Fire Brigade Training Centre at 0830 hours on the 15th March 1959. I was still undecided but had a further two weeks to make up my mind. I discussed it with some people whose opinion I respected and after weighing up the advantages and disadvantages as I saw them, I decided to join. After all I could always leave and revert to making tubular steel furniture.

My employer at the time accepted my notice to quit after first trying to convince me that I was making a mistake and telling me that after a month I would be asking for my old job back. Just the kind of encouragement I needed.

An early train took me to London Bridge Railway Station in plenty of time to walk the mile or so to the training centre in Southwark Bridge Road without having to rush. I felt a bit nervous, as I did before a boxing match when I was a teenager, collywobbles in the stomach, I really didn't have a clue what to expect.

I located the training centre office where I was directed to an adjoining room and told to wait. A few recruits were already there and it wasn't long before others arrived but nobody I knew. I expected to see the other two who were interviewed on the same day as I was. It was good to see that everybody looked as apprehensive as I felt, which had the effect of making me feel just a little bit less tense.

After a while an officer ushered us all outside; he lined us up sort of single-file facing the seventy foot high drill tower and told us that we were going to the brigade stores to be kitted out. My mind flashed back to being kitted out as an army recruit.

As we stood in the drill yard waiting for transport we watched a squad of advanced recruits undergoing training. I believe that was more by design than accident because they were practising hook ladder drill on the face of the drill tower. As we watched, open-mouthed and in silence, the recruits scaled the tower one by one. They were using a little hook ladder and by hooking it on to the window sills, they progressively climbed the outside of the drill tower, to the fifth floor. Now was the time to change one's mind. I could not in a million years see myself doing that. I don't know what the others were thinking but if one of them decided to walk out at that time I would probably have joined him. However, we were whisked away to the stores wondering what other acrobatic performances we were likely to have to perform on that lonely looking imitation block of flats. That tower stood proud and tall, scarred by the constant battering from the energetic and eager recruits, as they were repeatedly drilled. The purpose being, as I was to find out later, was to make them so familiar with their equipment and its uses, that handling it would become second nature.

After we had been kitted out with the essentials to begin training, we were taken to the Brigade Headquarters at Lambeth, where we were shepherded to a locker room and allocated a locker after first signing for the key. The room was long and narrow with fitted wooden lockers along the whole length of one wall, with windows on the opposite wall, the doorway was at the end leading to a long passageway. I particularly noticed the shiny wooden block flooring, it was so highly polished it resembled brown glass. Must be a conscientious cleaning lady, I thought. We seemed to have been allowed a little time to ourselves so we chatted, had a bit of a laugh and got to know each other.

The laughter and chatter ceased abruptly when a uniformed officer appeared at the doorway and shouted:

"Right you lot, all of you into the lecture room at the end of the corridor, come on, quickly now."

We all walked briskly along the corridor and sat down in the lecture room which was filled with rows of slatted fold-up chairs, facing a stage draped in long dark velvet curtains with matching pelmet, in the middle of the stage was a lectern. With the agility of an athlete, the officer leapt onto the stage and in one stride reached the lectern. Another squad of recruits entered the room and were told to hurry up and be seated. The officer, leaning slightly forward, placed both forearms on the lectern and clasped his hands. He stood frowning with his mouth firmly closed as he silently surveyed the sea of faces staring at him.

"My name is Bishop," he said as he continued to survey his audience as if he was looking for someone.

"Sub-Officer Bishop," he said. "These two chrome bars on each of my shoulders are Sub-Officer's rank markings."

He paused as he removed his arms from the lectern and stood erect.

"You lot call me 'Sir', I am one of the instructors at this training establishment, who will be trying to make firemen out of you."

He slowly looked around the room again, as his frown deepened and his lips tightened once more into a thin line. Bishop was about five foot eleven inches tall, weighing about twelve stone, with prominent features and fair to ginger hair brushed straight back. He had an air of efficiency and discipline about him, which as far as I was concerned was bad news. I had seen it before in a previous life in uniform.

Striding slowly up and down the stage Bishop continued to lay down a few basic ground rules. He paused once again and said:

"In a few minutes, the Divisional Officer in charge of the Training Centre and his deputy will come here to welcome you into the London Fire Brigade. He will tell you what is expected of you during your training and also what you can expect if you do not make satisfactory progress during your course."

He grinned as he said that, and seemed slightly amused at his thoughts. He was about to carry on when the lecture room door opened.

All the faces in the room turned towards the door to see a short plump man walk in; he bounced up onto his toes as he walked. Following him was a taller man who appeared to move only from the hips down, leaning slightly backwards as he walked with his arms straight down by his sides, he wouldn't have looked out of place in a troupe of Irish Jig dancers. He followed at a set distance as though he was being towed. We discovered later that the two officers were hardly ever seen apart, the taller one always trotting along behind the shorter one. They were referred to throughout the training centre as 'Pinkie and Perky'.

"Stand up!" shouted Bishop.

We all stood up.

"Sit down please, gentlemen," said Pinkie as he took up his position in front of the stage with Perky standing by his side but about one pace to his rear.

"Make your mind up," muttered someone behind me.

I wanted to laugh but I spotted Bishop who was still standing on the stage watching our every move.

When all the shuffling and scraping of chairs had stopped and everybody had sat down again, the Divisional Officer introduced himself and his deputy. He began first of all to tell us how good he and his training centre staff were and then proceeded, with some sarcasm in his attitude and tone, to tell us how useless we were to him and the fire brigade.

Of course he was right, none of us had a clue but with a note of confidence in his voice he indicated that we would all benefit from the intense training on which we were about to embark and become part of a skilled team of fire-fighters, fit to be called upon by members of the public to deal with any emergency. With the introductory speech over Sub-Officer Bishop took charge once again and ordered us to parade in the drill yard after lunch, dressed in our newly issued overalls, fire boots leggings and cap.

During the lunch hour we all gathered in the locker room to change into our fire gear ready for the afternoon session. What followed left me with tears running down my face and cramps in my stomach, I hadn't seen anything so funny for a long time. Very large overall trousers gathered around the waist and belted. With sagging crotches and a mass of spare material around our arses, we resembled a rear view of a herd of elephants. The waterproof leggings were made of a stiff black shiny waterproof material, which insisted on taking up the shape of the folds made during storage, poking out sideways resulting in us looking like mounted police, or in reality more like clowns. The knee-high leather fire boots were as stiff as boards, the soles wouldn't bend, it was then that I realised how Pinkie learned to bounce up onto his toes as he walked. I certainly wasn't looking forward to running around the drill ground wearing them.

No instruction that afternoon, most of the time was taken up by Bishop showing us around the establishment and outlining the routine for training. I suppose we had to wear the new fire gear to sort of break it in, some hope of that inside a month. We were handed some notes on the use and construction of equipment and told to study them and remember what we had read, because we would be examined on them at a later date. A few of the lads complained that it was like being back at school but I wouldn't know about that, all I had to learn from at school was a blackboard and chalk and the nearest I got to that was cleaning it at the end of a lesson.

Bishop showed us where the store was situated containing all the cleaning gear. He told us that the last hour of every day was spent cleaning the training centre, the term used for that interesting routine in the fire brigade was 'station work'. He also said with a smile on his face that the whole of Friday afternoon was taken up with station work and the care and maintenance of equipment, in other words 'Bullshit'. It was goodbye to the conscientious cleaning lady and hello to the army once again.

"You can start by polishing your locker room floor," Bishop demanded. "Those clumsy great boots you are wearing have ruined it, I'll inspect it in forty-five minutes and if it is satisfactory you can all go home, if it is not you will do it again."

He marched off leaving us all standing open-mouthed looking at each other, nobody taking the initiative, no one volunteering. Eventually we all meandered to the cleaning store, returning with a variety of cleaning materials and got to work.

Sure enough Bishop came to the locker room a while later and inspected the floor. He told us to be on parade in fire gear ready for training, at 0830 next morning, turned on his heels and walked out, leaving two nasty marks on our highly polished floor.

Our training began at the Brigade Headquarters at Lambeth and not at the Training Centre at Southwark, as we had expected. We were organised into groups of four, each four men forming a crew. One crew was selected to manhandle a fifty-foot wheeled escape ladder under the strict supervision of Bishop. Slowly the escape ladder was pitched to the third floor of the one hundred foot drill tower, with the ladder resting on the third-floor windowsill and the head of it poking into the window opening.

The one hundred foot purpose built brick drill tower was a free standing structure incorporating an internal staircase and a hollow core where the training centre's wet hose, used during drills, was hung up to drain and dry. The tower was also used by the personnel of Lambeth Fire Station which was housed on the ground and first floor of the Brigade Headquarters building. Many mornings during our training, recruits would watch and wonder what kind of fire Lambeth's crew had been fighting during the night, as the hose that they used, still smelling of smoke and covered in bits of debris, was scrubbed clean and hung in the tower. That gave us all a feeling of excitement and always prompted a barrage of questions and a discussion amongst the squad.

With the escape ladder in position, we were lined up in front of the tower. All eyes were gazing up at the third floor when Bishop shouted:

"Why are you all looking up in the air with your mouths open? I'm down here, look at me and pay attention."

He continued:

"When I give the order you will all turn smartly to the right and follow the leader up the ladder, climb into the third floor window, come down the internal staircase and get back in line, do you all understand?" he bellowed.

We all shuffled around a little and answered in what sounded like a lot of coughs and grunts. He paused for a moment as he walked along the line.

"Watch me," he said, "This is the correct way to climb a ladder."

He began to explain and demonstrate the fire brigade method of climbing a ladder.

"These are the strings," he said, patting the sides of the ladder. "And these are the rounds, most people call them rungs, we do not, they are rounds."

He went on to explain that the rounds must be grasped when climbing a ladder not the strings, and the hand and foot on the same side of the body should be moved together, left hand left foot, right hand right foot. He slowly climbed the ladder emphasising his movements and describing the reasons for his every move. When he reached the third floor window he climbed one round higher than the windowsill, placing both feet on the round before stepping down on to the sill. When he came out of the window on to the ladder, he stepped up one round, placing both feet higher than the windowsill, before proceeding to come back down the ladder, still demonstrating the correct method of hand and foot movements.

I realised at once that this was going to be a long sixteen weeks of detailed basic training. Bishop made climbing a ladder sound as though we were studying for a degree or something but I must confess that later on in the course, the reason for such detailed training became clear.

"Right!" shouted the instructor. "First one, away you go, next one, keep it going, come on next one, keep going, left hand left foot, up you go."

Gingerly the line of recruits began to climb the escape ladder. As the first man appeared at the door at the bottom of the tower the last man was just about to start to climb the ladder. We all lined up laughing and joking, feeling rather proud of ourselves when Bishop ordered us up again, and again, and again. No more laughing and joking we were too busy breathing.

"Away you go again," the instructor shouted, "And this time put some energy in to it."

Wearing those clumsy great stiff boots, the fun really started. It was like trying to climb a ladder in snow shoes. Legs started to ache, knees were bashed, fingers were bent backwards, and even the odd chin was bruised as those stiff new boots slipped off of the rounds, leaving the wearer dangling by his fingertips.

"Again! Again!" Bishop kept shouting.

Just when I was about to give up and collapse in a heap on the drill yard floor, Bishop told us to stop. We all lined up to the sound of coughs, wheezes and very heavy breathing. Some men were bending over with their hands on their knees gasping for breath, a couple were lying on the floor. Others including yours truly were walking around in circles with hands placed on hips and mouths wide open, searching for oxygen.

"Not very fit are we?" Bishop said.

Nobody argued with him.

"Come on!" he continued. "On your feet, stand up straight, if you want to change your minds about becoming firemen, you all know where the office is."

Nobody moved we were too knackered even to answer him.

As Bishop walked up and down the line explaining that the fitter we became the easier it would get and we might even begin to enjoy the training. As we began to recuperate he assured us that everything that we were required to do during training was for our own benefit and was absolutely necessary if we were to become fully-trained firemen, who the public and colleagues could trust and have confidence in. We were not worked too hard for the rest of that day but we still suffered from pains in the legs and buttocks from the exertion, for the remainder of the week.

The following week a new face appeared in front of the squad. We discovered that Sub-Officer Bishop was not our regular squad instructor, he was standing in for Station Officer Pearce who had been on leave. Pearce proved to be a bit of a pain, he had no sense of humour and didn't appear to enjoy instructing. There seemed to be a kind of barrier between him and us. He seemed to be suffering us, which caused a feeling of lack of belonging in the squad. Later on in my service I realised the reason for his attitude – he wanted promotion. Therefore, a spell in the Training Centre was an extra qualification that the promotion panel would consider. I believe it was a qualification he had to have and the sooner the better as far as he was concerned.

One morning soon after roll call we were all ordered to line up in the drill yard with three other squads of recruits for a physical training workout. Yet another new face appeared to put us through our paces. Sub-Officer Norman Rose introduced himself and immediately stamped his authority on the accumulation of not-so-fit recruits, as he put us through a somewhat demanding routine. At the end of the session we were all feeling good about our labours, only to be shot down in flames by Rose who described our efforts as being worse than a crowd of old women. Most of us took the remark as being his way of telling us to do better next time but one individual complained to the Training Centre Commandant, he objected to being compared to an old woman. Word went around that Sub-Officer Rose had been carpeted for the remarks so the next time that we paraded prior to our physical training session we didn't know what to expect.

Standing in silence all eyes were focussed on Sub-Officer Rose as he slowly studied the expressions on the sea of faces before him. That was the first time I noticed his ability to react to a situation with a mean look on his face. Little did I know that it wouldn't be the last time? After a lengthy pause, long enough to cause a little bit of anxiety among us, he said in a loud voice, "Right you lot, put your bloody handbags down and begin running on the spot."

Bishop was right, training was hard and we did begin to enjoy it, even though it became physically and mentally tiring. On the drill ground we worked hard, in the classroom and in our own time we studied hard. There was a great deal to digest and during question and answer periods, answers had to be speedily and correctly recalled. Individual progress was monitored by regular written examinations.

About three weeks into the course we began to show some noticeable improvement in our ability to use the equipment when fighting imaginary fires. We had progressed to the third floor of the drill tower on the dreaded hook ladder, the piece of equipment that sorted the men from the boys. All the men in the squad appeared happy at that point but we were all unsure about climbing the tower vertically to the fourth fifth and sixth floors, and to climb beyond that was unthinkable. Peter Pain, an ex-paratrooper in our squad, admitted that he would rather jump out of an aircraft than do hook ladder drill.

The hook ladder was thirteen feet four inches long, weighing between twenty-four and twenty-eight pounds. Protruding from the front, at the top of the ladder, was a high tensile steel ring which the climber could hook on to when wearing a hook belt. A steel hook with teeth on its underside, for gripping on to window sills and parapets, protruded from the back of the ladder behind the steel ring. The hook terminated with a six-inch bill at its end, to prevent it from slipping or being pulled from the sill as it was climbed and on each string at the bottom of the ladder there were toe pieces which rested against the building preventing the ladder from pressing against the building, which allowed space for the toe area of the climber's boots. The purpose of the ladder was for use in places where a traditional ladder could not be deployed, such as at the rear of a building with no access around the sides, or for an extra extension from the top of a traditional ladder, to gain access to upper floors that could not otherwise be reached. A climber always carried a lowering line on his back because the only way to rescue a person was to lower them to the ground on a line.

One of my many faults is to respond to anything that had a double meaning, with a stupid remark. I soon learned that Pearce didn't like any kind of joke and a couple of times when the squad responded to my stupidity with laughter, Pearce reacted with disapproval. One day after a lecture he held me back to tell me so while all the other men rushed off for their tea break. He often asked me difficult questions during training in the hope of belittling me in front of the others in the squad, nothing hard about that, so no points gained there, Mr Pearce. I believe, with hindsight, we had an instant dislike for each other the first time we met.

The time came when we were to be shown the correct method of carrying an insensible person down a ladder. The head of the escape ladder was pitched into the third floor window of the drill tower where we were all gathered inside. Pearce was standing on the windowsill, facing us, and holding on to the top round of the ladder with one hand. He began to describe the correct method of mounting the ladder when carrying a body. Then he decided to demonstrate how it was done with a body on his shoulders. I won't ask you to guess who he chose to be the body. Pearce draped me across his shoulders, stood upon the windowsill and began to demonstrate how to get the body in the correct position for carrying down the ladder.

He bumped me up and down on his shoulders whilst standing on the sill, my head hanging out of the window which presented a very unusual view of the drill yard below. Then he swung out of the window on to the ladder, talking all the time, then back in again, more bumping up and down, then out on to the ladder again. He then decided to demonstrate how to reposition a body if it started to slip during the carry-down, more bumping up and down. All the time I was staring at the ground from a height of thirty-five feet, hoping and praying that Pearce didn't slip or drop me. I believe he really got the message across that day that he didn't like me very much. I can assure you that the feeling was mutual. The carry-down method of rescue became the most practised. Incorporated in our training programme was at least one carry-down every day until it became such a routine that we didn't even think about it.

Because we were partly trained and had qualified in first aid, the squad was allowed to wear undress uniform outside the training centre. The first time I wore my uniform home, I found myself in an embarrassing situation. I was standing on a busy platform at London Bridge Railway Station feeling rather self-conscious because I was wearing my brand new cap, I didn't like caps. I was approached by an elderly lady who must have thought that I was a railway porter. She asked me the time of the next train to Dartford in Kent. I apologised and told her that I didn't know. When she started to tell me off, it dawned on me what had happened. Smiling and trying to be pleasant, I tried to explain that she had made a mistake and that I didn't work for the railway. The more I tried to explain the more angry she became. I then discovered that she was deaf and raising my voice made things even worse. It became embarrassing as people on the crowded platform began to stare, which made me begin to flush up. I remember thinking that all I need now is for her to whack me with her umbrella and that would really make my day.

From that day onwards I always tried to avoid travelling on public transport wearing my uniform especially my cap, so if I could not avoid wearing my uniform I would cover it by wearing a raincoat.

Pearce broke his hand whilst demonstrating how not to use the winch winding handles on the wheeled escape ladder. He was placed sick, unfit for work, so a third instructor took over our squad and we weren't even half way through the course. Sub-Officer Stollery took over the squad. His nickname was 'Horse', I'm not sure why but I believe it was because he was as strong as and built like one. The morale of the squad improved under the new instructor and our progress accelerated. We became more content and with that more confident and efficient. All but one man who failed the course agreed that it was worth the pain and suffering, from all the bumps and bruises. We enjoyed it and we felt good and fit with a sense of achievement. Horse Stollery was presented with a coffee percolator, probably to add to the other dozen from previous squads. We were all of the opinion that he had been a good instructor.

Our kit packed, we said our goodbyes and waited for transport to arrive from the respective divisions that we had been posted to. I was on my way to Old Kent Road Fire Station in the 'D' Division, South East London.

Old Kent Road was a two-appliance station housing a Pump Escape, that's the one that carried a fifty-foot wheeled escape ladder, and a Pump, which was a similar appliance but it carried a thirty-foot extension ladder instead of a wheeled escape.

The shift rota at that time was one week of day work followed by one week of night work with some rota leave days in between. There were two watches in those days, Red and Blue, working an average of sixty hours a week, over a six-week period. The pay was eleven pounds twenty-five pence a week, which included four hours compulsory overtime.

That's me, a long time ago.

No 1.

London Fire Brigade training squad passing out photograph.
I am second from the left front row, next to Sub-Officer Stollery.

Hook ladder drill.

Chapter 4

Red watch was on duty the day I arrived at Old Kent Road Fire Station to begin my career as an operational fireman. Filled with apprehension I reported to the station watch-room, the nerve centre in every fire station. I didn't realise it then but many long lonely wakeful nights were to be spent sitting in that watch-room. The duty-man phoned through to the station office to inform the officer in charge that I was on the station. Eventually a leading fireman came to the watch-room. He seemed quite old to me, I couldn't imagine him running up a ladder, or running anywhere really.

"What's your name mate?" he asked.

"Fireman Franks," I replied, "I was told I was joining the Blue Watch."

After looking me up and down he turned on his heels.

"Come with me," he muttered, beckoning me with a twitch of his forefinger.

I followed him across the appliance room, that's where the fire engines are garaged, into a room in the far corner. As I went in I noticed the sign on the door, 'Station Office'.

"This is Fireman Franks, Governor," he said to the station officer who was sitting at a desk reading a newspaper.

"Oh yes!" he replied, hardly raising his eyes from the paper.

"He's joining Blue Watch," continued the leading fireman.

"Oh yes!" said the station officer with the skill of a ventriloquist. In the same indifferent tone he mumbled, "Give him a locker and show him where to hang his fire gear."

After stowing my personal equipment in my allotted locker and hanging up my fire gear in the appropriate place, I returned to the station office. I knocked on the half open door but there wasn't a reply. I stepped inside and asked the station officer when I should report for duty. He mumbled his reply without raising his eyes:

"Ask the leading fireman."

"Yes, Sir," I said as I backed out of the office.

Walking back to the watch-room across the appliance room, I stopped for a moment to look at the two fire appliances (the public call them fire engines). Large shiny red vehicles with all doors wide open resembling wings, looking like a pair of huge dragons waiting to burst into life at the touch of a button, ready to roar into action in seconds.

It was then that I realised that I wasn't playing at being a fireman anymore as the squad did in the training centre, this was the real thing. Next time that I report for duty I will be a member of a proper operational crew, I thought. I wondered if the public would notice that I was fresh from the training centre and that I had never seen a house on fire, never mind dashing inside to rescue somebody. The thought of it gave me a touch of the collywobbles along with a feeling of great excitement.

The leading fireman was in the watch-room instructing the duty-man to record my arrival in the Station Occurrence Log Book. Everything that happens in a fire station is logged, including all visitors. I was told to report for duty the following Monday morning, early enough to be on parade in the appliance room, dressed in full fire gear, ready for roll-call at two minutes to nine.

The leading fireman showed me around the station and introduced me to some of the red watch men. They all appeared a lot older than me, especially those that joined at the end of the war and more so the Auxiliary Fire Service members who had served all through the war and were now full time London Fire Brigade members. I felt very inadequate amongst so much experience. We chatted over a cup of tea and I made the mistake of asking what the men on the blue watch were like. They set me up of course. I left the station believing that I was going to have to work with a bunch of crooks, gays and rapists.

I awoke early Monday morning, looking forward to my first day on duty as a fully trained member of a professional fire-fighting team. I arrived at Old Kent Road Fire Station with plenty of time to spare before roll-call, to allow myself to get rigged in my fire gear. Standing alone, fully booted and spurred in the appliance room, wearing my brand new shiny fire helmet, looking like something straight out of a Christmas cracker and feeling a prize twit as I waited. I couldn't help wondering if I had been set up. I was relieved when gradually the watch members began to assemble, similarly dressed but not so new looking, shouting their greetings to each other and some obscenities, at the same time giving me a nod and an inquisitive smile.

The duty-man gave four short rings on the station house bells indicating roll-call time, just as the sub-officer walked across the appliance room from the station office and shouted:

"Fall in!"

With a shuffling of boots we all formed a line between the two appliances in the centre of the appliance room.

Sub-Officer Carter was about five feet ten inches tall, good looking with large white teeth, a firm chin and a broad chest. He was about forty years old and as he walked I noticed that he was slightly pigeon-toed.

Blue Watch, standing in a single row between the fire engines with me tacked on the end, was called to attention. We began to answer our names as Carter called the roll. He then detailed the riders, driver and breathing apparatus wearers for the Pump and then the crew for the Pump Escape for that duty. I was detailed to ride the Pump Escape, the fire engine that carried the large wheeled escape ladder on its back, referred to as the P.E.

Station Officer Mullaney was the officer in charge of the Blue Watch, I could see him hovering in the background as the roll-call was being taken.

"I will see him in the office when you have finished with him sub," shouted Mullaney.

"OK, Guv!" replied Sub-Officer Carter.

"Oi! old Franksy," Carter shouted as he walked back to the station office.

"Put your gear in the back of the P.E. between the other two riders, then come and see me. Put it in the middle, it's no good you jumping out first because you won't know if your arse is punched, bored or countersunk when we get a shout."

There are many expressions in the fire brigade, some are old naval sayings and some are not, 'shout' means an emergency call.

I placed my fire gear in the rear cabin of the P.E. noticing that there did not appear to be very much room to get rigged, especially while being thrown about when driven at speed through heavy traffic.

I stood in the office in front of Sub-Officer Carter, as he went to great lengths to convince me that I was quite useless to him, like a piece of dead wood that had to be carried along with the flow, is how he described me.

"Listen to me," he said stepping a pace closer to emphasise his point. "I want you right up my arse when we get a shout, if I turn round and you're not there you will be in trouble, understand? We don't want to lose you because it causes a lot of writing."

"Thank you very much," I muttered.

"Now clear off upstairs and have a cup of tea, the Governor will see you later," he said over his shoulder as he walked towards his desk, where his cup of tea had been placed by the mess manager.

Station Officer Mullaney interviewed me and outlined what he expected from me. He reminded me that my first year was probationary and that I would be watched very carefully. I was told that a report on my progress would be forwarded to the divisional headquarters in six months and a final report after a year. After asking me if I understood, he told me to report to the sub-officer for station work.

Presenting me with a galvanised metal bucket, a large bar of yellow soap, a scrubbing brush, a kneeling pad and a tin of red cardinal polish, the sub-officer led me to a ground floor toilet and told me to clean it. He instructed me to scrub and polish the tiled floor and not to forget to polish the brass doorknob. He walked away leaving me with my jaw hanging open. My mind flashed back to the 'bulling-up' in the army and the boredom of the factory. I wasn't a happy fireman at that point.

I stood looking at the toilet bowl for a couple of minutes and wondered whether I would have to clean all the other toilets in the station. When I had finished that one I went upstairs to one of the other toilets and was surprised to see one of the older hands cleaning it, he even seemed to be enjoying it. Having seen some nasty tricks played on recruits in the army must have made me a bit wary of being set up. From then on I decided to show willing and get on with it.

All other jobs completed just before 1100 hours, I put the cleaning equipment away and went up to the mess room on the first floor for a cup of tea, just as the duty-man rang six short bursts on the bells to indicate stand easy. The areas of the station cleaned by the rest of the watch looked spotless. They obviously took a pride in how the station looked and, of course, the fire engines gleamed.

Feeling more relaxed during stand easy, I chatted to some of the others. I was told that another recruit, Tom Wade, had been posted in about two weeks before me but he was on rota leave. His brother-in-law, Harry Tobin, an older hand on the watch, reckoned that Tom would be 'over the moon' when he found out that he was not the junior buck any more.

Every day with the exception of weekends, as a regular part of station routine, the watch paraded in the drill yard for a drill session. The station officer or the sub-officer would detail a drill, incorporating the use of different items of equipment, so that we all remained familiar with its use and at the same time kept all the personnel on the nearly fit side of not very fit. The drill yard was very small at the Old Kent Road station and the drills that could be performed with ladders were limited. The speed at which the older hands did their drills was like a snail's pace compared to that in the training centre, so I found it strange at first, expecting the officer taking the drill to start yelling at us to get a move on. The drill period on my first day took us up to lunch time.

At the latter part of the lunch hour while we were all sitting around relaxing and chatting, well I was mostly listening, I had my first shout. The bells were so loud and sudden, I must have left a space between my arse and the chair, when I landed I was so startled that I just sat there for a few seconds, as all the others disappeared from the room. Realising that this was a real fire call I gathered my senses and ran to the sliding pole. I grabbed hold of the pole and before I knew it I had landed with a thump on the rubber mat at its base. A few large strides and I was clambering into the rear cabin of the P.E. where the other two crew members were already rigging in their fire gear. Actually all of the crew were on board before me and the driver had started the engine. The duty-man ran from the watch-room shouting the address and handed Sub-Officer Carter, whose riding position was in the front next to the driver, an order slip with the address of the fire written on it. After pulling the door release rope to open the appliance room doors of the P.E. bay the duty-man ran to the pump to repeat the operation for the pump's crew. The P.E. bay doors sprung open with a loud crash, and with my heart pounding I was on my way to my first real fire.

Fascinated by the sound generated by the revving of the engine as the driver changed up and down through the gears and the rhythmic clanging of the fire bell by Sub-Officer Carter, I was conscious of my accelerating heartbeat as we were being driven at speed along Old Kent Road. I couldn't get rigged quickly enough, a great surge of excitement flowed through me and then panic because I couldn't pull one of my leggings up properly, then I couldn't find my belt and axe. Finally fully rigged, I stared with anticipation past the driver trying to see ahead for any sign of a fire.

I noticed the public turning to look in our direction, as the sound of fire engine bells filled the air. I saw motorists giving way as we weaved our way through the traffic not knowing where we were going. I was a bit disappointed when we pulled up outside a house with not as much as a wisp of smoke in sight.

Those men sitting either side of me jumped out of the cab at the same time, the change in the engine tone indicated that the driver had engaged the pump ready to pump water. As I scrambled out of the rear cabin I heard the crash and bang from the lockers as equipment was being pulled out. I could see that the hose-reel tubing, that's the thin hose that is stored wound on a drum which is normally permanently charged with water, had already been taken into the house through the front door. The pump's crew had arrived and were busy assisting the P.E.'s crew. I had by that time already completed a couple of laps of the P.E., turned a couple of circles and was beginning to feel a bit foolish. Fortunately Station Officer Mullaney who was riding in charge of the Pump had not noticed my antics.

Fire engines have the habit of attracting crowds and the two from Old Kent Road were no exception. I felt that everyone was looking at me. It must have been written all over me that I didn't have a clue, everything that I thought of doing had already been done.

"Oi!" someone shouted from an upstairs window.

I looked up to see Carter looking at me.

"Blimey," I said aloud, "I'm supposed to be with him."

"What the bloody hell are you doing down there?" he shouted: "Get a bucket and bring it up here."

Feeling a prize twit and even a bigger twit, after opening three lockers on the fire engine before I found a bucket, I took it into the house, my face burning with embarrassment. Following the hose reel tubing I arrived upstairs in a room at the rear of the house. The smoke in the room made my eyes water and I began to want to cough. Doing my best to suppress my cough and trying to look as though the smoke wasn't affecting me I presented the sub-officer with the bucket.

"I thought I told you to stay with me, Franksy," Carter barked.

"Sorry, Sub," I spluttered.

"Help get this settee downstairs and into the back garden," he spluttered back.

The fire had been in an old settee which was stuffed with horse hair, it was a heavy old thing that gave off a dreadful stink as it still smouldered. We struggled down the stairs with it and into the garden where the job of extinguishing it was completed.

On the return journey to the station, Carter turned in his seat and peered into the rear of the cab, he looked at me and snapped:

"What the bloody hell happened to you then?"

"I don't know, Sub," I replied, "By the time I had got out of the cab you had gone."

"Well you had better make sure that you are a bit faster next time hadn't you, lad?" he said with the hint of a little smile in his face.

I looked at one of the older hands in the cab who also smiled and gave me a knowing wink of his eye.

As the days passed I gradually got into the routine of fire station life. I attended a few more calls, only to small fires but they served the purpose of breaking me in slowly. The other new recruit Tom Wade and I got on well together, when one of us was on rota leave the other would hope for a big fire so that he could boast about it. That little game developed into a kind of competition to see who attended the largest fire.

The size of a fire is classified by the number of fire engines that are required to deal with it. For instance, if ten pumps were required to deal with a fire, then that fire would be referred to as a ten pump fire. The senior officer in charge of the first attendance to any incident is responsible for assessing the number of crews that he requires to fight a fire or deal with the incident and as a general rule, one fire engine will provide one crew. If more fire engines than those ordered on a predetermined first attendance are required, then a priority assistance radio message is dispatched to the brigade's control. That message is generally referred to as a 'make-up'. The higher the number of fire engines attending a 'make-up' the higher the rank the officer in charge must be.

When a make-up message is received in the Brigade Control Room, the Area Controller is responsible for ordering the required number of fire engines to the fire and the appropriate number and ranks of senior offices.

My first make-up came one afternoon as a welcome interruption to station work. The officer in charge of New Cross Fire Station made pumps four, at a hairdresser's shop in New Cross Road. Our pump, with Mullaney in charge was ordered to the fire as part of the first attendance, along with the pump escape and pump from New

Cross, three fire engines being the normal first attendance for that area. The P.E. from my station was ordered on by control, as the fourth fire engine, on receipt of the make-up message.

The fire was just over the boundary of our station's area, about a mile and a bit away so it only took about two minutes to get there through the traffic. Thick black smoke was belching from the front of the shop and, as we arrived, it developed into a long tongue of orange flame shooting out about fifteen feet from the front of the shop and licking up the front of the three-storey building.

Two lines of hose, one being taken round the back of the shop and one lying in large flaked bights in the road in front of the shop, had been laid out from a pump which had been connected by two other lengths of hose to a street fire hydrant. As there was only one man on the branch (the branch is the piece of equipment connected to the end of the hose that forms the jet of water), I ran to back him up just as water burst with a splutter and a loud crack, from the jet.

The branch man directed the jet deep into the shop towards the seat of the fire, while I took the weight of the hose directly behind him. He knocked the flames back and we managed to work our way into what was left of the entrance of the shop. The branch man had taken quite a bit of smoke by that time and was out of breath from laying out the hose before Old Kent Road's P.E. arrived. He indicated that he needed some fresh air so I took the branch from him. I continued to hit the fire with the jet of water but I too began to feel the effects of the smoke and heat, plus the exertion of manhandling the charged length of hose on my own.

I could hear bangs and crashes coming from the back of the shop, along with more flames and dense smoke making it impossible to see. The weight of the hose suddenly got lighter, I knew then that someone was behind me backing me up, so I began to move the jet about and push forward.

"Hold it! Hold it!" shouted a familiar voice.

Nobby Pegler, a cheerful likeable man who had been a fireman for many years, was behind me. An experienced fireman, good at his job, he had noticed that I had been left on my own on the branch and that wasn't good fireman-ship.

"Knock that jet off!" he shouted.

The hand controlled branch that I was using, had the facility by moving a lever, to turn the jet of water off.

"Give me the branch," Nobby spluttered.

I didn't argue.

"Now get right down near the floor," he said, pushing down on my shoulder.

Nobby was obviously aware that I was having extreme difficulty in breathing and sure enough it was a bit more bearable lower down. Although the basic techniques of fire-fighting are taught during training, a lot of them do not really mean anything until they are experienced on the fire ground.

"Now take your time," he said as he directed the jet above our heads and across the ceiling.

"That's cleared anything that's likely to fall on our heads," he spluttered.

Systematically he worked the jet of water around the shop, gradually edging forward.

"Check the floor in front of you as we move forward," he shouted. "There's a basement under us and the floor may have gone."

We made our way to the back of the shop where we met another crew who had brought the second branch in from the rear of the shop.

Thanks to Nobby Pegler I learnt a lot at that first make-up. In the excitement and heat of the moment I hadn't remembered what I had been taught during my training. It was then that I truly appreciated the need for regular training and lectures.

I began to enjoy the brigade more after that job. I became more confident and started to feel that I was part of a team and not just a piece of dead wood.

The competition between Tom Wade and me was pretty even, sometimes he would edge ahead and then much to his annoyance I would attend a make-up when he was on leave, and so it went on. The older hands on the watch heard about our little contest and when one of us was away, they would talk about some fictitious heroic deed that the other had performed at a big fire. Each of us in turn went home believing that the other had become a hero overnight. Following that wind-up, the competition died a natural death.

Having a good idea of my own capabilities at that early stage of my service, allowed me to comfortably handle working with the men that I had got to know on the watch but I wasn't too keen on the thought of 'standing-by' at another station and working with an unfamiliar crew.

Whenever a station was undermanned, somebody from a neighbouring station with surplus riders would be ordered to 'stand-by' at the undermanned station to keep a fire engine on the run.

One day I was ordered to stand-by on the Massey Shaw Fire Boat, at Lambeth's river station. The Massey Shaw Fire Boat was an ageing vessel with a bit of history – named after a Chief Fire Officer, it took part in the evacuation of Dunkirk during the Second World War.

Now, I wasn't much of a fireman at that stage but I was even less of a sailor. When I arrived at the river station I was roped in for station work. I was detailed to clean out the skiff, the small rowing boat that was towed behind the fireboat. It was difficult to stand still in the little boat due to the constant rocking caused by the bow waves of passing river traffic. Every time I bent down to rinse my deck cloth, the water in my bucket slopped against the sides and up into my face. After being subjected to that treatment for about an hour I began to turn green. I'm probably the only person to become seasick in a boat on the River Thames, while it was still tied to its mooring. Fortunately the river station was not very busy. No emergency calls were received so I was able to recover on dry land. I never did find out whether or not I was set up for that treatment in the Skiff.

After several weeks of being at Old Kent Road Fire Station, it was easier to count the months to determine the time that I had been an operational fireman. I was getting used to station life but the fact that we were supplied with beds and bedding and were allowed to rest between the hours of 2300 and 0700 and get paid for it, was still hard for me to believe. After a quiet night it wasn't unusual to wake up refreshed and ready for the day ahead, even though a fifteen-hour night shift had just been completed. As a consequence of sleeping on duty, part-time work between shifts was widely practised and had almost become a tradition. Although illegal, as far as the brigade was concerned, most firemen did it.

A chap on the red watch had organised a job for Tom Wade and me to do between night shifts. It was a welcome boost to my income but being manual work, it was particularly hard following a busy night at the station. The reverse was also difficult to deal with. A busy night following a hard day's part-time work took its toll with regard to reserves of energy.

I reported for duty one evening after a particularly hard day, working part-time. It was my second consecutive night duty. The first night was quite busy, being turned out on two shouts during the early hours. However, I went to bed hoping for a quiet night and must have fallen into a very deep sleep. I recalled hearing bells ringing and even being aware of the station lights being switched on. The station lights are switched on automatically by brigade control, when they relay the emergency call to the station. Tom Wade told me that he saw me sit up and thought that I was awake but I couldn't have fully awoken. I must have laid down again. Suddenly I became aware of the sound of revving engines in the distance. Struck with horror, I jumped out of bed and ran to the sliding pole. I hit the rubber mat at the base of the pole with a thump and bounded across the appliance room. I scrambled into the rear cabin of the P.E. on the opposite side to my riding position, just as the driver began to pull away. I was horrified to see my door swing open as the driver turned left into Old Kent Road. Launching myself across the cabin, I managed to pull the door shut.

Relieved at not missing the call I began to get rigged. Missing an emergency call is the ultimate crime in the Fire Brigade, carrying a penalty just short of death. Suddenly I was stricken with panic. Horror must have been written all over my face because Tom asked me if I was feeling all right.

"Shit!" I screamed as I searched amongst the tools and equipment carried in the rear cabin.

"I've only got one bloody boot."

One of my fire boots must have fallen out as the door swung open. I shouted at the driver but I don't know what I expected him to do about it, because at that moment, the only thing on the minds of the rest of the crew, was the dull orange glow in the sky ahead.

Sub-Officer Carter turned in his seat and said through gritted teeth, "Franksy, you stupid idiot," or words to that effect, "Stay in the cab and keep out of sight, it looks like we've got a bloody make-up here."

Up to that time I had not seen him show so much aggression. Sure enough, when we arrived at the fire it had already broken through the roof and was belching out of the front first-floor windows of the two-storey terraced house. People were shouting at us that there was somebody in there, so a priority message "Make pumps four, persons reported," was dispatched over the radio.

When somebody is thought to be involved in a fire, the phrase 'persons reported' is always added to the make-up message.

Trying hard to stay out of sight and at the same time, desperate to see what was going on, I crouched in the rear cabin of the P.E. Within a few minutes the divisional officer arrived, the last thing I wanted was for him to discover me so I laid on the floor of the cab. I must have been there for three hours, cold, uncomfortable and thoroughly pissed off. What made things worse, was when I heard the end of a message sent to Control.

"One female found in back room on first floor apparently dead, request attendance of police."

I was very relieved when the crew eventually returned to the fire engine, looking worn out and probably even happier than me to return to the station.

Back at the station my boot had been placed right in the middle of the floor in the brightly-lit appliance room for all to see. A passing taxi driver had found it in the middle of the road and taken it into the station. The duty-man had displayed it and attached a note saying: 'Wanted, a one-legged Fireman.' I don't know what everyone laughed at because I didn't think it was at all funny.

Up to that point, I wasn't the sub-officer's favourite and that little mishap didn't help matters at all. He gave me a severe bollocking and Station Officer Mullaney reminded me of my pending probation report.

Time passed and that episode faded to the back of my mind. I was almost ready to be sent to the divisional headquarters to sit my watch-room examination, which I had to pass before I could take my turn as the duty-man, or take my turn in the 'Box', as it was known.

Unknown to me, while I was undergoing watch-room instruction one afternoon, Station Officer Mullaney arranged with brigade control, for a test call to be sent to the station. The duty-man Ted Woolhouse, who was instructing me, was aware of the set-up and at a given signal from Mullaney, he asked me to look after the watch-room while he went to the toilet. Before I could say anything he was gone and within a few seconds all hell broke loose. Bells started to ring, buzzers sounded, lights flashed, the whole switchboard seemed to light up.

My reaction to the situation was classic. I ran out of the watch-room to the toilet shouting:

"Ted! Ted! You've got a fire call."

He didn't answer so I banged on the door again, still shouting. Ted opened the toilet door a little and whispered. "Go and answer it, stupid, the Governor's watching you, it's a test call."

"Oh shit!" I said out loud, "I've done it again."

Dashing back to the watch-room I flicked the appropriate switches and took the call. Mullaney wasn't too happy with my performance but when I was able to tell him exactly how to get to the address of the imaginary fire call, he was very impressed. He thought I had been studying the local topography but by coincidence, the address of the imaginary fire call was to the road where I worked part-time. How lucky can you get? Soon after that I qualified in watch-room procedure and began to take my turn in the box.

Tom and I knocked off from our part-time job one afternoon and took a leisurely walk to the fire station to get ready for the night shift. We spoke about the incidents that we had attended since we had been in the brigade and what the night may have in store for us, it was the unknown that made the job so exciting.

Soon after reporting for duty that evening, at about twenty minutes past six, we received a call to a person trapped under a bus in Walworth Road near Carter Street Police Station. Before we left the station we had to load a special large heavy jack, known as the draper jack, onto the pump. The draper jack was the property of the London Transport Executive. The jacks were distributed to selected stations throughout London, specifically for use with London buses. Like some other specialised equipment the draper jack was not carried as a regular item but was classified as a 'Non Mobile Special'. It was only ordered onto an incident when it had been requested, or when it was known to be required. It took the strength of four men to lift and stow it on the pump and likewise to remove it.

I had attended a couple of minor road accidents that only needed our attendance to wash down and clear the road but I didn't know what to expect from this one. The three minutes that it took for us to arrive at the scene was enough for me to brace myself and prepare for the worst.

A double-decker London Transport bus was parked at an angle in the roadway, about five feet from the pavement. A crowd had gathered and were all jockeying for the best positions to see what was going on.

At first glance there didn't appear to be anybody involved. Mullaney ordered us to remove the jack and get it in position ready to jack the bus up. Leading Fireman Gifford, an old hand ready for retirement, crawled under the bus to assess the injuries of the casualty. As the bus was raised on the jack, I could see what I thought was a bundle of clothing. On closer examination I noticed a pair of legs and an arm protruding from the bundle and realised that the victim was a woman. Her shoes were missing and her stockings were almost non-existent on her badly lacerated legs.

One of the older and experienced hands on the watch, George White, muttered, "Poor old girl, she's had it." I looked at him a bit disapprovingly as he continued, "They rarely go beyond the front axle and live to tell the tale, Bob."

I didn't say anything, I just swallowed hard.

An ambulance crew prepared a stretcher and the woman, who was probably approaching eighty years old, was rolled on to a canvas salvage sheet and pulled from under the bus.

There wasn't a great deal of blood but by the shape of her limbs she suffered a lot of broken bones when she was hit and rolled under the bus. As she was carried to the ambulance her arm slipped from under the bright red blanket that covered her, and hung loosely from the stretcher. I happened to be nearest so I instinctively took hold of her hand and replaced it under the blanket, noticing as I did so, that her arm was bent in all the wrong places.

I didn't say much on the return journey to the station, but I remember wondering if there was an old man somewhere, waiting for his wife of many years to come home, only to be shocked by the bearer of bad news in a policeman's uniform knocking on his door. Or if she was on her way to visit her family and had left them wondering why she had not arrived. Although the incident was over for us and we were waiting for the next shout, the shock and upset was just about to begin for somebody else. I felt very sad about the whole episode. It was 2015 hours when we arrived back at the station, just in time for supper, anaemic meat pie soaked in insipid-looking gravy.

In the 'box' one night duty, sitting alone reading a magazine, leaning back in the watch-room chair with my feet on the desk, I heard someone walking along the passageway leading from the front door. Most of the men were upstairs either watching the television or lounging in the easy chairs, inspecting the back of their eyelids. I didn't take much notice even when the watch-room door opened because there was always someone wandering about the station. Aware of the silence, I glanced up to discover a very angry senior officer glaring down at me, tight-lipped and scowling. Recognising the erect figure as Assistant Divisional Officer Bowles, I sprang instantly to my feet.

When a senior officer visited a station the duty-man had a set procedure that he had to perform. That procedure included information that reflected the current state of readiness of the station. The duty-man should stand to attention and state his name, the fire appliances available and the name of the officer in charge of the station. He then had to ring one short blast on the station call bells to summon the officer in charge to the watch-room, and then inform the divisional headquarters that the senior officer was in attendance.

I stood looking at him, waiting for his reaction to finding me in such a relaxed situation, in the nerve centre of the station. After a short pause, while we stood staring at each other, he broke the silence. Speaking very slowly he said:

"What is your name, fireman?"

"Fireman Franks, Sir," I replied faltering over my own name.

Realising that I had not reported in the correct manner, I stammered through the reporting procedure ending with, "Station Officer Mullaney in charge, Sir."

Then I rang one short blast on the house bells.

The A.D.O. turned and walked to the watch-room door and stood with his hands behind his back, waiting for the officer in charge to appear.

I thought that I might just have got away with being caught out when Sub-Officer Carter appeared. I got a tingling feeling at the back of my neck when I remembered that Station Officer Mullaney was on leave.

"Crying out loud," I muttered, "I've cocked it up again."

"Are you in charge of the station?" asked the A.D.O.

"Yes, sir," replied Carter in a questioning tone, not knowing what had gone on previously.

Sub-Officer Carter glanced towards me as I stood staring at them both with my hand on my forehead and my mouth wide open.

"In the office!" the A.D.O. said abruptly to Carter as he marched off across the appliance room to the station office.

Sub-Officer Carter glanced at me curiously then followed the A.D.O. I sat down and put my head in my hands to await the worst.

All of the log bookings completed I waited for the inevitable. After about one hour I heard sounds outside the watch-room. I glanced towards the door just as Sub-Officer Carter burst in looking as though he was ready to kill.

"Book the A.D.O. out, you useless no good bloody idiot," he shouted. "What the bloody hell am I going to do with you?"

He tongue lashed me with every expletive that entered his head. Finally he walked towards the door shaking his head. He stopped for a moment, turned and shook his head again and in an exasperated voice he said:

"You could cock anything up, Franksy."

I couldn't help thinking that he was right. Thoroughly dejected, I sat in the watch-room looking at the clock on the wall – the time took forever to pass. My watch-room relief came in at 2300 hours, which allowed me to rest until 0300 hours, then back in the box until seven.

It seemed as though I had just fallen asleep when my relief shook me and said, "Come on, Bob, I've made a cup of tea, it's time to go down in the box again." I could have done without those few sweet words. I crept down the darkened staircase feeling cold and tired. After turning up the gas fire I sat down heavily in the watch-room chair to book myself on duty again in the log book. Looking up at the clock on the wall I stretched, yawned, shivered and said to myself, "Roll on nine o' clock."

Everything was quiet. All that could be heard was the slow even tick of the watch-room clock and I hate ticking clocks. I sat looking up at it watching the second hand jerk its way around its white face, again and again. Feeling thoroughly fed up I began to sort through various papers and magazines that had been secreted away in the first aid cupboard but my eyes were too tired to read. Sitting at the desk with my chin in my hands, I closed my eyes and thought about the events of the past day and the trouble I caused earlier in the evening, I almost nodded off. I woke up without any feeling in my right hand, I shook it and it began to tingle and feel very painful. Suddenly my arse left the watch-room chair as I was startled by the whole place erupting with bells and buzzers, the switchboard lit up and all the station lights came on.

I tried to pick up my pen but my hand was still numb and tingling, shaking it violently to get some life back into it, I managed to take hold of the pen. Grabbing the telephone with my left hand and throwing the switch connecting me with brigade control, I answered the call.

"Order your pump," a voice said, "to a fire."

Quickly I switched on the pump's indicator light which illuminated a green bulb in the appliance room. The voice continued at a fast dictation speed.

"In a shoe shop."

I was writing as fast as my numb hand would let me.

"Walworth Road near Camberwell Green, on Peckham's ground."

I dispatched the pump and returned to the watch-room where a couple of the P.E.'s crew were standing in front of the gas fire, warming their backsides. At least then I had some company, someone to talk to, to help pass the time. As we talked, control came on the line again to inform me of a message received from the officer in charge of Peckham's appliances. When appliances were at a fire, their home stations received all messages from that fire via brigade control, for entry in their station's log book. I accepted the message and told the two chaps standing by the fire that Peckham had made pumps four persons reported.

One of them remarked, "That's not very good this time of night," as they both walked from the watch-room into the appliance room to switch on the P.E.'s radio, to monitor follow-up messages from the fire.

They were not wrong. That fire was in a shoe shop with living accommodation on the two floors above. Starting in the shop on the ground floor, the fire spread up the staircase to the dwelling on the upper floors, whilst the five occupants slept. All five occupants died.

That was the general pattern of the job, one minute it was quiet and the next all hell would break loose.

With sixteen months service under my belt, twelve of them operational, everything seemed to be going well, a few little mishaps but no major cock-ups. I had been to many fires and special services and was learning fast. A 'Special Service' is an emergency call to anything other than a fire. Flooding, road traffic accidents, people trapped in machinery, they are all classed as special services.

I was waiting to attend a breathing apparatus course. As a qualified B.A. rider I could ride the pump more often. Because the station's three B.A. sets were carried on the pump, the B.A. qualification was necessary for members of that crew. It was the pump that was mostly ordered on to make-ups on other stations' ground so obviously, the pump's crew gained the most experience, and experience was what I wanted.

Station Officer Mullaney had completed my probation report and I had been to the divisional headquarters for my end of probation interview with the divisional officer. I was extremely happy with the way things were going, when one day during Mullany's annual leave, the D.O. visited the station.

The divisional officer was looking for a likely candidate to replace a man who had been promoted and posted from Lambeth Fire Station. During my training at Lambeth, I didn't like the look of the station and since I had been at Old Kent Road, I had heard stories about the place that I didn't like, plus the fact that I didn't think much of the place, when I had been there on stand-by duties.

Sub-Officer Carter didn't hesitate to put my name forward, a golden opportunity to get rid of me. I was summoned to the office and given the news, along with a load of rubbish about it being for my benefit and it could be easier to get promotion at Lambeth. My protest fell on deaf ears and I was due to report to Lambeth the next day. Carter did shake hands with me and he insisted that the posting was decided upon with my future in mind and the outcome would have been the same if Mullaney had been on duty but I couldn't help thinking that it was 'own back' time.

Lambeth Fire Station was large and unfriendly. It occupied the ground and first floor of the brigade headquarters building on the Albert Embankment, overlooking the River Thames. Housed in the basement was the main London Fire Brigade Control Room. There were scores of people working in the headquarters including non-uniformed admin staff, senior officers' families also lived within the complex. More than all those things, my main dislike was that it lacked the atmosphere that I had become accustomed to at the Old Kent Road Station.

Admittedly the scope for gaining more experience was greater at Lambeth. There were six appliances attached to the station, the pump escape and pump being the first line fire-fighting appliances; then there was the one hundred foot turntable ladder; my favourite the emergency tender was next in line as they were parked in the multi bay appliance room; then came the brigade's breakdown lorry and last but not least was the brigade's canteen van. The brigade's main fire control unit was also housed there, which was ordered to all incidents of eight pumps or more. Senior officers' official cars also edged their way into the appliance room but along with the control unit were not manned by station personnel. It was a big station and there were always a large number of bodies milling around.

The nearest that I had been to leaving the brigade at any time, was during the first few weeks at Lambeth. I became thoroughly demoralised by the place. It didn't even have a proper station mess room where we could all chat and swap stories, everybody had to use the main cafeteria, in a separate building. The men attached to the station were either older guys that had been there for years and would probably complete the whole of their thirty years' service there, or younger keen chaps, pushing for promotion, falling over themselves to get into the office to do the office work. That activity was purely to keep their names to the fore, so that they would be first in mind in the event of some acting up occurring, to cover sickness or courses etc. I was neither old nor keen.

It seemed to be a case of laugh at the governor's jokes if you wanted to get on, even if they weren't funny. It was like a boot licker's convention at times and very cliquey. As we paraded for roll-call one morning one of the older hands standing next to me happened to comment that I 'stood-by' there a lot. Indicating that I didn't understand what he meant, he repeated his question:

"You stand-by here a lot don't you?"

Suddenly it dawned on me that he and probably all the others, thought that I was performing regular out duties from another station, to make the numbers up.

I stared at him lost for words for a few seconds, and then with unintentional aggression in my voice I replied:

"Bloody hell, I've been posted here for the past three months."

"Oh!" he muttered raising his eyebrows and forcing a poor imitation of a smile.

That was what it was like in those days. The young men would push for promotion and move on to better things and the older men just carried on doing what they were paid for, not interested in anything or anyone new.

That was a very unsettling period and I began to dislike going on duty. It took me some time to come to terms with the situation but gradually I began to accept it, although I still would have liked a transfer out or back to Old Kent Road. There were three ways of getting out of Lambeth – leave the job, arrange a mutual exchange with somebody from another station, with similar qualifications, or get promotion.

The leading firemen and sub-officers that I came in contact with didn't appear to possess any special or outstanding abilities, so now and again the thought of sitting the leading fireman's written examination crossed my mind, perhaps seeing promotion as the best bet to get out of Lambeth. I didn't want to leave the job and there was no chance that anybody would volunteer to swap with me.

The best thing about being attached to Lambeth was the amount of calls that we received. Slum clearance in the area was in full swing. Tower blocks seemed to grow out of the ground almost overnight in the 1960s and families were moved from their two-up two-down terraced houses into those characterless monolithic structures. Streets of old houses were left empty for long periods, awaiting demolition. Inevitably, the less fortunate of our society made use of those old dwellings for shelter at night. They ripped up floorboards and pulled doors from their frames to use as fuel to keep warm. Consequently those old dwellings soon became dangerous derelict skeletons, especially at night, because of gaping holes and hundreds of rusty nails protruding from the exposed floor joists that were still in place. The painted front doors, displaying the numbers of the houses, that at one time shut out the world, were replaced by dark holes. Ugly emptiness replaced windows that used to be adorned with a variety of curtains and coloured drapes.

Generations had been born and raised in those old houses. I could imagine the sadness felt by some of the older residents, when the power of persuasion by the authorities beat them into submission and they finally and reluctantly moved. No garden out back, no vegetable patch, no flower borders, no little lawn, no cats, no dogs. That was the price paid to move into one of those vertical prisons, where if you were lucky the lift worked and you didn't have to climb the stairs to the fourteenth floor with your arms full of shopping.

Throughout London thousands of fires occurred in derelict premises and because of the unsafe structures of some of them, entering them was quite hazardous. However, those old buildings served a useful purpose to my generation of fire-fighters – they were ideal for serving one's apprenticeship. I believe that the experience I gained in one year fighting fires in derelict premises, would have taken about four or even five years, or possibly longer at a rural station. Those fires were mostly caused by children setting fire to rubbish inside and then watching the fire gradually spread, until somebody called the fire brigade. Tragically, on occasions there would be a drunk or a homeless person sleeping rough and firemen would discover a body or two inside, or they would be lying injured on the pavement outside where they had landed, after jumping from a window.

Out of the hundreds of fires that I attended during my first year at Lambeth, there is one that will always remain in my memory, probably because it was the first time that I actually had to rescue somebody on my own.

One morning, not long after roll-call we were called to a fire in Brook Drive, behind the Imperial War Museum, Lambeth. The P.E., pump and T.L. attended. I was riding the P.E. which was first to arrive at the scene. I saw smoke punching out with some force from a broken window on the second floor of a house, so I knew that a considerable fire was developing up there. Grabbing the hose-reel tubing, I ran to the front door, which was locked, so I opened it with my 'fireman's key', one thump from my size 10 fire boot to be exact. I bounded up the stairs to the second floor where I was met by a wall of smoke and heat.

Guided by the sound of spitting and crackling from the spreading fire as it was hungrily consuming the contents of the room, I crawled along the landing. Through a doorway on my right I could see a dull red glow which became brighter by the second, as it sucked in the fresh air that followed me up the stairs.

Lying flat on my stomach I could see into the room beneath the thick smoke layer which was down to about twelve inches from the floor, where I could just make out the figure of a man lying face upwards in the centre of the room. The acrid smoke was gripping my lungs but I knew that I had to try and get to him, that was my job, the public paid me and expected me and other firemen to help them in such emergencies.

The exertion of running up the stairs dragging the hose-reel tubing plus the shortage of oxygen began to tire me. The more out of breath I became the faster I panted and the faster I panted the more muck I breathed in. Common sense was telling me to back off and get out. I wondered where the rest of the crew were, why weren't they here helping me? With determination and an extra effort I crawled on my knees and elbows into the room. Coughing and almost vomiting, I spat phlegm from my lungs, my nose kept running as I continually tried to wipe the mucus away with the sleeve of my fire tunic. My eyes felt as though they were being bathed in a mixture of acid and grit. Grabbing the man by his clothing and mustering as much strength as possible, I managed to drag him out of the room and on to the landing.

Two other men arrived at my side and began to fight the fire. With a great deal of effort and determination, I managed to get the man, who could have been dead as far as I knew, on to my shoulders and carry him down to the first floor. Swiftly the remainder of the crew came to my aid and removed the man from my shoulders. I was then assisted down to the ground floor, still coughing up what felt like lumps of lung. I sat on the doorstep to recover while the crews of the other appliances that had arrived assisted in dealing with the fire.

The man involved, suffered from epilepsy. It appeared that he had a fit and knocked over a paraffin oil heater, which flared up setting fire to linoleum floor covering and the furniture in the room. Unfortunately the man suffered burns and a nasty gash above his eyebrow, which looked like a third eye. That was probably caused when his head made contact with the banisters as I carried him down the stairs. However, he did survive which made my discomfort and effort worthwhile.

From that day, it seemed that I was accepted more by the older hands, it was almost as though I had passed a test. In their eyes I had demonstrated that I could perform when faced with a difficult situation. They obviously didn't know that I was in two minds, whether to attempt the rescue or back off and that my instincts were telling me that I should back off. Anyway, I began to enjoy the job again and when after a while some younger men joined the Watch, life at Lambeth started to improve.

The date arrived for when I had to attend the breathing apparatus course that I was waiting for. After passing, I was qualified to ride the pump, which meant that I would be able to attend more fires, especially to make-ups, on other stations' ground.

On duty during an Easter bank holiday, we were all taking part in our favourite recreational activities like volley ball, snooker, darts or just watching television, when a call was received to train crash at Hercules Road, near Waterloo Station.

P.E., pump, T.L., E.T., and breakdown lorry – everything except the canteen van was ordered on to the incident.

Most of one side of Hercules Road consisted of railway arches and it was on the track above those railway arches that the collision occurred. The wheeled escape ladder was slipped from the back of the P.E. and pitched above the arches to the elevated track. Carrying selected items of equipment, several of us climbed up the escape ladder on to the track.

My first impression as I peered over the parapet was that the collision had occurred on the far side of a multiple track area and it didn't look too serious. Two trains, each about four carriages long, still upright, had locked together. The carriages seemed to be empty with only a handful of people standing on the track. The rear train had rammed into the back of a stationary train waiting at a signal, causing the second carriage of the rear train to jump the rails. The impact on the second carriage against the rear of the one in the front crushed the first compartment, reducing it to about a quarter of its original width. I made my way carefully across the track, taking care not to touch any electrified rails and watching for any trains still using the unaffected lines. I reached the damaged coach and climbed up to look inside the crumpled compartment.

A man was sitting on the far side of the compartment. To get in, I had to remove my fire helmet because the window opening had been reduced to a small gap. As I squeezed in, the man looking very pale and shocked turned his head and looked at me.

"Are you all right, mate?" I asked him, realising at once what a stupid question that was.

"It's my legs," he said, looking at his knees that were raised and almost in front of his face.

I have often seen the notices on trains asking passengers not to place their feet on the seats but apparently, that chap ignored the notice and it saved his legs and probably his life. He had his feet on the seat opposite him and when the impact came, the front edges of the two seats butted together and as the compartment was crushed, the edges of the seats raised under the man's knees, trapping his body on one side and his feet on the other, with his knee joints being prized apart, in the middle. As he was the only trapped live casualty, all of the available expertise was concentrated on his extrication. The E.T. crew, who were trained for just that type of incident, manhandled their equipment into position and with great care, prized the man free with jacks and levers. It took about thirty minutes to release him and more time to carry him along the track to Waterloo Station, where an ambulance was waiting to take him to hospital.

Exactly one year later, during the Easter holidays, I was on duty in the watch-room. A man limped into the station and handed me a five pound note. He said that he wanted to donate it to the Fire Services Benevolent Fund. He explained that it was in appreciation for the work done by the firemen, who rescued him from a train crash a year ago. I looked at him hard and realised who he was.

"Was the accident just outside of Waterloo Station?" I asked him.

"Yes," he replied looking at me. "You were there weren't you? I've got a photograph of you that someone gave me, I'll bring it in for you."

He went on to explain that he had received some compensation for his injuries and was lucky to be able to walk, but the case was still going on. He said then that had he been sitting with his feet on the floor at the time, he would have lost both of his legs from just below his knees. I told him how pleased I was to see him and after a while he left. I didn't expect to see him again but true to his word, he brought some photographs into the station a few days later and gave me one.

Like most firemen, the men at Lambeth worked part-time doing various jobs. Jock Pow, the organiser of part-time work on my watch, offered me the chance of earning some extra money, working in the carpet department of a large department store near Clapham Junction.

I jumped at the chance because I had given up my other job when I left Old Kent Road. The work involved handling large rolls of broadloom carpet, it was easier than my last job and it paid better. The trouble with working two jobs was that it didn't leave a lot of time for socialising or family life but I needed the money desperately at that time.

Jock Pow eventually transferred to Buckinghamshire Fire Brigade. A number of young married London firemen were tempted to transfer into the Bucks Brigade during the early sixties for the sole purpose of getting a nice new house that went with the job for their families. That was alright but for those destined for high places, promotion was much slower in Buckinghamshire. So they had to weigh-up the offer of a nice new house for their families against more prospects for promotion and a possible more affluent future in London.

Somebody had a great idea of having a watch outing to the coast. A trip to Littlehampton on the Sussex coast was arranged for a Saturday, following a Friday night duty. The idea was that everybody would be there after work, ready for a quick departure. Normally that would have been alright because we nearly always managed to get at least a little sleep during the night. That Friday night was worse than usual, we were all ordered to attend a twenty-pump fire at the warehouse of a company in Brixton, even the Canteen Van attended. We spent all night there, getting back just in time for breakfast. After showering and changing we boarded the coach and set off for Littlehampton. Before we were out of London the scene on the coach resembled a bus load of dossers, rather than a crowd of work mates out for a good time.

We arrived at Littlehampton and made a desperate attempt to brighten ourselves up. All agreed to be back at the coach pick-up point at five o'clock in the afternoon for the return journey, then we split up into groups. Tom Ford or Leading Fireman Ford the Fireman's Friend, as we used to call him, said that he would see us later and went to sit on a grassy patch under a tree for a rest. Off we went to have a good time in the amusement park and on the beach.

Time soon went by, as it does when you are having fun, so after a good day we made our way back to the pick-up point to join the others. It became the subject of great mirth when we discovered Tom Ford, lying where we had left him, sound asleep. His day out consisted of about a twenty-yard walk in Littlehampton, he only caught sight of the sea from the coach window.

Being a coach load of young men, the conversation on the way home was inevitably about women. Some of the lads called out or wolf-whistled at nearly every woman that the coach passed. By the time we approached London the driver had been persuaded to slow down so that a couple of the chaps could stand at the open door to invite some unsuspecting females into the coach for a lift. As a result of the consumption of a great deal of alcohol in a pub a few miles back, there was a lot of noise and laughter going on. During the hubbub the coach had stopped and two young women were persuaded to get on the coach. All eyes turned to the two female forms just as one of the instigators in favour of the idea, ran to the rear of the coach holding his forearm across his face. Those of us who noticed thought that he was feeling ill, until he started to pass the word along to turn the women off of the coach because one of them was his cousin and word might get back to his wife.

That was the worst thing that he could have said, everyone started shouting out, "Hello cousin."

I have never seen a man sober up so fast in my life since. I have visited Littlehampton several times since that day and every time I see that tree, I think of Leading Fireman Ford the Fireman's Friend. Although Tom passed away some time ago, it never fails to bring a smile to my face.

No 4.

**Train crash just outside Waterloo Station.
I am bottom left without my helmet.**

Chapter 5

Before I was allowed to drive fire engines I had to attend a brigade driving course, even though I had been taught to drive in a three-ton army lorry and already had a full driving licence, I still had to complete the brigade's driving course. After the course I returned to normal operational duties but my station officer would not allow me to drive any of the fire engines to an incident until I had learnt more of the station's ground and had become more familiar with the type of fire engines that we had on the run, which were not the same make as those attached to the driving school. That was understandable, so for a couple of weeks I was only allowed to drive our fire engines when returning from an incident, obviously within normal road traffic regulations.

When he had gained confidence in my driving ability, the governor allowed me to drive the P.E. to fires, probably because he always rode in charge of the pump. What a thrill it was to drive that ten-ton machine through the streets of London. Bells clanging, engine roaring, changing down through the gearbox at peak revs to negotiate bends, corners and traffic. I loved it, I did it thousands of times over the few years that I was a fireman driver, enjoying every minute of it, day and night.

The combined divisional headquarters building and fire station at Clapham was being rebuilt, so room to accommodate the divisional staff and their official vehicles had to be made at Lambeth. It was a convenient move, enabling Lambeth's drivers to be detailed to drive the senior officers' cars when the regular drivers were on leave or sick. That at least prevented the chore of carting fire gear etc, to Clapham on standby duty.

The stations that bordered Clapham's area, such as Brixton and Lambeth, each took a chunk of its fire ground to provide fire cover.

One particular day I was ordered to drive one of the senior officers' cars. In those days there were four senior officers running the division, two divisional officers and two assistant divisional officers.

I was standing in the appliance room going through the motions of polishing the D.O.'s car for about the third time, when the duty-man shouted from the watch-room door, that an ambulance had been requested for brigade personnel at an incident at Wyndham Road, on Old Kent Road's ground. Knowing that the D.O. would want to attend I went to the watch-room to get the details and then moved the car from the appliance room. I waited in the station yard with the engine running ready to go.

Within five minutes I was pulling up at the incident with a stern faced D.O. who didn't say very much on the journey. The incident was a small fire on the railway bridge over Wyndham Road. Old Kent Road's P.E. and pump and Peckham's pump were attending.

The wheeled escape had been pitched to the bridge and a hose-reel had been taken aloft. I saw Reg Webber one of Old Kent Road's crew and asked him what had happened. It didn't take any expert skills to notice that it was something very serious. Reg looking very grim and grey-faced he seemed to look through me rather than at me. He was in a shocked condition and just repeated.

"It's Tom Carter, it's Tom Carter." Then he walked away.

Looking around at some of the others I could see that nobody was in the talking mood and things were far from normal. My curiosity had to be satisfied so I climbed the escape ladder to the bridge and looked along to the track. The sight that greeted me could only be described as horrific. There were two bodies lying on the track, I recognised fire brigade clothing amongst the carnage and realised instantly what Reg Webber was trying to tell me.

Carter had recently been promoted to station officer and was in charge of Old Kent Road blue watch. His body was in a dreadfully mutilated condition having passed under the wheels of a speeding train, the other body was that of Fireman Bardens from blue watch Peckham.

My feelings at that moment could only be described as deep shock at the gruesome aftermath of the accident, especially as I had known the victims. Leading Fireman Joe Igglesden was also involved in the accident but fortunately he only suffered fractures and survived.

Fresh crews were ordered on to the scene to relieve those firemen traumatised by witnessing the accident. Because I was driving the divisional officer and he was in charge of the incident and responsible for recovering the bodies, I stayed until the job was completed.

The two bodies were wrapped in salvage sheets and placed on improvised stretchers made from short scaling ladders and carefully lowered to the ground using a T.L. rigged as a crane. As Station Officer Carter's body was being lowered, a torn, heavily blood-stained waist band of a pair of brigade uniform trousers hung from the wrapped bundle on the makeshift stretcher, indicating the severity of his injuries.

Station Officer Carter and Fireman Bardens died at Wyndham Road but fortunately Leading Fireman Igglesden recovered from his injuries. He did not return to operational duties but remained in the brigade for many more years. I believe that he completed more than thirty.

The shock of that tragic accident emphasised the dangers faced by firemen. The fact that even a small rubbish fire like the one at Wyndham Road could end in such a tragedy, should always be in one's mind. That incident brought home to me the fact that caution must be observed at all times for the safety of personnel, especially when working on or near railway tracks.

At that time the procedure adopted for such incidents, was to place two lookouts in safe positions, one each side of the incident. Their job was to look for approaching trains and to shout a warning to the crews working on the track, giving them plenty of time to get clear before the train reached them. I understand that on that fateful day, the correct procedure was followed and a warning was given as a train approached. The crew moved to a position between two tracks to wait for the approaching train to pass. Unknown to them a second train was approaching from the opposite direction on the track behind them. I believe that the lookout seeing the approaching train kept on shouting warnings at the top of his voice as the train got nearer, but his efforts to attract the attention of the crew standing between the two tracks were not heard over the noise from the first train passing. The carnage, hidden from view of the lookouts by the passing trains, was not revealed until both trains had passed by.

That accident resulted in a new procedure for fighting fires on railway tracks and the issue of a new piece of equipment known as the Railway Warning Horn. Two of the horns are carried on fire appliances for use by safety lookouts when working on or near railway tracks.

Although tragic incidents like that are not talked about very much, an image of such scenes remain permanently imprinted in the minds of those unfortunate enough to witness such an occurrence.

On the lighter side, something else I will never forget was when one of the older hands at Lambeth was jokingly told that the Queen was going to visit the station and a special display was to be staged just for her. That was without question believable for two reasons. Queen Elizabeth was going to be present at the London Fire Brigade's Annual Review that year and the crews at Lambeth often staged special displays for visiting dignitaries.

Having swallowed the story, he was told that he had been chosen to drive the E.T. and that he had to practise positioning it correctly in the station drill yard, then to dismount from the driver's cab, march smartly to a marked position beneath the balcony where the Queen was supposedly going to be sitting. He was to stand at attention for approximately three seconds and then salute. He got the performance off to perfection after practising it a few times over a couple of day duties. Then he was told to bull his boots up army-style and to have his best fire gear available for a dress rehearsal. He spent ages working on his boots that were deeply scarred and roughed up, as the result of tramping over debris at fires, but they eventually looked like glass.

Word went around that the dress rehearsal was imminent and almost everybody in the headquarters building and the station were hanging around not knowing what to expect. The victim, looking as smart as a guardsman, drove the E.T. into the station yard and parked it in the precise position. He dismounted and smartly marched to the predetermined spot, halted, waited for three seconds and smartly saluted.

At that precise moment, two firemen appeared on the balcony above him and each of them emptied a bucket of water over him. The shock of the cold water made him gasp and realising that he had been the victim of an enormous practical joke, he looked up and shouted long and loud: "Bastards."

Then followed up with three more short bursts of "Bastards! Bastards! Bastards!" As he attempted to shake some water from his tunic.

Nobody was safe after that little episode and one by one he got his revenge, just at the time when it was least expected. Things gradually settled down and in the end, he even saw the funny side of it himself.

The stories told by the older hands about emergency tender work fascinated me and made me eager to qualify to ride that appliance to widen my experience. At that time, the only special service calls that I attended were on Lambeth's own ground. One such call was to Waterloo Underground Station. A man had fallen, jumped or was pushed, in front of a tube train as it came into the station. He was a big man and he made a bit of a mess along the track. The largest part of the body that was in one piece was difficult to lift because of its weight and it was hard to manoeuvre in the restricted area between the rails. Added to that, because most of the his clothing had been ripped off there weren't many places to get a hand hold to lift him. Dave Crook, another young fireman, was told to go some way down the track to recover one of the man's shoes. His face was a picture when he returned with it because it still had the man's foot in it.

Eventually I attended an Emergency Tender course. That entailed more advanced breathing apparatus training, along with instruction and the practical application of all the tools, cutting gear, jacks, lifting and spreading gear and other specialised equipment that it carried. Qualifying was not plain sailing however. Station Officer Pearce, my training centre instructor for a time, was by then an assistant divisional officer and was one of the examining officers. He remembered me and it showed. I couldn't help feeling that he enjoyed putting the pressure on me during my tests.

As a trained E.T. man, I had what I had been looking forward to for some time – the opportunity to attend more special services and large fires anywhere in London.

There were only two E.T.s in the whole of the old London County Council's area at that time and the work load could be quite heavy. It wasn't uncommon in those days, to be ordered to an incident at the beginning of a shift and redirected to another one while on the way back to base. Sometimes that happened two or three times in succession and by the time we arrived back at the station it was often well into the afternoon or when on night shift the early hours of the morning.

Although there were many long runs to special services in the suburbs of London, it was surprising how many we attended quite close to the station. Amongst hundreds of run-of-the-mill calls to persons shut in lifts, minor road traffic accidents and spillage of chemicals etc., there were three that I remember quite clearly that happened almost on the station's doorstep, certainly within a very short walk.

The first call was from a man who came into the station at about eleven thirty at night. He said that he could hear a woman shouting for help in Whitgift Street, behind the station. We turned out and sure enough we could hear the feeble voice of a woman calling for help.

We pitched a ladder to the first floor at the rear of an old block of flats where we thought the call for help was coming from. In the beam of a searchlight we saw a woman, probably in her late seventies, hanging by her right leg from a row of old rusty iron railings. A spike from the railings had entered the back of her right thigh, about five inches from the cheek of her bottom. It had penetrated right through to the skin at the front, which was stretched tightly over the point of the railing, like canvas over a tent pole. While a couple of men supported her, others took turns in cutting through the railings with a hacksaw, being very careful not to cause too much vibration. She was talking all through the operation, only occasionally crying out with pain.

"I have been in the pub and I have lost my key, I was only trying to climb over the railings to get to my flat," she said.

Her main concern was not her injury but the fact that she wasn't wearing any knickers. As we worked in the beams of the searchlight and hand held torches, she kept repeating in a scornful voice.

"You boys stop looking at me, I've got no knickers on, you boys stop looking at me."

We talked and joked with her, she told us that her name was Kate and that she lived alone. When we had cut her free she was carried into her flat where ambulance men tried to dress her wound, before taking her to hospital to have the spike removed. While they were trying to dress the wound, accompanied by a yell from old Kate, the spike fell out.

A few weeks later, during the regular Saturday morning appliance room scrub-out using detergent and stiff bass brooms, I noticed old Kate hobbling past the station trying not to step in the streams of soapy water flowing from the appliance room into the gutter on its way to the drain in the street. I grasped her arm to assist her up on to the pavement and asked her how her leg was. She didn't answer my question she just raised her eyes and said, "Were you one of those naughty boys looking at me when I didn't have any knickers on?"

"Yes," I replied with a smile.

"Dear me," she muttered repeatedly as she toddled off along the road. "Dear me."

The second incident happened on a Saturday afternoon. We were playing volley ball in the station yard. Volley ball was the recognised method of fitness training in the brigade in those days and the teams took their games very seriously. We were in the middle of a close match, when a young boy about four years old came into the station yard. He ran on to the court and got in the way of the players, nearly getting himself knocked over. He was trying to say something but he couldn't be heard over the shouting of the annoyed players, telling him to go away. They didn't take too kindly to their games being interrupted by fire calls, never mind a small boy being a nuisance and getting in the way. The young boy persisted and someone shouted to me, because I was closest to him, to throw him out and close the yard gates. Taking hold of his arm I walked him out of the yard, telling him off in the process. He pointed down the road saying his friend was hurt. Because of his persistence I asked him to show me where his friend was. He ran about fifty yards along the road and stopped at the adjoining building. Pointing towards a short private access road, he kept repeating. "There! There!"

The road was only about 20 yards in length leading through an opening in the front of the building to allow access for vehicles to a loading bay. I couldn't see anybody in the access road but then the boy ran into the access road as far as the open door and pointed at the wall, still saying. "There! There!"

I walked to where the boy was pointing and realised that it was a recess, into which an automatically operated folding door concertinaed, leaving the road clear for vehicles to pass. I knelt on one knee and peered into the dark narrow gap between the folded door and the brick recess.

As my eyes became accustomed to the darkness I couldn't believe what I saw. I could just make out part of a little mauve coloured face and some fair hair. I ran back to the station as fast as I could to summon help and make a call of it. Some men grabbed what equipment they could carry and followed me back to the boy and the remainder brought the P.E. pump and E.T. to the scene and in a very short time we were battling away to release the poor little lad.

It took us about fifteen minutes to release the limp unconscious little boy, I was very concerned over the way he looked and when I saw him draw a breath I felt great relief.

I did not know for certain if he survived the ordeal or what injuries he suffered but I assume that he did survive because being the person who first discovered him, I would probably have been required to make a statement for the coroner and to attend an inquest.

It appeared that the two lads were playing in the access road, when a vehicle drove in, breaking an invisible beam which operated the folding door. On the sight of the approaching vehicle the two lads pressed themselves into opposite corners at the end of the access road, formed by the walls and the closed door. As the door opened it folded into its recess. The lad in the corner by the recess became trapped between the folds of the door and was dragged in, the driver thinking that there was only one child in the road, didn't realise what had happened.

The third local incident that happened during the early period that I spent at Lambeth in the rank of fireman, involved a man trapped in a lift. We received a call to a wine bottling company a short distance away from the station. I was driving the E.T. and had to get rigged in my fire gear directly we arrived, the crew being able to rig on the way. The E.T.'s crew had taken some equipment into the building with them, so I decided to take the portable gas cutting equipment in with me. Worn on the back haversack fashion, the cutting gear consisted of two small oxygen cylinders and a propane gas cylinder, secured in a carrying frame.

Inside the building the crews were trying to open the ground floor gates of a goods lift. The problem was a man was hanging upside down from the lift platform, which had stopped at ceiling height. He was jammed by his head and shoulders between the lift platform and the ground floor lift shaft gates, which were of a steel trellis construction. The metal gates and the steel gate runner were bowed outwards by the man's body, causing it all to jam and impossible to open without causing him further injury. The trapped man appeared to be motionless and we all thought he was dead, although nobody said it. Then he began to move the fingers of his right hand which was hanging down in front of our faces.

The trapped man began to regain consciousness and started screaming. Loud and continuous he screamed, kicking his legs in an attempt to get himself free. I was told to cut the top runner with the gas cutting gear and a wooden box was placed in position for me to stand on so that I could reach it without stretching too much. I selected the best position for the cut and began to heat up the runner. Through the dark lenses of my cutting glasses I could only see the cutting flame and the area where I was about to make my cut. The smell of burning hair filled my nostrils and with the victim continuously screaming, I didn't know whether I was burning him or not. I didn't want to stop the cut because it would have meant losing the heat from the steel runner, making the job take longer. I shouted that I could smell hair burning and was reassured that it wasn't the trapped man but Les Parks's hand that I had brushed the flame over. With the cut completed, the crew were able to remove the still screaming man.

What the crew didn't know at the time was that when I completed the cut the bowed steel runner sprang outward, knocking me off the box that I was standing on. Fortunately for me, the red hot end of the steel runner hit my goggles which probably saved me from serious injury. I didn't completely get away with it because later on, two bruises appeared in the shape of semi-circles under my eyes caused by the rims of my goggles. Unbelievably the man came out of that accident with only a small bone fracture in his face.

That accident happened because the man had broken the rules. He used a goods lift as a passenger lift, instead of using the staircase. He got into the lift and closed the floor gates to the lift shaft. There were no gates to the lift platform and no controls inside the lift, so he asked another person to operate it from the floor controls outside. As the lift slowly began to rise, the buttons on the sleeve cuff of the man's jacket, caught in the trellis construction of the fixed ground floor lift shaft gates, holding him fast as the lift continued on its upward journey. The person who had operated the lift from the floor controls heard the man's screams and managed to hit the emergency button. As it turned out, he saved the man from serious injury or even death.

Because Lambeth Fire Station was housed within the brigade headquarters' building, the personnel were often called upon to perform displays for visiting V.I.P.s. Both watches had a spectacular display routine that they performed with speed and skill. To keep up the high standard, rehearsals were often carried out as a normal drill routine. The female office staff from local buildings overlooking the drill yard, often watched us perform, of course we used to show off a bit and wave to them. In return they made paper aeroplanes, wrote messages on them and launched them from the high vantage points of their office windows. The paper planes would glide gracefully down and land in the yard. Some of the messages written on them were quite suggestive; unfortunately the writers could never be traced because the telephone numbers on them belonged to some other unsuspecting innocent office worker. I believe that some favourable responses were apparently obtained by a few chaps by ringing genuine telephone numbers that were written on one or two of the descending pieces of air mail.

Every few months a couple of community-minded firemen would organise a watch social evening. Those socials became such a success that they grew to a bit more than just a watch social evening. Wives, girlfriends and family members were all welcome. Inevitably women friends other than wives were brought along. That was alright until the firemen's children's Christmas party. When different women to those that some firemen brought to the social evenings arrived with their children, it became quite confusing, especially when trying to remember names.

Other activities enjoyed in those early days were the competition drills. Watches were allowed to enter more than one team. That had the effect of creating a competition within each individual watch to establish the fastest team to enter into the brigade competition. The drill for the four-man pump escape teams consisted of pitching the escape to the third floor window of the drill tower, two men climbing the ladder and entering the third floor, then one carrying the other back down the ladder again, connecting the P.E. to a fire hydrant, laying out one length of hose and knocking over a target with a jet of water. Rolling up the hose and placing it in a marked area, then replacing the wheeled escape ladder on the back of the fire engine, climbing aboard and driving it over the finishing line. That drill was a really exhausting exercise.

The pump competition consisted of laying out two lengths of hose, connecting to a fire hydrant, knocking down two targets with jets of water, then making up all gear and driving over the finishing line. It was very tiring performing those drills and the teams had to be very fit to be among the winners. Although those drills were enjoyed by many, the competitions and displays were gradually phased out due to union pressure and in the interest of safety, after a fireman was killed and another seriously injured, when they fell from an escape ladder during a practice for a competition drill.

Chapter 6

The swirling spray surrounded me like a mist causing droplets of water to settle on my fire helmet. The collection of droplets on my helmet trickled down to its rim and gradually formed a row of small crystal clear stalactite-like icicles, which sparkled in front of my eyes as the emergency lighting illuminating the area refracted through them. I had been holding a branch for about an hour and a half, directing its steel-like shaft of water towards the blazing stacks of waste paper. My hands were numb and I only believed that I had feet when I looked down and saw my fire boots. It was about 0300 hours in the morning in the middle of February. I gripped the branch in the crook of my right arm and jammed it against my body, then tried to draw my hands as far up into my sleeves as possible, in an attempt to warm them. Gritting my teeth to stop them chattering I looked around me, the roadway was like an ice rink and other firemen manning jets, sparkled like diamonds. The emergency lighting reflected on their frozen images, giving the impression that they would snap if they moved.

The long solid stream of water from my jet broke up as it reached its target and cascaded over the burning waste paper bales. All there was to relieve the boredom was the sound of the high revving engine of the pump, forcing the water through the hose and the occasional voice of the control room radio operator, communicating with some other unfortunate crew who happened to be out on that bitterly cold night. My thoughts reflected on the past and I wondered how I happened to be standing there dressed as a cartoon character in the middle of the night, freezing to death. Unfortunately that job wasn't unique, waste paper and rag warehouses often went up in flames and they always took a long time to extinguish and were hard work.

In contrast to that kind of boring job I found emergency tender work very interesting and at times demanding. I was always pleased when I was detailed to ride the E.T. at the beginning of a duty and even more pleased when I was detailed to drive it. Lambeth's E.T. was a large walk-through vehicle, it resembled a bus at the front where the crew sat and a storage room at the back where all the equipment was stowed. Because it was ordered on to jobs that required specialist breathing apparatus crews, fires of eight pumps or more and most special services, long journeys through London were quite a regular event, which I enjoyed immensely.

One Saturday afternoon there was a fire in a building used as offices in Lombard Street in the City of London. As far as I can recall, the building was about five floors with a basement and a sub-basement and a frontage about one hundred feet wide.

The officer in charge asked for assistance and requested breathing apparatus crews. Lambeth's E.T. was ordered on and the crew rigged in B.A. on the way there, except for me because I was driving. After booking the E.T. in attendance with the brigade's control unit, the crew was quickly deployed inside the building. By the time I had rigged in fire gear, donned my breathing apparatus set and reported to the control unit, the E.T.'s crew was already working inside.

Smoke, heat and fire had spread throughout the building by means of the ventilation system, therefore all the work inside had to be undertaken by B.A. crews. When I reported to the control unit I was immediately recognised as an E.T. crew man because E.T. crews wore yellow-coloured B.A. sets and pumps' crews wore blue sets. I was told to join a pump's B.A. crew which had a station officer in charge.

Our task was to search the sub-basement which was heavily smoke-logged. A hose-reel had been taken some way in by a previous crew but they had since been withdrawn. We were told to make our way further into the sub-basement to look for the seat of the fire, the station officer leading the way with me behind him followed by two other men. Unable to communicate, other than by touch and unable to see because of the thick black smoke, we shuffled our way further into the unknown, hearts pounding and minds playing tricks in the blackness. Arms outstretched feeling for obstructions, adrenaline flowing. Conscious of the proximity of the other men, only from the clicking sounds of the thin mica breathing tube valves in their self-contained oxygen B.A. sets, as they lifted and fell in rhythm with the wearer's breathing.

As we progressed further into the sub-basement it began to get very hot, my ears felt as though they were being cooked and the skin on my face started to sting. The goggles and mouthpiece worn with oxygen sets didn't give much protection to the face. Suddenly there was a great surge of heat and a deep orange glow appeared in front of us then disappeared for a second before reappearing even brighter. The station officer leading us reeled backwards and fell. In his efforts to remain upright he crashed into me, almost dislodging my mouthpiece. I went reeling backwards into the other two crew members. All four of us finished up scrambling about on our hands and knees, which probably saved us from being caught in the flashover that went across the ceiling. I was completely disorientated and with that came a feeling of sheer terror and panic. As I tried desperately to get to my feet I grasped hold of the hose-reel tubing that I had released instinctively as I fell, so that I had two hands to save myself. Knowing that one end of the tubing was outside the building, I had to decide which way to crawl. The trouble was, the tubing was lying in coils on the floor where we had dragged a long length inside, to make it easier to pull further into the building as we moved forward.

Crawling around in circles on the floor, following the hose-reel tubing, I eventually found the door to the staircase leading up to open air. The smoke was thinner by the door and it was possible to see about two feet in front so I stood up and began to clap so loudly that my hands stung from the impact. Clapping loudly was the recognised way of attracting attention when rigged in breathing apparatus, because trying to shout would cause a break in the mouthpiece seal and allow toxic fumes to enter the set. Pure oxygen B.A. sets that we used, were self-contained and any poisonous gases that entered them could not be expelled. The gases would continue to circulate through the set and the wearer, until he had absorbed all of the poison or had collapsed from the effects of it. The sets were only designed to extract the carbon dioxide from the exhaled breath, leaving unused oxygen to mix with fresh oxygen from the cylinder, to be breathed again.

My clapping was heard by the remainder of the crew and they made their way towards the sound and out into fresh air.

I am pleased to say that we all came out of that situation without any physical injuries. Once out we were able to talk and laugh about the experience, which helped us to accept it as just part of the job. That job was hard and long. The oxygen B.A. sets that we used were of one hour duration, depending on the amount of work performed by the wearer and the amount of oxygen demanded by his body. At that job we had to recharge our sets twice.

Another interesting fire that occurred around that period was the fire in the second Blackwall Tunnel for road traffic, during its construction under the River Thames. The contractors had extended the bore to approximately half way under the river when fire broke out at the cutting face.

Hydraulic equipment and timber staging was involved. The absence of any form of ventilation caused a massive build-up of smoke, which gradually rolled along the tunnel, making it impossible to work in the atmosphere without the aid of breathing apparatus.

The situation that developed underground, presented a problem to the brigade that I do not believe it had experienced before. The tunnel workings were pressurised to limit water seepage from the River Thames above. Therefore, access had to be made through a pressure chamber and an air-tight bulkhead. Also the oxygen breathing apparatus which the brigade mainly used could not be safely worn in the pressurised atmosphere of the tunnel.

It was explained to me that when pure oxygen is breathed, while in an environment where the surrounding pressure is much higher than atmospheric pressure, a dangerous medical condition is created. The pressure of pure oxygen drawn into the lungs would equal that of the pressure outside of the body. Therefore, the volume of oxygen absorbed by the lungs would be much higher than that absorbed under normal atmospheric conditions. That results in not only the red cells in the blood absorbing oxygen but the plasma too. Therefore the blood becomes completely saturated with oxygen to a maximum capacity. In simple terms it appears that blood in that oxygen-enriched state has no space to absorb carbon dioxide from the body tissues and subsequently discharge it through the lungs. Consequently, carbon dioxide builds up to a dangerous level in the body.

All available open circuit compressed air breathing apparatus sets were transported to the scene but that presented another problem. The C.A. sets used in those days were only thirty minutes' duration, but considerably less than that if the wearer exerted himself.

By using twenty minutes as a guide for the average duration of the compressed air sets and after calculating the time it took to reach the working face through the smoke-filled tunnel and return to comparative clean air, the time allowed for fire-fighting was very short, making that tunnel fire a very hard drawn out job.

On the day of the tunnel fire I was driving the E.T. and I enjoyed a good clear run from Lambeth to the tunnel workings.

When we arrived at the tunnel we were informed of the problems that existed and told to go down in the contractor's lift to the forward control point, which had been set up at the foot of the lift shaft, just inside the tunnel bore.

First we had to enter a cylindrical steel chamber where the air pressure was raised to equal that of the tunnel. That wasn't without a problem; one of our crew suffered pains in his ears so we had to be decompressed to let him out. Once the pressure was equalised we went through a door in the bulkhead into a lift cage. At a given signal we were lowered to the working level where the air was smoky but breathable.

Benches had been set up for crews to service their compressed air breathing apparatus sets before returning in relays to the working face to fight the fire. We were briefed again on the working procedures and told that a small electric train had been made available by the contractor to transport us along the tunnel. One of the workmen had volunteered to drive the train for us, so he was shown how to wear a full face mask compressed air breathing apparatus set.

To make the sets last a little longer we were told to have them ready as we progressed into the tunnel and only to put the face mask on when the smoke was unbearable. That could be done with the compressed air sets, because unlike the oxygen breathing apparatus sets, the C.A. sets had full face masks and were open circuit, any foul air in the lungs was discharged from the set on exhalation.

The air temperature was high and it was very tiring work. We all had just about enough of that job by the time we were ordered out. On the way out we went through the reverse procedure by being slowly decompressed to atmospheric pressure before being allowed out into fresh air.

I didn't feel too well when I booked off duty and that evening, I suffered with the mother of all headaches. I wasn't aware at the time but some men had to be taken from home, back to the tunnel site, to be put back in the compression chamber again for treatment, they were suffering from the bends, decompression sickness. My problem was probably caused by the inhalation of carbon monoxide, the result of not wearing my C.A. set all of the time.

As time passed I attended many more fires and special services, I was gaining a good deal of practical emergency tender work and fire fighting experience.

Whilst I was reading the latest issue of Brigade Routine Orders posted on the station notice board, it made me wonder about my future. B.R.O.s were regular bulletins that were published to keep personnel informed of events within the brigade or the introduction of new instructions etc. I was browsing through the alphabetically arranged list of names of the successful applicants who had sat the last leading fireman's written examination. I thought that maybe it was time for me to sit the next examination. When I saw the name Wade at the end of the list I was surprised. Tom Wade who was a recruit at Old Kent Road the same time as me, had started on his quest for promotion while I was content to just be a member of a crew. That kick started me into action making me determined to begin to study for the next leading fireman's written examination.

I opened my eyes and my mind to my dormant situation. Deciding to apply to sit the next examination and take a serious look at the promotion trail made sense. I felt at that time, as far as the practical side of the job was concerned, that I had gained a good deal of experience. More so than a man at a quiet station, without an emergency tender. The admin side of the job I would have to learn but that had nothing to do with the written examination for leading fireman rank. Fortunately and much to my surprise, I managed to pass the leading fireman's written examination the following year, and the subsequent practical examination.

Just after lunch one day, the E.T. was ordered to a man trapped in machinery at a tannery in Bermondsey. The tannery building was old and the machinery appeared antiquated, probably the same age as the building. By the look of it, it didn't appear to have been modernised in any way. Protruding through a hole in the wall of an adjacent engine room a common drive shaft was suspended just below the ceiling, about twelve feet from the floor. The shaft spanned approximately eighty feet across the width of the factory. Fixed along the shaft were a number of pulleys, around which a number of continuous thick webbing belts revolved, transferring the power from the shaft to large revolving drums directly below on the factory floor.

The scene that greeted us was a bit gruesome to say the least. A limp and battered body of a man was partly suspended from and partly wrapped around the horizontal steel drive shaft, close to the ceiling.

During the lunch break the man, who had apparently worked at the factory for many years, had evidently been doing some maintenance work. He had been standing on a machine, working close to the revolving shaft. The surface of the shaft had become very rusty and rough over many years. The probable sequence of events leading up to the tragedy was that his body accidentally brushed against the revolving shaft and its rough surface gripped the woollen jumper the man was wearing. He was whipped into the air and forced through the small gap between the shaft and the ceiling about once every second.

It didn't take very long to release him and get him down, just a matter of supporting his limp body and cutting away the offending woollen jumper. He had suffered appalling injuries, his arms and legs were broken and lacerated in several places exposing his bones, his chest was crushed and his head was just a mass of featureless bloody pulp. His rubber boots were thrown from his feet by the centrifugal force of his revolving body and were lying several feet away. The floor beneath his body was heavily bloodstained, thinning out to just a few spattered drops at the extremes on each side of the revolving shaft.

The accident was not discovered until another employee, who was on the floor above the factory having his lunch break, went down to the factory to investigate a continuous knocking under the floor.

Work continued to be varied and the incidents that I attended I found interesting. I was keen and eager to learn more about fire ground procedure and about running a fire station. I was given the opportunity to act up to leading fireman for a short period to cover sickness, which I willingly accepted. It was a little bit of encouragement that I was grateful for.

The thought that my officer in charge had enough confidence in me, to allow me the opportunity to demonstrate my potential as a junior officer pleased me, or was it because I had joined the others and began to laugh at his unfunny jokes. I had never held any kind of rank before, not counting being elected milk monitor at school, so it was a real boost to my confidence.

While riding in charge of the P.E. during my short period as an acting leading fireman, I found myself being left in charge of the station. The other appliances with their officers were ordered on to an incident over the other side of Lambeth Bridge on Westminster's ground. I could have bet on what happened next. We received a call to a fire and I was in charge of the initial attendance.

I loved going on a shout but now I was looking at it from a different angle. I had to make the decisions on this one, I was the officer in charge, I was sitting in the number one's seat, and it was a bit worrying. My heart was thumping inside my chest all the way there. I could not afford to make a mistake, not on my first shout, I had to get it right.

The door slammed shut behind me as I leapt from the fire engine.

"It's in the back room," shouted a distressed women with a smoke-blackened tear-streaked face.

"Is there anybody in there?" I asked firmly, making sure she understood what I was saying.

When she told me that nobody was in the house I felt immediate relief, it was only the fire that had to be dealt with, thankfully no rescues. The P.E.'s crew made short work of the one-room fire with a couple of hose-reels and I had the 'stop' message back before the next fire engine arrived from a neighbouring station, with a station officer in charge. A 'stop' message is sent over the radio from all incidents to inform the control that no more mobilising of fire engines to the incident is required.

Even though that was only a small fire I was inwardly pleased with myself. I didn't show it but it marked a milestone in my brigade life, I liked being in charge on the fire ground. At that time John Hurcombe was the station officer in charge of the watch. I learned a good deal of office routine from him and found him to be a first class officer, a very good manager of men and an excellent leader on the fire ground. Under Station Officer Hurcombe's command I began to put a lot of missing pieces together. I learned how to liaise with other brigade departments and how to deal with problems at station level and when to involve divisional and brigade headquarters. I watched and learned how to deal with the public and studied his technique in man management. It was a very valuable learning curve.

With a station officer in charge, there were two sub-officers and two leading firemen attached to the blue watch at Lambeth, as opposed to one of each officer rank, at smaller stations. The reason for that establishment was the number of fire engines attached there, that had to have an officer riding in charge and because of the large number of men on the watch. Norman McKnight and Ted

Kinmonth were the sub-officers but because they were pushing hard for promotion they were often on detached duty, acting up to station officer rank to cover sickness and courses, or vacancies caused by any other reason. By out-posting the sub-officers it gave the leading firemen the chance to act up and gain experience in the rank of sub-officer, which gave a fireman the opportunity to act up and gain experience as a leading fireman. The system made it possible for men such as me to try their hand at junior officer's work and responsibilities.

I was proud of my first experience in charge of a fire but when a similar situation occurred the next time I was acting up, I was a bit overwhelmed just hearing the address. We were ordered to a fire on the roof of the Royal Festival Hall, South Bank. After climbing all over the roof to investigate, the alarm turned out to have been caused by volumes of black smoke, issuing from the boiler flue. I felt instant relief at discovering that cause.

All kinds of activities went on during stand down time, especially in the evenings because only essential work was done after 2000 hours. One evening a fireman arranged for a blue film show to be staged; word spread and on the evening of the show we even had pumps from other stations arriving, supposedly to play an inter-station volley ball match in the yard by floodlight. The place was crowded and buzzing with excited firemen full of expectation of a good evening's entertainment. Suddenly a cheer went up as a stranger walked in carrying a film projector, screen and a brown paper parcel containing the films.

"Be with you in a moment," he said, blowing hard from the exertion of carrying his equipment.

Meanwhile, the fireman who had arranged the show announced that he would be going round with his hat, to collect two shillings and sixpence (twelve and a half pence) from everybody who wanted to see the films.

The room was alive with laughter and chatter and when the projectionist shouted loudly that he was to start, the room was suddenly cloaked in silence. Dozens of pairs of eyes gazed with anticipation at the screen to watch *The Sexual Exploits of a Maid*.

"Lights!" shouted the projectionist.

Suddenly the room was shrouded in total darkness. Click! The sound of the switch on the projector broke the silence, followed by a whirring sound. Complete darkness except for the glowing ends of a couple of cigarettes and the flash of a cigarette lighter. We waited in silence for a few seconds when somebody shouted:

"I've seen it!"

Everybody laughed.

"Lights!" shouted the projectionist as he fumbled with the switches on the projector.

The lights were switched on and all eyes were fixed on the stranger fiddling with the projector. Looking rather uncomfortable he sort of half smiled and said in a nervous voice, "I think the bulb has gone."

After all the shouting and abuse had died down, the man who had arranged the show suggested that we have another collection and he would drive to Piccadilly Circus and buy a new projector bulb from the all night chemist. That suggestion caused more shouting and abuse but eventually it was agreed and off he went.

One member of a visiting crew, who happened to live fairly close by, volunteered to go and get his projector, in case the chemist didn't have the right bulb in stock. He didn't have any transport because his car was parked at his home station, so brigade control was told that a member of the public had reported a fire hydrant leaking badly, in the road where the chap lived. Permission was given for the pump to go and check the hydrant, so it left the station with the chap on board, to collect his projector.

The pump returned before the man who went to the all night chemist, but without the projector or the chap who went to get it. There seemed to be a lot of whispering going on and eventually it became known that the chap had gone to his house to pick up the projector and found his wife, who obviously thought she was safe because he was on night duty, with another man. All hell broke loose and he refused to return to the station. Arrangements were made with the officer in charge of my station to make an entry in the station's log book, showing that the man went off duty feeling unwell after playing in a volley ball competition. That made an official reason to get a stand-by from another station to prevent the fire engine being taken off the run because of a shortage of riders.

Finally the new bulb arrived and was fitted into the projector, accompanied by cheers the show got under way. The first film was just getting interesting, the humpy pumpy bit was about to start, when we got a fire call. To the cries of dismay and annoyance we departed until the early hours of the morning and of course, the film show was over when we returned.

During the following year or so, the watch attended hundreds of fires and other incidents. With almost five years' service I was packing plenty of experience under my belt. I had sat my leading fireman's written and practical examinations and was waiting for the results of my promotion interview. The normal procedure was for a few men to get immediate promotion, filling existing vacancies, and the remainder of successful candidates to be placed on a panel from which future positions would be filled as they occurred during the year.

Station Officer Hurcombe must have given me a good confidential report with a recommendation for promotion, because I was one of the fortunate candidates who were promoted on publication of the results. I was also happy with my posting. The vacancy on the red watch at Lambeth was mine. All I had to do was change watches to start my new job, I didn't even have to change my locker. I never thought that I would ever admit to being happy about staying at Lambeth. When I was first transferred there more than three years ago, I was so depressed that I almost resigned.

Most of my on-duty time was spent in the station office cursing the typewriter because it couldn't spell. I worked with another leading fireman, Nobby Clarke, I never did know his first name. Nobby was very knowledgeable and a good mainstay to have around. More than once he prevented me from dropping clangers that would have earned me the wrath of the governor, George Hunt. Guided by Nobby, I soon became familiar with the red watch routine and the finer points of the office work.

Station Officer George Hunt had for years written and produced pantomimes and was preparing the final one before his forthcoming retirement. The pantomimes were performed by the members of the red watch, with some help from the control room staff. For years the pantomimes were staged to entertain underprivileged children from orphanages and children's homes and of course the firemen's children. No women were in the cast, all parts were played by firemen. George Hunt's final production was to be *Beauty and the Beast*.

The professional skills of two dance teachers taught the cast of firemen to perform dance routines. All the costumes were borrowed from a theatrical costume supplier, which made all the so-called actors look the part. In fact, for a bunch of firemen the cast looked quite good, especially the hairy chests of the chorus girls.

As a new member of the red watch I was roped in. The thought of performing on a stage in front of an audience terrified me. I was given the part of the Beast to play and fortunately I had to wear a head of a beast mask for most of the performance. Thankfully my blushes could not be seen. Beauty was played by Arthur Jackson, known as 'Jacko', a control room operator – he was a very large man weighing at that time about two-hundred and eighty pounds, he made an excellent Beauty.

Although we had bouts of fits of laughter throughout rehearsals, the funniest part was during the first performance. As a matter of convenience all of the pantomime music was recorded on an old reel-to-reel tape recorder. At the end of the pantomime, when I changed from the beast into a prince, I invited everyone to my castle for a celebration, where we all had to dance a minuet. The problem was, the old tape recorder had been working for so long that it began to malfunction when the music for the minuet was played. The sequence was supposed to be danced at a very slow pace, striding about the stage bowing to our partners and raising our flamboyant feathered hats in much exaggerated effeminate movements but the recorder began to speed-up and play the music at about three times its normal speed. Consequently we were all moving around the stage in jerking movements, trying to keep time with the music – it was rather like the actors in a very old silent film. It was embarrassing but very funny.

The time came when Station Officer Hunt's retirement was imminent. The word on the grapevine was that Station Officer Mullaney was to be transferred in, to replace him. I felt a little apprehensive about that, because I didn't exactly have a satisfactory start in the brigade as a recruit under him at Old Kent Road.

The rumour materialised and Mullaney arrived to take charge of the red watch. I soon realised that my apprehension was unnecessary. Within a short time most of the station management staff had changed, we all worked well under the command of Mullaney and the new Sub-Officer Doug Bailey. Everybody enjoyed practical jokes, there was always something or somebody to laugh at, providing that you could take a joke and didn't mind being the victim occasionally.

It was my turn to be the victim one day duty when Doug Bailey told me that there was a call for me on the exchange pay telephone. Because I had the job of driving the two dance teachers to their homes after rehearsals for the pantomime, twice weekly for a number of weeks, rumours were rife and I became the victim of a lot of leg pulling. Men being worse than washer-women for gossip, it appeared that according to the stories being put about, that I had been having an absolutely wonderful time twice a week, for the duration of the pantomime rehearsals.

Unknown to me, Mullaney had primed Bailey and told him to keep an eye out for my reaction when I answered the telephone. In a disguised voice Mullaney introduced himself as a partner in a firm of solicitors and said that he was acting on behalf of the husband of one of the dance teachers and that I was being cited as co-respondent in his divorce petition. I was shocked to say the least. I couldn't think straight for a few seconds, all kinds of things went through my mind, including not wanting any of that kind of aggravation during that period of my married life. Mullaney must have realised the state of mind that I was in because I slammed the phone down and dashed to my car without saying a word to anyone. Bailey didn't even see me leave. I was in my car about to drive out of the station yard when I saw Mullaney running towards me waving and shouting:

"Stop! It was me! It was me!"

I don't believe that I have ever been so angry and so relieved at the same time, as I was at that moment. I just sat in my car feeling completely drained, listening to Mullaney telling me what a wonderful joke it was.

The reason that I took that joke badly was because my home life could have been a lot better at the time. Since leaving the army I had been facing up to the reality of life, working for a living in mundane welding jobs and feeling trapped in a basic existence without a future. I liked my job but my wife didn't like me being in the fire brigade, she was not happy about me having to work night shifts and it caused problems.

My second daughter Bonita Jane was born on the 23rd July 1959. With four of us living in one room it became a bit stressful and arguments began to occur ever more frequently, mainly about money but also about me having to do night work.

Maureen didn't like me being a fireman, if I wasn't at home then according to her I was out enjoying myself. She made no distinction between being away from home socialising and being away from home working. She always worked hard, part-time when the children were young and full-time thereafter but she had a peculiar attitude with regard to the money that she had earned. She would always spend it on things for the home or what was needed but whatever she bought, she would regard it as her own.

For those and many other reasons, married life after leaving the army was a bit of a let-down. My feelings had changed and I felt that the spark had gone out. I often reflected on the remarks that were made when we decided to get married so young. Therefore, I didn't need any added aggravation or accusations poured on already troubled waters, thus my reaction to Mullaney's joke phone call.

I did try and make the marriage work because we had our two daughters Beverly and Bonita to consider. We managed to get a flat in Beckenham and later got a mortgage for a house in Gravesend, Kent. Unfortunately that didn't compensate for the deterioration in our marriage. In fact it made matters worse by increasing my journey to work by one hour each way. On reflection I believe my marriage to Maureen had been on a downward spiral for some time. We had grown up and were paying for the errors of our teenage years. Going on duty was something that I enjoyed and I used it to compensate for my unfulfilled home life.

Enough of that and back to the interesting part of my life. Promotion was what I wanted, but the part of a fireman's job that I missed most was driving the fire engines. Junior officers were only allowed to drive if the officer in charge of the appliance was of a higher rank, but normally the job of a junior officer was to ride in charge. The duty that I enjoyed most as a junior officer was riding in charge of the E.T. I had gained a lot of experience on that appliance and I enjoyed the work.

The majority of fires were extinguished by means of the hose-reel tubing using water from the one hundred gallon tank incorporated within the bodywork of the old Merryweather fire engines. As a routine drill, a line of hose was laid out from a street fire hydrant and connected to the pump to augment the water supply, in case more water than the hundred gallons in the tank was required, or a larger diameter hose line was required to deal with the fire. The well-practised and proven method of fire fighting that we adopted was for the P.E.'s crew, who were normally the first to arrive at a fire, to attack the fire either with one or two hose-reels, or a jet from a line of hose. The pump's crew on arrival had to augment the water supply to the P.E. from a street fire hydrant, before the water carried in the P.E.'s tank was used up, which could of course put the men on the jet in danger, especially if they were inside a building. That worked well on most occasions but sometimes fire hydrants were situated some distance from the fire and that used up precious time, so a relay from the pump's tank would be set up into the P.E. to maintain the water supply a little longer. Later the more modern fire engines incorporated a four hundred gallon water tank which made a big difference to the initial attack at a fire. Another routine that we adopted was for me to have a quick look around inside the building on fire, to assess the situation confronting us. I would then pass the information on to Mullaney when he arrived and he would take the decision whether to 'make-up' or not. Mullaney became fully confident in my quick assessments of the type and potential spread of fire, he trusted my judgement. It made the job easier for him and I gained a lot of useful experience from working that system.

All the incidents that we attended seemed to go particularly well and after a very busy period Mullaney called me to his office. He surprised me by telling me that he was satisfied with my standard of work and progress, and that if I passed the forthcoming sub-officer's written and practical examinations, he would have no hesitation in recommending me for promotion. That had the affect of giving me a massive ego boost, so I decided to go for it.

Studying Manuals of Firemanship was something that I did during my spare time but by no means on a grand scale. Motivated by Mullany's pep talk, I now had something realistic to aim for. I knew that I was capable of doing a sub-officer's job but the examinations were obstacles that I did not know whether I had the ability to overcome. I pulled out all the stops and attended a study class twice a week in my own time. I learnt about examination technique and brushed up on my mathematics, especially hydraulic problems.

The day of the written examination arrived and apart from being late, thanks to public transport, it all went fairly smoothly. I enjoyed meeting other examinees and seeing some old acquaintances. I was quietly confident after the examination, but as time went by I began to go over the questions and answers in my mind and the more I thought about it the less confident I became.

After a few weeks the postman popped the long-awaited envelope through my letter box. The word that stood out was 'Successful', I was very relieved. That was one obstacle out of the way so the next part of the procedure was to concentrate on passing the practical examination.

The practical examination included the drilling of a squad of raw recruits. The task was to recite in detail, every movement that the squad had to perform, and guide them safely through a selected drill. Two senior officers watched and listened to every word and marked the candidates accordingly. The examination lasted all day and I was glad to get it over with.

Again there was a waiting period of a few weeks before the results were known. I felt fortunate to receive the favourable news of a pass mark. The next crucial part was to get through the 'dry mouth' part, the face-to-face promotion interview.

While anxiously awaiting a date for my interview, I studied as much as I could about brigade procedures, all the latest operation notes and brigade orders. There was a vast amount of material that the interview board could question me on and encourage me to talk about.

On the day of my sub-officer's interview I prepared myself by bulling up army-style. It was always a bit hit and miss keeping to a timetable because of the unpredictable London traffic conditions so I left home in plenty of time to meet the interview board. I was within about one mile of the Brigade Headquarters when I felt my car wandering on the road accompanied by a vibration and a rumbling sound. Realising what the cause was I was horrified at the thought of changing my punctured front wheel with only about fifteen minutes to go before my interview time.

Changing my wheel in record time I finally parked my car and raced to the interviewee's waiting room which was empty. I began to get worried at this stage so I left the room and almost bumped into D.O. Rose, who was a member of the interview board. That was my first encounter with him since he was a sub-officer instructor at the brigade's training school.

"Where the hell have you been?" he barked. Out of breath, I stuttered and panted as I tried to explain my predicament.

"Never mind that now, get yourself cleaned up and settle down, I'm taking a short break so when you're ready report to the general office and someone will announce you."

I did some deep breathing and calmed down and when I was ready someone announced me before I walked smartly into the interview room. As I sat in that lonely chair before the board, I remembered what a colleague had told me. He said that he was

116

convinced that the chairman of the promotion board switched on a powerful heater that only heated up the interviewee's chair. He could have been right I could feel the beads of perspiration forming on my forehead and top lip, as soon as I sat down. The chairman began the interview by trying to put me at ease; it didn't work because the first word I uttered came out as a pathetic squeak, but a quick cough and a shuffle in the interviewee's chair cured that 'lady luck' was with me, once again I was successful but London being a large town raised the question, what station would the powers-that-be post me to. The brigade could post me to any station within the London area, where there was a vacancy for a sub-officer, without consideration of where I lived or the difficulty in travelling.

Again I was very fortunate, I couldn't have been posted to a better or more convenient station. I was to report for duty at Brixton Fire Station, South London. At that time in my career I was very satisfied with my progress and good fortune, I was keen to get on and enjoyed my work. Job satisfaction was something that I had not experienced at any time in my life before. Although I enjoyed my time off duty I always looked forward to going to work.

Chapter 7

Brixton Fire Station housed three fire engines, pump escape, pump and turntable ladder. An old four-storey building that had undergone quite a few alterations in its time, resulting in the accommodation being spread out on three floors with senior officers' quarters on the upper floor. I could never understand how anybody out of choice, would bring his family to live over a fire station in Brixton south London. I suppose that if you want promotion that badly, then you have to accept what goes with it, whatever that may be.

My accommodation was a room on the second floor, next to the station officer's room, two leading firemen shared a room along the corridor, on the same floor. The firemen's locker room was on the first floor along with the kitchen and mess room. Three appliance bays, plus the watch-room and station office occupied the ground floor. Brixton was a sprawling station with a free-standing drill tower situated in a large drill yard surrounded by a high brick wall with two heavy timber gates leading into Gresham Road.

A large population of immigrants had settled in the London Borough of Brixton during and prior to the 1960s, mainly of West Indian origin. Large old Victorian houses that were built during the eighteen hundreds formed the main type of available rented accommodation. Landlords were cashing in, by converting large old houses into multiple occupancy dwellings. Large rooms were converted into small flats and small rooms were converted into bed sitting rooms. Heating facilities were either inadequate or non-existent which encouraged a good trade in paraffin oil heaters, new and second-hand. Problems arose because some of those heaters only received a minimum of maintenance to keep them working, and many only received the daily top-up with fuel. A very high percentage of fires attended in that area during the sixties were either caused by or involved a paraffin oil heater.

An additional problem created by the cramped conditions that people had to live in was the storage of the flammable fuel. Nine out of ten of them placed the storage container, made from various unsuitable materials, next to the heater for convenience of refuelling. A practice that was invariably carried out whilst the heater was still alight, a potentially dangerous practice. Over filling and spillage was frequent and free-flowing paraffin, alight in a house, was the cause of many serious fires and tragic loss of lives.

Another problem encountered when dealing with a fire in a house of multiple occupancy, was caused by the actions of the tenants, who feared losing all of their hard-earned and treasured possessions. Quite often we had to negotiate an obstacle course of furniture in the entrance and passageway of a house, before we could get to the fire.

When a person's room or small flat was on fire, the priority of other tenants living in the house was to save as much of their own personal belongings as possible. The order of priority for saving possessions seemed to be, television sets, record players, settees and wardrobes. It wasn't unusual in those days to discover a body, or a 'stiff' as it is known in the job, in just a small one-room fire. A lot of people and sometimes whole families lost their lives in fires caused by or involving a paraffin oil heater.

A scene indelibly marked in my memory is the sight of four firemen each desperately applying mouth-to-mouth resuscitation trying to revive a young child laid out on the pavement outside of a burning house in the early hours of the morning. As it turned out their efforts were in vain. All four children died, a tragic loss of young lives and a traumatic experience for the firemen.

It wasn't necessarily the larger fires in houses that cost lives. One incident I attended on Brixton's ground only involved a heater and a small boy who had fallen on to it. When I saw him he was lying on his back, with the whole of his abdomen so severely burned that only raw flesh could be seen. All of the skin from a large area of his abdomen was burned, some of it could still be seen stuck to the heater.

Every day, all kinds of accidents and tragedies are dealt with by firemen who are not immune to the normal feelings of sorrow, sadness or shock. They may become used to controlling or hiding their feelings when dealing with tragic incidents by putting on a brave face, or even appearing callous by their attitude or behaviour. Their true feelings are often hidden and may only be shared by those closest to them. Among the worst experiences a fireman can suffer is to discover the charred remains of a baby or young child who had suffered a slow agonising death by breathing in poisonous

119

fumes and smoke, its struggle for survival indicated by the final position of its distorted little body as it fought for life. Another is to lose the battle to resuscitate a child, or an adult, who has been overcome by smoke. I have heard firemen question themselves about their unsuccessful efforts to resuscitate. When you hand the victim over to an ambulance crew for removal to hospital, you just hope you have maintained a little spark of life for the medical teams to work on.

The majority of deaths at fires are caused by the inhalation of the products of combustion. Not many people are burnt to death, most die before the fire reaches them. That can be ascertained at a post-mortem, even the cause of death of the most severely burned victims can be established.

Don Brown, a newly promoted station officer was my governor at Brixton. I had been attached there for only one week when he was placed sick and unable to report for duty. I was given the opportunity to act-up to station officer which seemed a rapid rise to fame, considering that I was only a Leading Fireman a little more than a week ago.

Taking the work and responsibilities in my stride I soon shook off the inevitable anxious feeling and found the position interesting and challenging. I liked making my own decisions and when Don Brown returned to duty I felt very frustrated for a time. That short stint in charge motivated me to keep up my studies to prepare for the station officer's examination, in an attempt to secure a station officer's position for myself.

A lot of fires occur after school hours especially the days building up to Guy Fawkes Night. As with most young children, impatience and excitement eventually gets the better of them and those in the Brixton area were no exception. Despite all of the warnings of the dangers, lighted fireworks were still thrown in the air or at other children. Stacks of rubbish and other children's bonfires were set on fire before the big event on November 5th. Because of the high number of calls received on Guy Fawkes Night the normal attendances to fires are generally reduced to one pumping appliance. On one memorable firework night Don Brown had taken his pump to attend a list of about four addresses to calls to bonfires out of control and I was left in the station in charge of the P.E. Shortly after the pump left the station, control ordered the P.E. to an address, to assist the pump's crew.

When I arrived at the scene I found Don Brown sitting in an ambulance holding a pad on his head and a crowd of angry young men and women standing some yards away shouting obscenities and abuse at the pump's crew. Don had approached the bonfire party to assess the situation, not necessarily with a view to extinguishing it, when someone ran up behind him and knocked his fire helmet off and another person hit him on the head with a bottle, gashing his head. The crew withdrew under a hail of missiles, ordered an ambulance for Don over the radio and asked for the attendance of the police.

The arrival of the P.E.'s crew gave the impression that reinforcements had arrived, the crowd took that as a challenge and began throwing more missiles at us. The police eventually arrived and we all withdrew from the scene, the fire having died down substantially. The fact that the fire would probably not have been extinguished didn't occur to the crowd but we had to attend because we were called by a worried nearby resident.

Most stations had their resident practical jokers and firemen who are always game for a laugh, accepted the antics of jokers as part of station life. Brixton was no exception and although some of the tricks that the members of the watch got up to could have had serious consequences but I could often see the funny side.

I heard shouting coming from the drill yard one lunch time and went to investigate. Calls for help seemed to be coming from inside the drill tower. I discovered the junior buck hanging in the darkness, swearing his head off, about twenty feet up inside the hollow core of the drill tower, where wet hose was hung up to dry. Another time someone reported his bicycle stolen, only to find it parked on the fifth floor of the drill tower. Sometimes tempers were lost but mostly it was all taken in good part.

One evening, in the absence of Don Brown, I was ordered with my pump and turntable ladder, to a fire in a derelict house on Peckham's ground. When we arrived Peckham's crew was dealing with the small outbreak, which was probably caused by children playing with matches. On this occasion a small crowd had gathered, as they normally do when fire engines are working, and among them was a startling looking blonde woman. She was heavily made up and wearing a snug-fitting evening gown, which showed off her ample figure to the extreme. A couple of Peckham's crew were dealing with the small fire while the remainder were chatting to the blonde, who appeared to be enjoying every minute of it. My T.L. driver, being a bit of a 'Jack the lad' pushed himself forward to talk to the raving beauty, who responded readily to his advances. Egged on by the others, he dated the woman, just as the station officer in charge of Peckham's appliances told him that the T.L. wasn't required and to return to Brixton. The woman asked him for a kiss goodbye and not believing his luck, he willingly obliged. He really made a meal of it, giving her a long passionate kiss, accompanied by a roar of approval from the remainder of the firemen and the public. Full of the joys of spring, he leapt into the cabin of the T.L. and left the scene, waving and blowing kisses as he went.

We all stood laughing for a few seconds when the beautiful blonde shouted, "Oi!"

As all heads turned towards her, she removed the blonde wig and continued in a deep manly voice, "Tell that stupid bastard that I'm a bloke, I'm part of a drag act from the pub next door."

Well, we nearly collapsed with laughter as the drag queen tottered off in his high heel shoes, back to the pub. On our return to the station, the T.L. driver gagged and almost vomited when he was told the truth about his new found love, amid much more raucous laughter of course.

Everything was going well for me at Brixton; we had a good team which was unfortunately broken up when Don Brown was suddenly transferred to Lambeth. There were many upheavals going on at that time. The expansion of the London County Council into the Greater London Council and the forming of a third watch in the brigade, created many vacancies and movement of officers.

A lot of those changes that took place during the nineteen sixties were to incorporate a three-watch shift system that was introduced to include the new white watch. The new Greater London Council took over many fire stations that bordered the old London County Council area when the Greater London Council was formed. A very large fire brigade was created and predicted by some at that time, to be too large to be managed efficiently.

Soon after Don Brown was transferred, I was also posted back to Lambeth but not on the same watch as Don. Jack Stacey was my governor, a well-known character within the brigade set in his ways, he had been in the Brigade for many years. Having served in the army during the 1939–1945 second world war the subject often came up when talking to Jack. Most of his war was fought in the desert and he was fond of spinning a yarn about it. It wasn't unusual for him to receive photographs or cuttings from newspapers and magazines from colleagues, posted to him through the brigade's internal postal system, of camels, views of the desert or soldiers marching over sand dunes, all with a suitable and witty caption added. One day a large envelope arrived on his desk containing a couple of handfuls of fine dry sand and nothing else.

He always saw the funny side of those jokes and demonstrated his pleasure by laughing heartily and using a string of well-known adjectives in his broad northern accent, describing the unknown sender, who according to Jack was born out of wedlock.

I only spent eleven months as Jack Stacey's sub-officer but during that time we picked up some good working jobs. We were called one day to a person under a bus near the Oval Cricket Ground, Kennington. I arrived first on the P.E. followed by Jack on the pump, with the E.T. bringing up the rear. The scene that greeted us was a bit gruesome to say the least. I laid down on the roadway to look under the bus and saw the motionless body of a man positioned just behind the front wheels. A lot of blood was draining towards the gutter and as I examined the body more closely I discovered that it didn't have a head.

Jack took charge of the incident in his own inimitable way, shouting to the crew:

"C'mon, drag 'im out he won't bloody 'urtya."

The body was rolled on to a salvage sheet and dragged from under the bus while another couple of salvage sheets were held as a screen to prevent the public from witnessing the gruesome scene, or 'rubbernecking' as it is known. Jack beckoned me to him and told me to give him a hand to pick the body up and place it on a stretcher. He promptly grasped the feet and left me the mucky end. I took hold of the shoulders of the man's jacket and as I lifted with Jack, a large piece of flat skin with hair on it, hung from the neck of the body which I had to flip over on to the victim's chest to prevent it from hanging from the stretcher. Police marked the position of the bus on the roadway before it was removed, so that we could hose down the bloody mess, into a nearby drain. One of the crew remarked:

"This gives a whole new meaning to the term brain drain."

Apparently the man was running to catch the bus and just as it began to move away from the bus stop, the man, who was approaching the bus from the front, tripped over and fell head first in front of it. Before the bus driver could stop the bus, one of its

123

front wheels went over the man's head, bursting it and spreading its contents over the road.

Another job that I recall clearly was early one morning, we were called to a fire at Waterloo Railway Station and on the way there, we could see an ominous orange glow in the sky. I briefed my crew, preparing them for action because it looked as though we had a decent job on our hands. As we turned into Waterloo Station I heard Jack's unmistakable voice over the radio sending an assistance message to brigade control, making pumps six. I thought at the time that it was unusual for the governor to 'make up' on the strength of a glow in the night sky. We drove as near as possible to the platform where the fire was and as the crew laid out the hose I made my way along the platform to the scene of the fire. Burning merrily at the far end was a guard's van loaded with daily newspapers. Looking back I saw my crew rushing along the platform with a jet, and Jack strolling along behind them as though he was on a Sunday afternoon walk, looking as though he didn't have a care in the world.

The jet soon knocked the flames back and it was almost all over before the 'make up' appliances arrived. Most of the burnt bundles of newspapers were pulled out of the guard's van and were being spread out and dampened down. When the assistant divisional officer arrived Jack was standing in the damaged guard's van, urinating out of the opposite door on to a still smouldering bundle of papers that had fallen on to the track.

"Good morning, Station Officer Stacey," the A.D.O. said in a sarcastic tone.

Jack turned to face the A.D.O. and saluted him with his right hand whilst putting himself away and zipping up his fly with his left. I walked away unable to control my laughter.

"Good morning sir," answered Jack.

From a distance it looked as though Jack was being criticised so I moved a bit closer and heard Jack say, "I don't care what you say, the radio operator must have been hearing things, I didn't make pumps six, I made pumps four."

Jack knew full well that the job wasn't even worth four pumps but he was doing a good job of wriggling.

At a twelve pump fire a few weeks later, I was called to one side by my divisional officer and told that I was transferred to Clapham Fire Station beginning on my next night duty. D.O. Norman Rose was a tall upright man whose facial expressions depicted his mood, at that time he was wearing his mean look. I was astounded by what he said and showed it by strongly protesting and demanding the reason for the transfer. He didn't give me a reason, he just pointed at me and said slowly, "Be there."

Strange coincidence, once again a person with the surname of Rose was giving me grief, just as Sergeant Rose did when I was in the army.

I was fuming over the order but there wasn't anything that I could do about it, so I had to pack my equipment and personal effects the following night duty and report to Clapham Fire Station.

The rebuilding of Clapham Fire Station had been completed sometime before I was posted there. Station personnel occupied the ground and first floors and the divisional headquarters staff occupied the second floor. Senior officers' living accommodation had been built at right angles to the station, along an adjacent side road, backing on to the enclosed station drill yard. The station housed a pump escape and pump plus the brigade's breakdown lorry, which had been transferred there from Lambeth as part of an earlier reorganisation.

Because I was not very happy about my sudden transfer, I asked for an immediate interview with D.O. Rose. After almost an hour of arguing my case against my transfer I left his office without any satisfaction. I was there to stay.

The station officer in charge of the watch at Clapham was fond of bellowing over the station tannoy system. Sure enough, as soon as I came down from my interview he was broadcasting a message telling me to go to his office.

He began to chastise me for bypassing him and going direct to the D.O. with my grievance. He was absolutely right of course, that's what the chain of command was for but the mood I was in I was ready to bust down anyone's door. The last thing that I wanted at that time was a lecture and when he launched into one, I almost lost control. We had a shouting match which finished up with me demanding that he accompanied me upstairs to the D.O.'s office once again. He declined so I told him in no uncertain terms what I thought of him and his attitude then refused to work with him and stormed out of his office.

Unknown to me at the time, my antics were being watched by some of the station personnel. The station officer's desk was positioned in front of a large observation window on the mezzanine floor overlooking the appliance room and my efforts to get my point across must have looked rather threatening. I was told later that because of the way that I was gesticulating, the men thought I was going to hit the station officer and they were willing me to do so.

Feeling absolutely furious, I went to my room to think and to decide what my next move should be when almost immediately there was a fire call. I responded automatically by reporting to the appliance room, via the sliding pole. Only the pump was ordered with the station officer in charge, leaving me in charge of the station and the P.E., therefore I had no choice but to ride, otherwise the station's area would have been left without fire cover. Soon after that there was another fire call and I was ordered out with the P.E. It was late in the evening when the station officer and I met again and to my surprise he spoke to me in quite a civil manner. Anyone listening would never have thought that we were at each other's throats earlier in the evening. That earlier episode was never mentioned again but I remained alert and ready to react to his mood for some time until we became used to each other's way of working.

For most of the time the station was run on an even keel but it was common knowledge that the members of the watch were not keen on the station officer but as he admitted, he was there to run a fire station, not a popularity contest, he was quite right of course.

During their quieter moments, firemen had the practice of listening to the radio messages from incidents attended by other stations in the brigade, it kept them informed of what was happening in and around London. On the 5th November 1967 an interesting message was intercepted in the station's watch-room, it concerned a train crash at Hither Green, South East London. It was particularly interesting because the officer in charge had sent a radio message stating that he was attending a major accident. That message indicated that there were many live casualties involved.

Communications equipment at stations had been modernised over the past few years and messages from fires and the ordering of appliances to incidents were received from the brigade control by teleprinter. Some watch-rooms at stations, especially divisional headquarters stations like Clapham, were fitted with radio receivers.

As word about the train crash spread around the station, all ears were trained on the radio waiting for the informative message from Hither Green, describing the extent of the incident. A priority message came over the air requesting heavy duty oxy-acetylene gas cutting equipment and heavy duty lifting gear.

126

Fireman Bill Harding was driving the breakdown lorry and Leading Fireman Ron Bentley was riding in charge of it that day. The men reacted immediately by not waiting for a message from brigade control ordering the cutting gear on to the incident. They removed it from the non-mobile special store and loaded it onto the lorry even before the order came through on the teleprinter. The station officer was aware of my experience using breakdown lorry and emergency tender equipment and that my knowledge of oxy-acetylene cutting gear dated back to my army days, so he suggested that the spare leading fireman that we had that day should ride in charge of the P.E. and I should go with the B.L. crew to the incident. When the brigade control order came through we were ready for an immediate turn-out.

Crammed in the cabin of the breakdown lorry, which was designed to carry only two crew members, we made our way to Hither Green as fast as Bill Harding could drive the old beast. As we turned into Brownhill Road Catford, a procession of ambulances were speeding past us in the opposite direction, ferrying those casualties to hospital that the brigade crews were able to remove from the wreck. We continued along Brownhill Road towards the scene of the accident, more or less in silence, each of us creating mental pictures in our minds of what might be ahead. We knew what we were going to, so I suppose unintentionally we were preparing ourselves for what we may encounter later.

The accident had occurred on an elevated part of the track including a bridge over the roadway. Below the bridge uniformed figures were running about doing their specific jobs. To the right of the bridge men were scrambling up and down the embankment assisting injured passengers and manhandling heavy equipment. On the bridge, visible from the road, there was a railway carriage perched almost on end, in a near vertical position leaning against another one that had overturned. It was an unbelievable sight, it looked so unreal. It was as though I was looking at a film set and all the people running about were actors.

After parking the B.L. as near to the incident as possible for ease of moving heavy equipment, we reported to the brigade's control unit, then we removed the cutting gear and jacks from the B.L. ready to haul up the embankment. I didn't appreciate the full extent of the disaster until I went up the embankment on to the track.

Buckled and overturned coaches were spread along the track. Firemen and medical teams were working in desperation to reach trapped victims. Bodies were caged in tangled masses of steel wreckage but it wasn't possible to count them because of the mutilation. I walked along the top of an overturned carriage, in fact I walked along its side and had to step across open doors of the carriages where there were dead victims, the compartments were appropriately marked with chalk. It was live casualties that the wreck was being searched for; the priority was to remove them or get them immediate medical attention, before they died from their injuries and shock.

Some of the bodies were in a dreadfully mutilated condition, especially those that had spilled out of the train windows and were squashed and rolled between the overturned carriages and the rough stony track. Parts of bodies, torn bloodstained clothing, an assortment of damaged shoes, ripped open suitcases and handbags, damaged train seats, all those things littered the track. I remember drawing Ron Bentley's attention to a bundle of clothing and a wig that I could see under part of the wreckage. On closer inspection I realised that the bundle of clothing was a legless torso and the wig was the complete hollow top of a skull from the forehead down to the back of the head. It was a dreadful accident in which about forty-nine people died and about eighty were injured.

During that period of my career, I allowed my concentration on the forthcoming station officer's examination to lapse. Although I was ill-prepared for it, I still sat the exam but without success. That had the effect of waking me up and renewing my determination. I again attended a regular study class in my off-duty time and was better prepared for the next examination. The centre where the examination was held was like a reunion party, loud laughter and handshakes, men waving and calling to each other. It was worth attending just for the pleasure of seeing old friends.

A few weeks later the results were published and I was pleased to have been successful. My concentrated studying had paid off.

Divisional Officer Rose and I passed on the staircase a few days after the station officer's examination results were known. He was wearing his mean look once again but I had got to know him better by then. I had discovered that behind that hard exterior was a caring man who was always ready to help anyone with a genuine personal or brigade problem.

"Be outside my office directly after lunch," he said hardly glancing towards me.

"Yes, Sir!" I answered, "But what for?"

Rose stopped at the top of the short flight of stairs, turned and said in a loud voice:

"Bloody well be there and you will find out, won't you?"

Then he carried on up the next flight of stairs to his office.

Wondering all through my lunch break what I had done wrong, I asked my station officer if he had any idea what the D.O. wanted to see me about. He had no idea and was just as inquisitive as I was. Still baffled I went up to the D.O.'s office and was about to knock on the partially open door when he looked up from his desk and told me to come in and shut the door. I stood in front of his desk licking my dry lips while he read and signed a couple of papers. His technique for making a person feel intimidated was second to none. Finally he put his pen in a desk tidy and looked up at me. He leaned back in his chair and momentarily studied me through squinting eyes. I just stood in front of him feeling a bit stupid, still wondering what it was all about. Then he said very slowly, "How would you like to be considered for temporary promotion at Dockhead?"

I was so surprised at the question that I felt my head jolt backwards and my mouth momentarily drop open. I had heard that Station Officer Fouracre attached to Dockhead Fire Station had fallen through a floor at a fire and had landed astride a heap of old iron, severely injuring himself, a very unfortunate accident that could happen to anyone, especially when working in thick smoke.

I quickly gathered my thoughts and accepted the offer, I was told that it was a long-term temporary promotion which was to begin the next morning and it carried more responsibility than just acting-up. As I was about to leave his office he said, "By the way…"

I turned to look at him, he smiled and continued:

"Muck it up and I'll have you back here as quick as a flash."

No 5.

I am on the right at the Hither Green Train Crash
when I was a Sub-Officer.

Chapter 8

Dockhead Fire Station housed three fire engines, Pump Escape, Pump and Turntable Ladder. Convenient for some, it was positioned next door to a pub. The building consisted of three floors, all of which was occupied by station personnel. Situated near the docks among large Thames side warehouses and cold stores it was not one of the busiest stations in the Division but could boast its fair share of large fires. Thirteen men, including a sub-officer and two leading firemen made up the watch. None of the members of the watch with the exception of Sub-Officer Les Whyte were known to me. I met Les Whyte about nine years previous, at the interview session when we applied to join the fire brigade when he, John Davis and I were accepted.

The first thing I did as a priority was introduce myself to the men and talk to them to try and judge the level of morale on the watch. I didn't lay down any rules or demands, I just told them to carry on as usual and I would observe points and raise anything at a later meeting that I didn't like or wanted to change. My second priority was to have a frank and private discussion with Les Whyte. Because he was the sub-officer attached to the watch, it would have been quite normal for him to have expected to act-up in the absence of his station officer. I needed to know what his feelings were towards me being transferred in. After all said and done, it was my future that was at stake, I was going to be kept under close observation so I didn't want any unnecessary aggravation. I put the question to him, asking whether I had his support or not. Les told me that he was not interested in further promotion and that he had allowed his feelings to become known, therefore, he was never asked to act-up. He told me that he had become disillusioned with the brigade and that he would be leaving when he felt the time was right. He assured me that meanwhile he was quite content and would support me during my stay as officer in charge.

I soon settled in and was able to plan my daily routine to include drill periods, lectures and fire prevention inspections. Having to organise all the necessary activities were to my advantage, doing the job was in my mind better than studying for my forthcoming interview for substantive station officer rank. Les and I got on better than I really expected, despite his loss of interest. He was fairly efficient about the station and a good officer to have on the fire ground, mainly because he still enjoyed that essential part of the job.

Although I realised the convenience of the station being next to a pub, in my ignorance I didn't place much importance in it, probably because I have never been a regular drinking man. One evening, as I took a stroll around the station, I suddenly realised that I was the only person in the building. I looked in every room, the radio was talking to itself in the mess room and the television was doing likewise in the T.V. room. It seemed like the fire brigade's version of the *Marie Celeste*.

It didn't take long for the probability of the whereabouts of the men to come to mind, so I decided to sound the emergency call bells. After first locking all the doors to the station, I stood in the watch-room with a smug look on my face as the call bells rang, waiting for the panic to start outside when the men realised that they couldn't get in the station.

Within a few seconds, to my amazement, I heard the sound of voices and footsteps running down the stairs into the appliance room. A bit puzzled I sent them all upstairs to the mess room where I could talk to them. As they walked past me I could smell beer so I knew that my theory was right. Still puzzled I walked slowly up the stairs behind them. Halfway up the stairs was an open window leading to a flat roof at the rear of the station. I leaned out of the window and saw that the flat roof adjoined the flat roof of the pub next door. Then I heard the voice of a woman coming from the darkness of the pub's roof:

"You alright, lads?" she called in a high-pitched cockney voice.

"Yes thank you," I replied, smiling to myself. Then I carried on up the stairs to the mess room, much the wiser.

After a long discussion which included some frank speaking, it was revealed that a visit to the pub was a regular event just before closing time in the evening. The call bells could be heard in the pub and the recognised route back to the station was, around the back of the bar and up the stairs to the living quarters, out on to the flat roof, across the roof and in through the window on the station staircase. Need I say that they didn't need that escape route again while I was the officer in charge. While I was on leave one Saturday night duty, Les received a call to a warehouse in Shad Thames. I was sorry that I missed that fire because that warehouse was six storeys high and was stacked on all floors with containers full of boxes of matches. It proved difficult to extinguish and was classified as a thirty pump fire. The first I knew of it was when I saw it reported on national television news. However, I didn't miss it completely because I had to visit the scene every duty for the next three weeks. When I was happy that it was safe I closed the job down to allow workmen to remove the debris. Then I had to complete a detailed fire report. Les didn't stay with me for very long, he had applied for a posting to a station nearer to his home and a few months after my arrival he was transferred.

John Goodson replaced Les Whyte as my sub-officer, we had not met each other before he was posted into Dockhead. John knew all of the firemen on the watch and was closer to them than I was. For the first time in my career I was experiencing a barrier between myself and the men. I began to sense that they preferred it when I wasn't around, a feeling that I was unfamiliar with. I noticed that the atmosphere that had developed assisted me to run the watch more efficiently. Any unpopular decisions that I had to make were more readily accepted. I soon began to realise that the rank of sub-officer was by far the best. Any mundane tasks could be handed down to the leading fireman to deal with and anything too difficult could be passed to the station officer to handle. However, I was quite happy to be in charge.

During a period of unrest within the brigade, the Fire Brigade's Union organised an emergency calls only demonstration. That meant that no work would be done in stations and the men would only be available to attend emergency calls. The industrial action was in support of a claim for shorter working hours and more pay. The firemen occupied themselves by standing outside the fire station collecting signatures and drumming up support from members of the public.

Typical of most stations, the firemen having no direct access to their Chief Officer or members of the Greater London Council aimed their frustration at their station officer. As the frustration built up around the brigade the only support that station officers received from their seniors at divisional headquarters was a telephone message telling them to 'play it cool'. What interpretation they expected to be put on that statement was anyone's guess.

It was strange that the firemen reacted in that way, because nobody wanted shorter hours and better pay more than I did, and probably every other officer in the brigade. I suppose, human nature being what it is, they decided to knock authority while they had the chance, knowing that there would be no comeback by way of disciplinary proceedings because the industrial action was official as far as the London Fire Brigade and the Fire Brigade's Union were concerned. What mattered though was the fact that when the fire-call bells sounded, all the men on the watch reverted to their normal working procedures. Things soon got back to normal when the industrial action was called off but I certainly learned a great deal from the experience.

Along with my efforts to study for my forthcoming station officer's promotion interview, likewise, John Goodson was also swatting for his station officer's promotion interview. That situation was very useful to me because we were able to discuss a variety of brigade matters which helped to broaden each other's knowledge and opinions.

I thought it very strange when I was asked to submit a confidential report on John's suitability for promotion though. I wouldn't have thought many people have been asked to write about somebody else's suitability for a job, that they wanted for themselves. As it turned out we were both promoted, John was transferred and I remained in post at Dockhead.

To have been promoted to the rank of station officer within ten years of joining was not a record by any means but I felt happy and lucky, even privileged. At last I could take a rest from studying because I felt quite satisfied at that moment. When I was promoted to leading fireman I looked directly to the next step up the ladder to sub-officer and then to station officer. However, on promotion to station officer I became more relaxed and happy with my lot because looking at the next rank and the working conditions that went with the job, I couldn't visualise myself working within those conditions. To set my sights on the rank of assistant divisional officer would have meant making up my mind to accept a complete change of lifestyle. To have to move into a brigade tied house or flat over a fire station and to accept the current working conditions at that time, which included working a seventy-six hour week, did not in any way appeal to me. I considered that any job that encroached on my leisure time, interfered with my independence or clashed with my private life and almost doubled my working hours, was not for me.

Completely satisfied with the situation that I was then fortunate enough to find myself in, I was happy to settle down and run my watch.

Many strange requests are made to fire brigades under the heading of 'Special Services'. On one hot summer's day in July 1968 I was ordered to a special service on Tower Bridge. The River Thames formed the boundary line between the division that I was in and the division north of the river. My crew arrived and dismounted on the southern side of the bridge and another crew did the same on the northern side. The bridge had been raised to allow a ship to pass into the Port of London. The ninety-two degree heat of the day had expanded the steel structure so much, that when it was lowered it wouldn't close properly to allow the road traffic to pass over it.

I walked to the centre of the bridge to where the two halves were jammed. The station officer from the other side of the river met me there. We stood discussing the situation for a few minutes, each of us standing on our own territory, rather like two land owners arguing about their boundary. We decided that the only action we could take was to try and cool the structure with water spray until it contracted enough for the two sections to close properly. The brigade's fire boat, Sir Eyre Massey Shaw, was ordered to spray water from the underside of the bridge and the crews from both sides of the river sprayed water over the road surface. Incidentally the Fire Boat Sir Eyre Massey Shaw, took part in the evacuation of Dunkirk. After about three hours of spraying, the bridge finally closed and traffic was allowed to travel over it once again. I don't know if that had ever happened to the bridge before or since but it made the headlines on that hot summer day.

After a couple of years at Dockhead I heard that the station officer at Old Kent Road Fire Station was due to retire. A new station had been built to replace the one where I had begun my operational career as a raw recruit. It was a modern open-style construction of two floors; on the ground floor was the appliance room which housed two fire engines, a P.E. and pump. Adjoining the appliance room was office accommodation, junior officer's locker room and the station officer's office and bedroom. The first floor was taken up by the firemen's locker room, kitchen, mess rooms, and the recreation room.

At one of the regular meetings of station officers with the divisional officer, I mentioned my desire for a transfer to D.O. Rose, I thought I would plant the idea in his mind with the hope that my name came up in the frame when the position became vacant. Following a round of promotions and postings two newly promoted Leading Firemen joined my watch at Dockhead, both arriving on the same night duty. I hadn't met either of them before so I had no idea of their brigade background. During their introductory interview I discovered that neither of them had much to offer and I considered that some of my firemen were better qualified by way of experience, to ride in charge of a fire engine.

That very evening we were called to a fire in a refrigerated warehouse. As we arrived at the address I could see that the fire was on the top floor of the five-storey building which was approximately two hundred feet long and one hundred and fifty feet wide. Being a cold store, I knew that it had the potential of becoming a serious fire. The thick cork insulation lining the cold rooms and lack of ventilation in the virtually windowless building, along with the impregnated animal fat in the old timber flooring deposited during years of storing meat, meant that it had the potential of a massive build-up of volatile gases and heat, just waiting for the introduction of air to complete an explosive mixture. Those conditions presented a potentially very dangerous situation for the fire-fighters and could result in severe damage to the building or even complete destruction.

Considering all of the potential hazards I dispatched the following priority message to brigade control prefixed with the address of the incident: Make pumps ten, turntable ladders two, breathing apparatus required.

During the initial fire fighting operations, I ordered one of my new leading firemen who was riding in charge of the T.L. to supervise the pitching of the ladder to the roof, then to climb up it to confirm my suspicion that the fire had broken through the roof. He seemed to turn white before my eyes. I am sure that he had never seen a building of that size on fire before and had never had to climb a T.L. during fire-fighting operations, especially one that disappeared into the darkness and smoke above.

The reason that I told him to climb the T.L. was that when working under those operational conditions, the priority is for the man's safety. Because he would be in charge of his own progress up the ladder into the unknown, he could stop and climb down if conditions were intolerable. If he stood at the head of the ladder whilst it was being extended mechanically by the T.L. operator, he could be placed in danger by entering excessive heat and smoke and would be powerless to do anything about it.

When he reported back my suspicions were confirmed. I was relieved because I knew that the potentially disastrous conditions that had been building up inside, had been vented through the roof making it safer to work inside of the building. The size of the fire went up to twelve pumps and we were able to contain it in a central cold room on the top floor, using six jets. We spent most of the night cutting away and damping down the smouldering cork insulation before the relief crews arrived. Visits were made all through the following night duty to ensure that it was completely extinguished.

The two new leading firemen told me later that they had wondered what they had let themselves in for, after such an action packed first night duty. They settled down after a while and soon became useful junior officers.

Unexpectedly one day I received a telephone message from divisional headquarters telling me that I was to be transferred to Old Kent Road. I was pleasantly surprised because I thought my request some months previously had fallen on deaf ears. The transfer meant that I had to change watches but I didn't mind that. I even had time to square things up at Dockhead, ready for the next officer in charge to take over.

I had a couple of leave days before my first duty at Old Kent Road, so I took all of my personal and brigade gear with me after my last duty at Dockhead and called into Old Kent Road on my way home. I met one of my opposite numbers on one of the other watches, stowed my gear and was ready for my first duty two days later.

As far as busy stations go, Old Kent Road was amongst the top few within the brigade, not necessarily for shouts on its own ground but for the total number of calls attended. The station was closely surrounded by five others – Dockhead, New Cross, Peckham, Lambeth and Southwark. All within a few minutes driving distance. Therefore Old Kent Road's appliances especially the pump were often ordered on to neighbouring station's ground, either on the initial call or to assist at a 'make-up'.

The mobilising officer in the brigade's control room, whose responsibility it was to maintain fire cover throughout the brigade, was continuously aware of the location of all fire engines. He only had to glance at his frequently updated appliance situation board, to see which station's appliances were available. Because Old Kent Road's ground was so well covered by surrounding stations, he would often select its pump to attend large fires anywhere in the brigade. That made Old Kent Road a desirable station to be attached to, so I was looking forward to a new station and a new challenge.

Within a couple of weeks of being transferred to Old Kent Road I had settled in and had already noticed how much busier it was compared to Dockhead. The men on the watch were a mixed bunch, some experienced and some not long out of the training centre. I was surprised to see Larry Case there. If I had not met him at the Job Centre at the latter end of 1958 I would probably not have joined the London Fire Brigade. I certainly didn't expect to meet him again in the circumstances of me being his governor, he only lived a few streets away from the station and he knew the area well, along with two or three of the other drivers. Having drivers who knew their topography, took quite a lot of pressure off and it was even better when I had gained confidence in their driving ability.

It was not unusual to be ordered to a large fire in another division, especially if breathing apparatus was required. Some jobs could be long and arduous and would require servicing an exhausted breathing apparatus set ready to enter the building more than once.

During school lunch break and just after school closed were the main times for false alarms and rubbish fires, both of which we had our fair share. Even if it was suspected that a call was a false alarm, we had no way of being certain, so we responded with the same sense of urgency as for any other call. I had by that time in my career seen the results of so many tragic fires and accidents, that I felt that nothing would surprise me anymore.

Having attended probably thousands of calls by that time I still enjoyed the thrill of the chase. The thrill of being driven at speed through the streets of London in a fire engine could only be beaten by being in the driving seat. Of course I realised that my thrills were other people's disasters, so sometimes to discover that the call was a malicious false alarm, was a relief. Contrary to that I felt sorrow and sympathy on the many occasions that I saw somebody's family home on fire. The priorities in those cases were to find out if there was anyone still in the building and to get a crew around the back of the premises, just in case there was someone hanging unnoticed and unheard, from a rear window or flat roof etc.

An interesting part of fire fighting is the investigation into the cause of an outbreak, which has to be established. In most cases the occupier or person who discovered the fire can be very helpful. Otherwise, a process of elimination will determine two, or perhaps three, probable causes. If arson is suspected the police are informed and as in the case of fatalities, they take over the investigations.

I had a rule that I always kept to. Whenever I had somebody dead, injured or overcome at a fire, I always made notes and sketches of the situation. People have a nasty habit of dying, occasionally weeks after being involved in fire or accident. It is very difficult to try to recall past events with any accuracy, or to write a statement for a coroner sometimes long after the incident had taken place, especially when so many other calls had been attended since the one in question.

One such case that comes to mind was a shout to a fire in an electrical sub-station. As we pulled up at the incident we were met by a member of the public who directed me to the sub-station where a young boy, aged about ten years old, was lying on his back near the electrical apparatus. The man who met us had removed most of the boy's burning clothing, which was still smouldering nearby.

His poor little trembling body was badly burnt so I knelt down beside him and spoke to him to establish whether he was conscious or not.

He told me his name and said that he couldn't see anything. In a very feeble voice, he explained that he climbed on to the electrical equipment because he and his friend thought it was switched off because they couldn't hear the humming sound that they had heard before. When he mentioned his friend I immediately ordered a search of the sub-station and surrounding area to try and locate him. It became known later that he was uninjured and had run home, frightened after the accident. The pathetic little burned figure kept repeating that there was a bright flash.

The unlucky young boy was quickly removed to hospital where unfortunately he had to have an arm amputated. About six weeks later his luck completely ran out, the poor lad died of septicaemia. If I had not taken notes and made a sketch of that incident, it would have been difficult to have made a factual statement for the Coroner. I was amazed when about three years later, I was asked by solicitors acting for the boy's parents to submit a further statement. From the hundreds of jobs that I had attended since that incident, it would have been difficult to have recalled all of the details without the notes that I still had, although I will always have a mental picture of the scene.

Once again due to the shuffling around of personnel I had a vacancy for a sub-officer on my watch and to fill the vacancy Eddie Blackhall my leading fireman, had been acting-up for a while.

Ron Brown, a sub-officer who had transferred from the Surrey Fire Brigade, was due to fill the vacancy, after first spending a couple of weeks at divisional headquarters, familiarising himself with London Fire Brigade procedures. On his arrival, Eddie of course reverted to his substantive rank of leading fireman.

Ron and I had a long talk on his first day. He told me about his previous experience in the Surrey Fire Brigade. Six years as a training school instructor and six years in the fire prevention branch. If I remember correctly his operational experience amounted to a period at Leatherhead Fire Station as a leading fireman, not a great deal of experience at the sharp end. I appreciated his frankness so we decided to do something about it by way of our own debriefing session after every fire. That gave Ron a chance to examine and question my actions and decisions and comment on my technique of command and management on the fire ground. It also allowed me to monitor and comment on his actions and reactions and offer advice and some guidance, to assist him in updating his own fire ground technique.

Ron, Eddie and I were a great team, the time we spent working together was enjoyable and we had a lot of fun between the serious bits. I still smile when I recall the banter between us during that period. They were both big men, over six feet tall and each weighing around sixteen stone. I being less than five foot eleven was often the subject of ridicule from the two big guys. As I was eating my supper one evening, Ron and Eddie were having a deep and serious conversation in the officers' mess. They were standing by the door and now and again one of them would point to a position on the door, about three feet from the floor. I wasn't too interested in what they were discussing so I didn't take much notice of them. Becoming aware of some disagreement between them I finally asked them what they were up to. I shouldn't have bothered, I fell right into their trap as one of them replied:

"We are trying to work out the best position to fix your coat hook, Sir."

I always enjoyed a good laugh and I thought that was well worked out and very funny. Another time a mysterious parcel appeared on my desk containing a small wire coat hanger about three inches wide. A note attached indicated that it was a new issue for the uniform jackets of small officers. And so it went on.

After a few unusually quiet duties, which helped Ron settle in and get to know the station and the men on the watch, we were ordered to a fire in a derelict house. That was to be Ron's first taste of the type of work that we had to deal with in the areas of Bermondsey, Southwark, Lambeth, Dockhead and Peckham. We arrived to see smoke drifting gently out of the first-floor windows of one of a terrace of about ten derelict two-storey houses, awaiting demolition.

The hose-reel tubing was taken into the house to tackle what was clearly a small fire, indicated by the way the smoke was drifting lazily about. The fire was in a back room on the first floor, it had been lit in what was left of the fireplace and had spread to the timber floor boards.

Sprawled on a dirty old mattress on the floor were four men. As the fire was being extinguished they began to mutter and swear. They were all alcoholics, absolutely stoned, well on their way down to rock bottom.

"Come on then, wakey! wakey!" I shouted, "Come on, out of it or you will all be burnt to death, quickly now, the place is on fire."

As I expected their reaction was typical and predictable:

"Fuck-off!" one of them muttered, raising his head and peering at me through sunken red slits in his dirty unshaven face.

"Piss-off and leave us alone," he mumbled.

"Come on," I said. "You and your mates get out before the police arrive."

"Fuck the police," he said as he laid his grimy head down again.

I looked at Ron who was standing behind me, the expression on his face said it all. I got the impression that Ron did not believe what he was seeing.

I jokingly commented. "Not quite the same as Leatherhead is it, Ron?"

Eventually the four drunken men made their way down the staircase to the street. One of them, who they called 'Wingy' only had one arm, he couldn't make it without my help. In fact I carried him down the stairs and into the street. I stood him by a lamp post which he leaned against, draping his one arm around it for support.

As a contribution to Ron Brown's introduction to life in the back streets of London, I started a conversation with 'Wingy'. He proceeded to tell us, in a stuttering and repetitive way, why he was in that down-and-out situation. Standing unsteadily without the support of the lamp post, he slowly and deliberately searched his pockets with his one hand. He produced a medal, which appeared to be his only possession. I couldn't see it clearly because he was waving it about but I got the meaning of his ramblings.

He told us that he lost his arm when he was blown up in a submarine during the war He said that he was given a medal then but nobody has cared about him since. I asked him why he was drunk so early in the day and before he could gather his thoughts to reply, one of the others butted in saying, "The only way to look at this rotten world is through the bottom of a bottle."

I don't believe Ron will ever forget that day and those four unfortunate men.

A few weeks later, two bodies were discovered at a fire in the same derelict house. They were in the upstairs front room. One of them was sprawled in a grotesquely distorted position in the middle of the floor. When the undertaker's men tried to fit the body into a metal coffin for removal, the lid wouldn't shut because of a leg protruding above the top of the coffin. I believe I speak for all who were present, even the undertaker's men, when I say that we were all a bit sickened when, as they tried easing the burnt leg down below the coffin lid, it snapped off at the thigh with a loud crack, exposing a clean white broken bone, contrasting against the remainder of the burnt and blackened leg.

The other body was situated below a window and was not discovered right away because it was covered by debris from the collapsed roof. The staircase was unusable so access had to be made by ladder, through a first floor window. What we didn't know at the time was, as each of my crew was going in and out of the window, they were continually stepping on the undiscovered victim below the rubble. Eventually the body, which was not as badly burnt as the other one, burst open at the abdomen. The gruesome sight drew the attention of a crew member as he climbed in through the window. When the debris was cleared it was discovered that the body was 'Wingy'.

Ron soon adapted to his new brigade and after handling a few good jobs in my absence and having passed his station officer's examination whilst in the Surrey Fire Brigade, he was given the opportunity to act-up at another station. He didn't return to me as a sub-officer, he continued to act up at different stations until he was promoted to substantive station officer.

As I mentioned earlier, practical jokes were natural time fillers during the quiet periods and at some time or another most brigade members have been the victims of the ingenuity of bored firemen. Some of the capers that they got up to were absolutely hilarious, but occasionally they got carried away and their antics were not at all humorous. When their jokes involved operational gear it was potentially dangerous, or at the very least could have caused a loss of valuable time if the equipment was required in a hurry. I have seen men frantically trying to put their fire tunics on at a fire, when they should have been already fully rigged, because someone had clipped together the sleeves of their fire tunics with a mass of staples. Another nasty trick was to steal an egg from the mess cupboard and place it right down in the toe of a man's fire boot or sprinkle a few little pieces of coke or other small hard objects in fire boots, then watch the unsuspecting wearer hobble around in pain until they had time to empty their boots.

On my way to a fire on one occasion, I was fastening my fire tunic when the first button came away in my hand, not an unusual thing to happen. When the second, third and fourth buttons came away I couldn't believe it. I finished up with a handful of chrome buttons and none on my tunic to keep it fastened. It was an old trick irresponsibly played. What some prankster had done was to dip a matchstick, or similar applicator, into a lead acid battery in the battery charging room, then drop a small amount of acid on the threads of the buttons of my tunic. After a time the threads rotted and the inevitable happened.

Many varied and sometimes unusual events take place within the confines of fire stations and also when attending emergency calls. I learned a long time ago that it was always advisable to have your wits about you and to expect the unexpected.

I received a telephone call at the station one evening from a man speaking with an Irish accent, he claimed that he had placed a bomb in the fire station. In an effort to keep the man talking I suggested that he was a friend of mine playing a practical joke and I could tell that he was putting on a false Irish accent. With my hand over the mouthpiece I quickly whispered to my sub-officer to contact the police and ask them to trace the call. Meanwhile the man lost his temper at my suggestion that he was not an Irishman and was desperately trying to convince me that he was a born and bred Irishman. I kept laughing and telling him his accent was good but it didn't fool me and that I was too busy to talk to him. That had the effect of making him even more determined to convince me that he was a genuine Irishman. I was sure by then that the man was the worse for drink and he was obviously not aware of the time he was spending talking to me. He was on the line long enough for the call to be traced so I was expecting the police to arrive at the phone box, or wherever the man was telephoning from, and arrest him.

To my astonishment, instead of ordering a mobile unit to respond, the police butted in on the call with the obvious result of the man hanging up. I had to take the threat seriously because the Irish Republican Army was active in London at that time. I had attended an I.R.A. bomb attack on the Houses of Parliament only a few weeks earlier, so anything was possible.

I carried out the procedure for dealing with bomb threats by informing control and ordering my fire engines and personnel out of the station. When the appliance room doors were opened to drive the fire engines out, we found a man lying on the ground moaning. At first I thought he was a drunk but when I took a closer look I could see that his face was covered in blood and was badly swollen and cut. He asked us to help him on to his feet because he thought his arms were broken as they were too painful to lean on. He had obviously been in some kind of an accident or had been badly beaten up. At a guess, I would suspect the latter. The police were informed again and an ambulance asked for.

With the fire engines parked in the roadway, at a safe distance from the station, we could hear the sound of approaching police cars. I asked the occupants of the first police car whether they were there to deal with the bomb threat or the injured man, they chose the man. When the second police car arrived they also said they were there to deal with the injured man. It seemed that nobody wanted to deal with the bomb threat.

Eventually a police inspector arrived and because of his supercilious attitude the arguments started. He told me, in a demanding sort of way, to accompany him on a search of the fire station, so that I could identify any unusual objects or any items that shouldn't be there. That would have been a fair request and in accordance with normal police procedure at such incidents, but my latest written orders on the subject did not differentiate between brigade premises or any other premises.

I reminded him, after he became agitated at my refusal to comply with his request, which was more like an order, that I was also a member of a disciplined service and had orders and procedures to comply with.

I explained that it was my job, along with my crews, to stand by at a safe distance ready to perform any rescue and fire-fighting operations in the event of an explosion. If I contravened those orders and was either killed or injured, it could be claimed that my actions were a contributory factor and any pension or compensation award to my dependants could be affected. I knew I was being a bit over the top but I wasn't going to have that officious individual quote his procedures and try to impose his will, or intimidate me and get away with it. Anyway, I was pretty sure that there wasn't a bomb in the station and if the police had done their job correctly in the first place, they could have apprehended the culprit. He didn't like my remarks about that either.

It was all sorted out, when Jim Gurney an acting A.D.O. turned up and agreed to accompany the police on a search of the station. Nothing was found but it was a good exercise, which I believe showed up an oversight in the brigade's procedure for suspected explosive devices on fire brigade premises.

Looking back I consider that the most enjoyable time that I spent in the Brigade was in charge of a watch at Old Kent Road Fire Station, there was always something going on, some funny episodes and some tragic.

I recall that we all felt as though we were experiencing a personal tragedy when the wife of one of my firemen was dying from cancer. He tried to put on a brave face when he was on duty but I could see that he was going through absolute hell. I explained his situation to D.O. Rose who gave me permission to give him as much time off duty as was necessary for him to be with her. I kept a close eye on the man's worsening situation and as requested, regularly reporting back to the D.O. All the men on the watch were extremely saddened when the news was received that the man's wife had died. It took him some time to adjust to life without her.

On the happier side there were a lot of laughs, especially when the men let the station rat out for a run. It was cleverly made from the bristle end of an old toilet brush. A tail replaced the handle and a couple of beads were tied in with wire, to look like eyes. It was attached to a long length of nylon fishing line and at around the time for the pubs to close, it was placed outside the station.

The station frontage was about thirty feet wide across the forecourt and pavement to the kerbstone. After dark, a street lamp post, cast a long shadow across the forecourt to the front door of the station. For the best results the rat was placed at the base of the lamp post, in its shadow. The nylon line, undetectable in the dark, was threaded through the front door letter box.

Late in the evening when people were making their way home, probably after having had a drink or two, the rat operator would pull on the nylon line and move the rat short distances with sharp jerking movements across the footpath towards the station. The reactions of the passers-by when they first noticed the strange looking animal were so funny that when I first discovered my fireman doing it, I laughed so much that I had difficulty breathing. I saw old men take a swipe at it with their walking sticks, young men running after it trying to kick it, but the expert timing by the rat's operator was so good that nobody ever caught it. Women would scream and cross the road rather than walk near it.

One particular chap hid behind his girlfriend while she tried to feed it with chips. Sometimes a small crowd would gather and attack it together, they would chase it towards the station where it would run up the front door and disappear through the letterbox, to the astonishment of its pursuers. Once a woman rang the enquiry bell and reported it. She was thanked and assured that no fireman's boot would remain unturned until it was found.

One day my pump, with myself in charge, was ordered to stand by at Peckham Fire Station for fire cover during a make-up fire elsewhere within the division, which had left some parts of the division short of fire and officer cover.

During that stand-by duty we received a call to a fire in a house on the outer perimeter of Peckham's ground. When we arrived at the address a member of the public shouted that they thought that there was someone in the house which was a large three-storey property. Automatically I dispatched a message to brigade control making pumps four, persons reported. I could see smoke percolating through cracks in the glass of a heavily smoke-stained window on the first floor directly above the ground floor entrance. Hose was taken in through the front door and up the stairs to the front room where the fire appeared to be contained. The door of the room was locked so it had to be forced open. Meanwhile a ladder was pitched to the first floor window which had to be broken to allow the thick smoke to be ventilated to open air, which made it a little easier for the crew inside the house to enter the room.

The fire was quickly brought under control and as the smoke gradually cleared the extent of the damage could be assessed. Sadly among the debris a body of a young child aged about five was discovered. I inspected the body and was convinced that all life was extinct so I left it in the position that it was found to await investigation by the police and for photographic records to be taken.

A police doctor attended and while he was examining the body I noticed that a bubble of mucus appeared from the child's nose and for a few seconds I thought that the child was still alive but the doctor, probably sensing my concern, said that it was the release of a build-up of gas within the body.

It transpired that the child had been locked in the room on its own, with some food and drink, while the mother had gone to work. Presumably she had inadvertently left a box of matches within reach of the child who decided, probably out of complete boredom, to play with them with disastrous results.

During my stay at Old Kent Road I had several changes of firemen, leading firemen and sub-officers. Some passed through on the road for promotion and others moved on to gain more experience or just for a change of station. During their stay, each individual added something to the watch; an impression was made one way or another. A sub-officer that was with me for a time certainly made an impression, by way of demonstrating his sexual prowess.

I often turned a blind eye when my sub-officer had a visitor in his room. In fact on occasions when we had a call in the late evening, I sometimes noted one or two chaps, single men of course, running into the appliance room, from the station yard. They had obviously been making use of their cars to get a little privacy. Morale was high on the watch and I didn't consider affecting it by playing the moral guardian to a bunch of grown men, because I wasn't exactly the innocent bystander, as I will explain later. All the time that there were no problems, then my blind eye continued to be turned. Anyway, the men concerned were not aware that I knew what was going on.

Alerted by the conspicuous absence of firemen around the station one night duty, I went for a walk around the building. I discovered the men in the yard, gathered outside the window of the sub-officer's room. When I asked them what was going on I got the joint whispered reply, "Shush, Governor!" At the same time they were waving their arms indicating that I should keep my voice down.

The curtains of the room had been arranged to hang about one inch from the bottom of the window, allowing a perfect view into the room. From the wide open window of the television room directly above, came the sound of a conveniently loud T.V. programme, drowning out any uncontrolled giggles or whispers, made by the men as they gazed into the room.

I stooped to peer into the room and saw that the sub-officer's bed had been repositioned so that the foot of it was butting up against the wall beneath the window. What I saw was the most explicit scene of a couple indulging in sexual intercourse that could have been imagined or that I am likely to ever see again. Although I couldn't see any faces I accepted that one of the naked bodies on the bed was my sub-officer. The men could hardly contain themselves so when any one of them couldn't hold their laughter any longer he would run away from the window and just burst into hysterical laughter.

I know of at least two other occasions when the show was repeated and I suspect that when I was on leave, there were probably Oscar winning performances.

A book could be written solely on the antics of what went on at Old Kent Road. Unfortunately like all good things they eventually come to an end. Nothing lasts forever.

No 6.

Tower Bridge being cooled with water spray.
Massey Shaw Fire boat cooling the underside of the structure

Chapter 9

My life changed dramatically from the beginning of the 1970s. To explain how and the reason why, it is necessary for me to return to the events that occurred during 1965 when I was attached to Brixton Fire Station. I had made the remote acquaintance with a young woman named Rosemary Browne, she was a member of the Brigade Control Room staff. It began with the sound of her voice on the telephone which I instantly recognised whenever she answered my telephone calls when I had cause to contact the control room.

As time passed we became telephone friends, I began to look forward to talking to her when our shift duties coincided. We treated our conversations as just a bit of innocent fun, we were just two voices exchanging views which served the purpose of breaking the monotony during slack periods, mainly during night duties. Neither of us knew anything about the other or what we looked like.

Curiosity took over one day. Rosemary, enticed by her friend Ann who also worked in the control room, surprised me by telephoning me at the fire station when she was on leave. She pretended that she was in a telephone call box just up the road from the fire station and that she wanted to meet me. I believe that she expected me to make excuses and put her off but I was quite pleased at the thought of meeting her so I told her she was welcome. That called her bluff because she was actually telephoning from the West End of London, even so she decided to put me to the test and said that she and Ann were coming to see me anyway.

After a couple of hours, two giggling girls arrived at the station asking for me. When I saw them I was pleasantly surprised, they both seemed very young and very attractive. One had longish fair hair and one had short dark hair but I didn't know which one was Rosemary. I remember thinking and hoping that she was the little one with the short dark hair. It turned out that she was indeed the little one that I was instantly attracted to. They waited for a short time until the end of my duty when I walked them both to a bus stop. I was very impressed and wanted to see Rosemary again but was doubtful about her response now that she had met me. After all, she was only eighteen and I was eleven years older than her, married with two children.

Being married with children was a big deterrent, constantly nagging at me in the back of my mind, making me wonder in what possible direction my friendship with Rosemary could be heading. I did not need telling that the association was likely to cause grief and unhappiness to either Rosemary, my family or myself, probably all of us. To heal the self-inflicted wound I knew that there was only one sensible action to take and that was to nip the friendship in the bud.

When our night duties clashed which was about once in ten days, we talked a lot on the telephone, sometimes well into the night. We both knew that our friendship was not going anywhere and on that understanding we agreed to meet for a coffee and talk face-to-face. I met Rosemary near her home in New Kings Road, Fulham, South West London one morning after a night duty.

That meeting nearly didn't happen because I had a fire call just after 0800 hours that morning. Fortunately it was only a very small fire that the occupant of the flat managed to extinguish before we arrived. After opening all the windows so that the smoke could disperse and making sure that the fire was completely extinguished, I and my crew made a speedy return to the station.

I didn't have time to take a shower so after a quick wash and brush up I drove as fast as the traffic would allow me, in an attempt not to be late. Fortunately Rosemary was well aware that emergency calls can happen at any time of day and night so she didn't mind that I was a few minutes late and she didn't even mind that I still smelt of smoke. We walked for a while, over Putney Bridge to a coffee bar in Putney High Street where we sat chatting for some time. We then walked back to her house and before parting she gave me her home telephone number in case I wanted to talk to her when she was off duty. That was a temptation that I found almost impossible to resist.

During the next few years Rosemary and I became very close. Because of my responsibilities I was still living with my family, but living a lie. The situation within my marriage, which had begun to worsen long before Rosemary and I met, wasn't getting any better. On reflection, it began to falter as long ago as when I left the army, and over the years the decline in our relationship was hard to live with for both of us.

The cause I believe was due to getting married at eighteen years old and being in the army for three years. The fairytale image in our minds of being together probably distorted all of the facts associated with the real world, and as our true personalities developed it became obvious to me that the incompatibilities in our relationship was causing a lot of tension between us.

As the years passed the whole regrettable situation began to affect me and it also caused Maureen to become quite ill. As far as I was concerned and for the benefit of all, there could only be one remedy. The best for everyone involved was to end the farce that my marriage had become. My association with Rosemary was known only to some close friends and work colleagues. I believed it was necessary to protect her until we were absolutely sure of what we both wanted and had made some outline plans for our future.

I knew that once Maureen had discovered that I was seeing Rosemary her bitterness would surely develop into an obsession to get revenge, a natural reaction for some people. If I had decided to stay with Maureen and she had discovered that I had been seeing Rosemary, I am certain that she would never have forgotten it. She would have used it as a weapon by bringing the subject up at every opportunity. The knife would have been plunged and I knew that it would have been twisted for a very long time in the future. I am sure that ultimately, being married to each other would become even more intolerable, causing us to part even without a third person being involved. The bitterness inside her would gradually eat away at her because it was not in her nature to forgive or forget.

I had no grounds against Maureen for a divorce so I decided as a means to an end, to agree with and co-operate with anything that she demanded. I paid for her divorce costs and for the house to be transferred to her sole name. During 1971 I left with only the clothes on my back. I rented a single room in Tooting South London, drastic action but necessary for us both to sort out our lives.

Of course I had to pay maintenance for Beverly and Bonita and an amount for Maureen. One day Beverly said that she had a message from her mother. She told me that Maureen's car had broken down and that she couldn't afford to have it repaired so could I advance her some maintenance money so that she could get the repair done. I do not remember how much money I gave her but I do remember that I had trouble raising the amount. I discovered later that she played me for a sucker, because about two weeks after I gave her the money, she remarried.

In 1973 I managed to arrange a mortgage for a house in Crawley West Sussex. I moved there to live on my own in December that year. That presented me with a journey to Old Kent Road Fire Station that took at least two hours by car and sometimes longer, depending on the traffic density.

On March 2nd 1974 Rosemary and I were married in a registry office in Horsham West Sussex.

The Control Room at the Brigade Headquarters Lambeth had closed and Rosemary was transferred to the Croydon Control Room, so her journey from our home wasn't too bad.

After a few months of endless hours of wasted time and car running costs by burning fuel in traffic queues, crawling along in low gear trying to keep calm and not letting frustration affect my patience, I began to think how nice it would be if I was attached to one of the fire stations that I passed on my way to Old Kent Road. Reluctantly, because I was very happy at Old Kent Road, I made up my mind to apply for a transfer, simply because it made sound economic sense.

A vacancy at Norbury Fire Station near Croydon was offered to me. I accepted it because vacancies for station officers in the areas that were suitable for cutting my travelling time did not appear very often. The journey to and from Norbury cut my journey time by two hours each day compared to travelling to Old Kent Road.

Built to similar specifications and housing similar types of fire appliances as those at Old Kent Road, Norbury was quite an acceptable modern station as far as accommodation was concerned. It wasn't as busy as I would have liked but it had its moments. My watch was made up of mostly young men, all of them being an unknown quantity to me. Not knowing or working with any of them before I had no idea how they performed on the fire ground. Until I had gained confidence in their ability I had to keep my wits about me at all times. Sub-Officer Colin Crabb was in post and seemed to have a pretty good knowledge of the station's ground. Colin briefed me on the area and the type of risks and their locations. He appeared to be an efficient Sub-Officer who knew the watch personnel quite well. As my confidence in Colin and the watch members grew, I allowed myself to gradually relax.

153

I am now at a stage in my memoirs where my opinions and criticisms become a bit boring to express and probably even more boring for a reader to digest. In this and a couple of the following chapters I make reference to the methods of selection of officers by the senior management of the London Fire Brigade. All of my comments and opinions originate from my experiences and opinions, which were formed over many years following the creation of the Greater London Fire Brigade.

A rumour that blossomed and grew increasingly interesting on the grapevine, suggested that the brigade was to review the senior officers' working hours and that they were changing to the watch duty system. That was the same system that the rest of the brigade were working, up to and including the rank of station officer. The senior officers' residential duty system which demanded living in brigade accommodation and being on call from home was hopefully to be phased out.

Up until that time, as far as I and many others who preferred to keep their home lives separate from work were concerned, further promotion was out of the question. What the rumours suggested appeared to be very encouraging but because of the 'perks' that went with the residential duty system, I found it hard to believe that those working it, would ever let it go. It suited a lot of people and those already in post would not give it up without a fight, or at least the guarantee of a non-worsening clause in their conditions of service.

It had been my opinion for many years that the London Fire Brigade had been managed by senior officers, who may not have been the best men for senior management positions. I believe that a question mark hung over them, simply because the brigade was not able to select its senior management from all of the officers that it employed. Rarely at that time, were officers imported from other fire brigades. Selection for promotion above station officer rank could only be made from those prepared to accept the residential conditions. Some of the living accommodation that went with the appointments were situated in areas of London that I would not add to my list of preferred locations to live. I certainly would not wish to reside in some of the tied dwellings available and at the same time double my working hours.

I could not convince myself that for the remainder of my service, the conditions that went with higher rank would be worth the gains that it attracted. There were of course, many candidates who would welcome free accommodation and free fuel and light. Combining all the perks along with the boost to their ego made further promotion for some officers, even under those existing conditions, attractive and worthwhile. That was their business and their personal choice. I could accept their judgment but it was not for me.

I knew a number of dedicated station officers who would have made excellent senior officers. But their understanding of what was expected of them, combined with consideration for their families regarding neighbourhood, housing and schools, outweighed any desire for promotion to a senior rank. Unlike some they could not be influenced by delusions of grandeur. Inevitably, there were those who would take promotion at any price and there always will be, in any occupation. In my opinion, weighing up the performances of some of those in the category of 'promotion at any price' that I have worked with, very few have demonstrated the skills required to do the job efficiently or even show potential for further promotion.

As time passed I became more familiar with my new area and more aware of the potential and skills of the men on my watch. It was a nice relaxed life at Norbury, with just enough work to prevent me becoming too bored. The senior officers in the division seemed a bit laid-back, which made me realise why the rest of the brigade referred to the 'H' Division as the 'Lazy Aitch'.

In February 1975 a serious underground train crash happened at Moorgate Underground Station. A train crowded with commuters crashed into a wall at the end of a dead-end tunnel. The two front coaches and half of the third coach were compressed into about seventy-five feet of the blind tunnel. There were many trapped, dead and injured people involved. Control continually ordered fresh relief crews from all over London, for the duration of about four days, to relieve exhausted personnel. Emergency Tender crews applied their skills, extricating live victims for hours on end and typically, their attitude to their work and their devotion to duty at such disasters they were reluctant to leave so they had to be ordered back to their stations to allow fresh crews to take over the rescue operations. About forty-three people were killed and a further seventy-six injured. Firemen had to work in close proximity to many trapped and mutilated dead bodies, to enable them to remove the live injured, a priority to prevent them from suffering further trauma or even death.

The media focused attention on the last two trapped passengers that were still alive, an off-duty police woman and a man. As crews worked in relays to release them it became a race against time. It took many hours of hard work and crew changes before they could be extricated. My pump was ordered on to the job as a relief, at the time when the decision was made by the medical team to amputate the woman's leg from below the knee. Because of concern over the deterioration of both victims, amputation was the only sure way of releasing her and the man, since he was trapped beneath her. Crews were lined up along the narrow space that had been made between the tunnel wall and the tangled wreckage, in preparation for a speedy removal of the last two casualties.

After the amputation was made, the two injured people were passed on stretchers along the chain of men, towards the platform. The man was first and as he passed me he turned his head and looked at me, we spoke briefly and he appeared to have his wits about him. I was shocked to learn that he died the following day. The woman was brought out next and in her anaesthetised state, she slipped slightly from the stretcher. Her leg minus her foot was hanging down and as she was passed up to the platform level, from the track, I instinctively grasped the bloodstained gauze-covered leg to support it and to prevent it from being knocked, not that she would have felt anything, but it just seemed a painful and unnecessary thing to happen at the time. The working conditions became quite appalling because of the heat and the stench from the decomposing bodies, still trapped at the compacted front end of the wreckage. Towards the end of the incident all work had to be performed by men wearing breathing apparatus.

In contrast to disasters attended by fire brigade personnel, I remember feeling a bit of a fool when I attended a special service call to a woman locked out of her house. Because she had a young baby waiting to be fed, we turned out to gain entry for her. She had left her bedroom window open on the first floor, so it was a simple job to pitch a short extension ladder to get in.

I must have been feeling energetic on that day because I climbed the ladder, opened the window fully and stepped on to the window sill. As I lowered myself to the floor of the bedroom, I didn't notice that one of the buttons on my fire tunic became entangled in a hole, which was part of the design in the pattern of the net curtains. Thinking that the curtains would just brush over me I walked towards the bedroom door. I was very embarrassed to find that the curtains came with me. I ripped a large hole in them which didn't enhance the pattern at all and almost wrenched the curtains from the window. The woman was grateful for our services and was very understanding when I told her what I had done. In the background I could see my firemen nearly bursting trying not to laugh. On the way back to the station they went into hysterics, and so did I.

Eventually the time came for applications to be submitted for promotion interviews for the rank of assistant divisional officer. Attracted by the proposed new senior officers duty system, like many others I handed in my application. Interviews were held and after about twelve months of discussions between the Fire Brigade's Union, the National Association of Fire Officers, the London Fire Brigade and the Greater London Council, the promotions were made.

Existing assistant divisional officers, working the residential system, were upgraded to divisional officer rank and continued to work the residential duty system and the newly promoted assistant divisional officers worked the watch related rota. I am pleased to say that I was promoted and posted to the 'H' Divisional Headquarters at Croydon. I couldn't have wished for a better posting because Croydon was very convenient for travelling from my home in West Sussex.

My last duty at Norbury Fire Station was a night shift. We didn't turn a wheel all night and by about 0800 hours the following morning I had packed all my personal effects and equipment, ready for my move to the A.D.O.'s accommodation.

At that stage in my career I was never surprised when something unexpected turned up at any time during a duty. My duty man phoned me from the watch-room, to tell me that a policeman was with him and he wanted to borrow a ladder. I went to the watch-room to speak to the constable and to explain that we did not loan equipment but if he had a problem that we could deal with, we would be pleased to help.

After informing brigade control I ordered my appliances to the address that the constable had given me, where the female occupant had not been seen for a few days. It was in a block of flats, whose residents had been complaining of a foul smell which appeared to be coming from the drains. The policeman told me that he had responded to a telephone call about the smell which the residents said had been hanging around for a couple of days. He was then informed by a resident that her neighbour, an elderly lady, had not been seen for a few days.

I ordered my crew to pitch a ladder to a small open window at first-floor level but told them not to climb it. Taking the constable to one side to talk to him, I explained that I was leaving the station and if, as I suspected, we were going to discover a body, then we must agree then and there, that he would make the discovery and be responsible for writing all of the reports and the statement for the coroner. He agreed, so I sent a man up the ladder to enter the flat, after instructing him not to look for anyone but to make his way directly to the front door and open it.

The policeman and I waited at the front door of the flat. My fireman quickly opened the door and ran out with his hand over his mouth, violently heaving and gagging. The smell that came out with him was the worst that I have ever had the misfortune to draw into my nostrils, it was a really foul stink, absolutely diabolical. The policeman and I reeled backwards and automatically placed our hands over our noses as the contents of our stomachs hit the back of our throats.

Making our way into the flat we discovered the body of an elderly woman lying on her side in her bath. The hot tap was turned on and being supplied through a gas water heater, of the type that continued to heat the water, all the while that the water was flowing.

The poor old dear had been immersed in scalding water for about three days. The submerged part of her body was virtually cooked, with the flesh breaking away and the part above the water was bloated and green in colour. The bath water, which was running out of the bath overflow into the drains, was causing the disgusting smell. The flat was neat and tidy, even her slippers were neatly placed at the side of the bath with her stockings rolled up and placed inside them. Presumably, she had slipped in the bath or had suffered some kind of attack whilst in the bath. Whatever, it was a very sad job to end my stay at Norbury, marking the end of my few years in the rank of station officer in charge of a watch at a station.

It didn't take long to realise that the brigade was not geared up for the newly promoted A.D.O.s. Even after the prolonged period of negotiations prior to the promotions, there were no proper office facilities and no quarters available for night duty. It became a case of make do, totally unsatisfactory and a typical example of senior management's efficiency at that time plus the fact that it did not affect any of the original residential officers.

Because divisional officers and the ranks above were still working the old residential duty system it seemed to create a 'them and us' situation. The A.D.O.s were treated as the poor relations and had to make do with surplus office equipment and old unreliable transport.

Although the A.D.O.s were in the front line and were the first senior officers to attend 'make-ups' and special services it didn't seem to matter. Only occasionally did a D.O. attend an incident and in the majority of those occasions, the job was virtually all over by the time of their arrival. Even so, in their eyes, having a brigade car parked outside of their brigade accommodation, was an entitlement. It seemed that their perks, rank and status was more important than their duty to the public. As I understood it at the time it was a brigade problem, not a local divisional one that had to be resolved. The D.O.s were not going to lose their entitlements and perks no matter what. So that was the position, poor and inadequate office accommodation and the oldest and most unreliable fire cars were all that were available for use by the A.D.O.s. I suppose that it all added up to the same old story – lack of preparation and finance.

At the time when the new watch-related A.D.O.s were promoted another anomaly occurred. All of the in post residential A.D.O.s were automatically upgraded to D.O. rank, which must have made them feel particularly fortunate because they didn't even have to attend a selection interview. I believe the ability or suitability of some of them for automatic promotion to those posts was questionable. The whole charade seemed to develop into quite a ridiculous set-up and after only a few months, I was regretting ever applying for and accepting promotion. I was missing station life and feeling a bit surplus to requirements.

After a good deal of pressure and complaining, the A.D.O.s were eventually provided with office and on-duty living accommodation. One reliable fire car was also made available for the on-call duty A.D.O. We became much more organised which in turn led to better continuity and efficiency.

In the past station officers did not have much opportunity to get to know their senior officers who only seemed to visit stations when there was a problem or to look for problems. Therefore, up until the time that I was attached to the divisional headquarters my relationship with my senior officers as working colleagues was almost non-existent.

Working from the divisional headquarters and supposedly being part of the divisional management team, I was able to see individual officers in their true colours. It didn't take long to discover how the residential duty system was, in my opinion, abused by some officers working it. A typical working day for a D.O. in the 'H' Division in the middle of the 1970s, was for the officer to arrive at his office at about 1000 hours and have a cup of tea and a chat until about 1030 hours. He would sort out any work that had arrived in his in-tray and place it in the relevant watch A.D.O.'s in-tray. Re-direct any paperwork completed by the watch A.D.O.s, to the relevant brigade headquarters departments, after sometimes having the work retyped and adding his own signature, giving the impression that he had done the work. Then he would struggle to look busy until lunch time. They seemed to bumble their way through part of the afternoon until about 1500 hours then leave the office to go home under the pretext of visiting a station.

I wasn't very popular when, at a divisional management meeting, I said that the divisional officers didn't do much more than push pieces of paper around the office and that the watch A.D.O.s were doing the majority of the D.O.'s work, as well as their own, which included first line operational cover.

Contrary to my principles and my opinion of the residential duty system, I applied for further promotion to divisional officer. I can only say that I wanted to keep my name in the frame in case the system changed for the better. For me, the existing residential duty system was definitely not something that I would seriously consider accepting.

I was not expecting to be shortlisted but I did get an unexpected bonus. Perhaps bonus is the wrong word but the powers-that-be, thinking that I was on the promotion trail, gave me the opportunity for temporary promotion to divisional officer. The opening was in the 'H' Division Fire Prevention Branch, which meant that I would be mostly desk-bound. The only chance of being involved in the operational side was when I was the duty D.O. and in my experience, as I mentioned earlier, there was only a remote chance of a D.O. attending an incident in time to have any useful input. Although I had to work the residential hours, I was allowed to live at my home in West Sussex during out-of-office hours, and ride from there if I was required to attend an incident. In a full year I was called upon to attend an incident on only three occasions, not counting the duration of the firemen's strike which I will mention later. My life revolved around my paging device and the telephone, both of which always had to be available, just in case.

Although I was enjoying that period of temporary promotion as a change of routine, I much preferred the A.D.O.'s operational reference. Shoving pieces of paper around an office wasn't really my scene and fire prevention work was all paperwork.

During that period of temporary promotion the Fire Brigade's Union called an all-out strike. The National Association of Fire Officers, of which I was a member, did not support the firemen's strike. Therefore, N.A.F.O. members worked as normal, or as normal as possible given the circumstances. The non-supportive decision by the N.A.F.O. camp caused a lot of bad feeling amongst the F.B.U. members which grew progressively worse as time went on. Some officers were F.B.U. members and they stood on the picket line with the firemen. Bad feelings generated between N.A.F.O. members and F.B.U. firemen and between N.A.F.O. officers and F.B.U. officers.

The government mobilised the troops and brought old Home Office 'Green Goddess' fire engines out of storage, to put on the streets of London. It was agreed with the representative bodies and management, that officers may attend fires, but they were not to do the work of firemen. They were only permitted to advise the troops on the best way to tackle the fires, and that was all. Striking firemen monitored calls on their V.H.F. radios and turned up at fires with banners of protest and making their feelings known in other ways, but they did not hinder the operations in any way.

Some officers had to spend nights at Territorial Army Centres where the Home Office appliances were situated. I personally did not appreciate the reminder of years past. It was bad enough trying to rest on a camp bed amongst a load of squadies but the memories that it brought back were enough to give me nightmares.

Croydon control ordered me by radio, to attend a fire at a large country house on an outer station's ground near the border of the divisional area. I arrived to find the troops pouring four jets of water over the building as flames continued to belch out of the windows. An army captain was in charge of them and as I approached him, he expressed his amazement at the fire not being put out by the large quantities of water being poured on it. I felt a bit uncomfortable having to explain that roofs were designed to keep water out and that was where his troops were directing their jets. I secretly enjoyed telling him though.

I coaxed the soldiers inside the house with their jets and directed them in a little bit of on-the-spot fire fighting, all the time being aware that I was constantly being observed by other striking officers and firemen, watching to see if I actually took a physical part in the operations. However, after a bit of guidance, the squadies didn't do too badly for men not trained for the job.

For a long time after the firemen's strike, visiting a station was like walking on egg shells. Discipline seemed to be deliberately disregarded and there was a lot of noticeable dislike of N.A.F.O. members, for not supporting the strike. After all, most of the union members had families and mortgage repayments to maintain. The long strike took its toll and large debts were accrued by the strikers, while N.A.F.O. members and other non-union personnel received their full pay.

The post-strike attitudes of bitter F.B.U. members forced N.A.F.O. Officers even more distant from station personnel. The effect on officers who worked from divisional level was minimal but for those in charge of watches, life was difficult for a time. For the few firemen who were non-union members, it must have been hell, I know of at least one who was forced to resign and others who conveniently developed medical problems and had to be discharged from the Brigade.

The only guidance that filtered down from the hierarchy was the old phrase 'Play it cool'. Problems that did occur were classified as 'grey areas' and were ignored. It seemed as though senior administrative officers at the brigade's headquarters had taken up the pose of the proverbial ostrich and buried their heads in the sand. The brigade appeared to just bumble along aimlessly for some time. Fortunately the public did not suffer, firemen continued to provide first-class fire cover and to perform the tasks that they were paid for. Discipline seemed to be maintained on the fire ground, where it mattered.

Reorganisation took place once again. The green watch was created, making four watches along with the red white and blue watches, each working an average of a forty-eight hour week over a six-week period. The rota, which was the best thing to emerge from the turmoil of the strike, was two days on duty from 0900 hours until

1800 hours, then two nights on duty from 1800 hours until 0900 hours, followed by four leave days. The extra watch and shorter hours obviously meant more personnel, which created an accommodation problem. The existing locker and sleeping areas proved to be inadequate and overcrowding became a problem in some stations.

Competition amongst officers heated up as they jockeyed for positions. It seemed that new jobs were being created weekly, causing the endless scramble by applicants, almost pleading for promotion interviews. The trend was to apply for any position in any department at the brigade's headquarters, get your face known by those that mattered and in a very short time reappear at a divisional headquarters, one or two ranks higher.

It was quite obvious to individuals who worked under some of those rapidly promoted men, and I emphasise some of them, that their abilities as operational fire officers and their leadership qualities were never taken into consideration at their promotion interviews. That in turn, reflected on the quality of the brigade's senior management of the day, who made up the panel of interviewers.

Perhaps it was considered that the ability of the senior officers, with regard to the operational work, didn't matter anyway because the officers and firemen at station level did the operational work. A cynical view perhaps but station personnel were the experts, they did the job every day it was their bread and butter. Crews from stations are the backbone of the service. The operational deficiencies of a few of the rapidly promoted 'whiz-kids' did not readily show up, purely because of the skill and courage of the front line crews. Some officers chose to ignore that important fact, and didn't even offer the slightest encouragement by way of even a pat on the back or a 'Well done chaps', following a particularly difficult job.

After more than a year of temporary promotion, I reverted to my substantive rank of A.D.O. Following that I had three interviews for promotion to D.O. during a period of about three years. Every one of those interviews seemed to focus around the question of where I was prepared to live and each time I explained my reluctance to buying a house in London or moving into brigade accommodation. It seemed that candidates that were prepared to submit to the demands of the brigade, in respect of accommodation, were home and dry. I know of several men who agreed to move house as a condition of promotion but played for time by claiming that they couldn't find a suitable property. Some of them were put under pressure to move and had to camp out with relatives while they were on duty. That way of life I considered being completely alien to my way of thinking.

Divisional officers being in charge of divisions had been a thing of the past following several reorganisations and reshuffles of ranks and officers over a few years. A new rank of Deputy Assistant Chief Officer had been introduced for officers in charge of divisions and they were given the title 'Divisional Commander'. They had a staff of four divisional officers, working the residential duty system and eight assistant divisional officers, two on each of the four watches.

At times it was like a game of musical chairs without the music, divisional commanders and divisional officers being transferred in and out, in rapid succession. During the last eight years of my service, ten divisional commanders passed through the division. Each one brought with him his own personal answer to the brigade's problems, each one thought he was God's gift to the division and the 'Lazy Aitch' would be no more. Each one held his own style of divisional management meetings. All officers on duty in the division and others that were not on duty but wanted to be seen as dedicated servants, obediently attended. Only to be bored out of our minds as we listened to the same old ideas along with the same old threats of reform and other useless utterances. To be fair, I suppose some of those commanders could have made useful contributions to the division, had they been around long enough to make an impression.

Lack of backing for station officers and assistant divisional officers who were trying to maintain a level of discipline on their stations was an underlying problem. It was inevitable that at times some personnel would need a bit of pressure applied to keep them toeing the line. For some obscure reason, probably the fear of somebody at brigade headquarters forming the opinion that divisional commanders couldn't maintain discipline within their divisions, everything was kept on the island and smoothed over. That gave the impression to senior brigade management that all was being managed well and was under control. The men knew it and some took advantage of it. Several occasions that I can recall, some officers in charge of stations were left with egg on their faces because of lack of support.

I did my best not to allow the negative support by my senior ranking officers affect the way I did my job, or to let it influence my actions or decisions. I adopted a policy of reporting the facts and then ignoring the progress, or lack of progress that the case made. That attitude gave me the satisfaction of knowing that I was doing my job with minimal frustration from the action or inaction of others. I must admit though, I did turn my blind eye on some occasions when my morale bottomed out.

Officers continued to be promoted, moved around the brigade and slotted into a position somewhere. Overall, morale was not very high and there didn't appear to be any magical cure for it, even on the distant horizon.

Chief officers came and went, six of them during my service. Not only did they have to run a very large fire brigade but they had to please the Greater London Council, by way of the Fire Brigade's Committee, who were the paymasters, from public funds of course. The result was that any changes for the better were very slow to take place.

Verbal outbursts of frustration, expressing my dissatisfaction at the direction the changes were taking the job, seemed to be happening more frequently. The root cause being the system of management that had allowed the brigade to deteriorate to a level that I had not seen before. I was beginning, for the first time since I was transferred to Lambeth as a young fireman, to dislike reporting for duty.

Although the brigade employed a high number of personnel, occasionally it happened that paths crossed over the years. Sub-Officer John Bishop, who was my first instructor in the training centre, became my partner as an A.D.O. for a time before he retired and was re-employed by the brigade as a civilian technical officer, within the Fire Prevention Branch at Brigade Headquarters.

John Hurcombe, who was the station officer who recommended me for promotion to leading fireman when I was on his watch at Lambeth, was also an A.D.O. and worked for a time on one of the other watches in the division before his retirement. In my opinion, he had all the qualities required for a senior post but I believe that the bottleneck caused by the residential system that went with further promotion prevented him from applying until the introduction of the watch related A.D.O.s.

Amongst the many responsibilities of the rank of A.D.O. was the duty of carrying out the initial investigations into offences against the Fire Services Discipline Code. Sometimes the alleged offence would involve non-uniformed staff. The abolition of station work was one of the improvements introduced by management. Contractors were hired to clean the stations and some of them employed a team of male cleaners who travelled around by van to clean several stations. Others hired local people as cleaners.

I became involved in a case when a fireman telephoned his officer in charge to inform him that his wife wouldn't let him leave the house to report for duty, because she had heard stories about firemen playing around with the female cleaner at his station.

It transpired that the man's wife had been told that the cleaner at the station where her husband was attached, was young and sexy and that she had been tempting the firemen. She wasn't wrong, I discovered that the cleaner was indeed quite a sexy-looking woman and that some of the young firemen were doing their best to win her favours. One chap even said that he was performing a humanitarian service. Apparently, the story that went around suggested that there was almost a continuous queue outside of the broom cupboard, an obvious exaggeration but typical of fire brigade humour. She also visited the station some evenings, accompanied by a female friend. I handed the problem over to her employer to deal with. When he reported back he told me that she left his employment voluntarily when he confronted her, and that her husband wasn't happy about her working in a fire station full of red blooded males anyway.

Another time a firemen was attempting to have his way with a temporary cook in the watch food store. The store was a very small windowless room, more like a large cupboard. During their passionate gyrations they dislodged a large tin of custard powder which descended upon them in the darkness. It exploded over them and everything else in the store. They were discovered by the sound of coughing coming from the store and the sight of a yellow cloud creeping under the door.

Out of all of my dislikes, my pet hate was the sale of alcoholic drinks in fire stations. That was something that I couldn't accept at any price. The introduction of bars under the guise of social clubs was in my opinion a big mistake. Station personnel constructed the most elaborate bars in the most unlikely places – they could be found in station basements, in outbuildings or in full view in lecture rooms, large enough to hold a social evening or a retirement party.

Stocked with all kinds of booze, some of them were on a par with many a private club. Senior management had full knowledge of the creation of those drinking dens. Some senior officers openly used the facility to satisfy their own desire to indulge in cheap booze. Being only a social drinker, I found it difficult to understand that a person had to have a supply of alcohol every day but I soon found out that some did, and they were the men guilty of reporting for duty already smelling of drink. Others indulged just because it was available.

The club-type atmosphere that was created at some stations attracted more than the occasional female visitor, at some stations partying went on until the early hours. Someone eventually came to their senses and moves were made restricting the use of bars to off-duty personnel only. Eventually I was pleased to see them phased out altogether.

The operational side of the job continued as ever and it wasn't unusual for an A.D.O. to be ordered to large fires many miles away on the other side of London. I remember being ordered to a fire in an area of north London that I wasn't too familiar with. I knew how to get to the area, so I decided to drive there before I consulted my road atlas for a more precise location of the fire. When I was quite close to my destination and about to consult my atlas, I noticed a water trail on the roadway. I relaxed, knowing that fire engines often left water trails on the roadway especially as they sped around corners. With two-tone horns blaring and my blue flashing warning lights on I automatically followed the water trail thinking that I was home and dry. Can you imagine my embarrassment as I sped around a corner and pulled up behind a ready-mix concrete lorry on a building site.

Rosemary operating the Brigade Radio System.

Rosemary updating the Appliance Situation Board
in the Brigade Control Room.

Chapter 10

It is said that time heals most things. Either that was the case or conditions began to get a little better, or maybe I began to accept everything in its deteriorated state as being the norm but I am not sure which.

I accepted that there would always be a difference depending on experience and the ability to handle certain situations by officers as they made their way up through the ranks. Having occasionally found myself thrown in the deep end I recognised from personal experience that you must be ready for the unexpected. What I do not accept is that it was possible in those days to hold a senior rank with an operational reference simply by attending college courses and working in non-operational departments within the headquarters environment without a proven background of experience in man management and operational technique, developed by being in charge of a fire station and work on the fire ground.

I was told that because I was not prepared to attend meetings during my off-duty time I lacked dedication. In my mind dedication was proven by the conscientious way that an officer carried out his duties while on duty, something that I always tried to do to the best of my ability and not by trying to impress by being over keen in other areas. One particular 'high flyer' that passed through the division on his way to higher things, left a desk drawer containing a quite a lot of unprocessed work, for someone else to sort out. His formula for progression through the ranks was 'Make no decisions, make no mistakes'. That drawer became known as the 'too difficult drawer' and was referred to many times by the divisional staff when one of us had to deal with something out of the ordinary. If a problem was being discussed at a meeting or casually over a cup of tea, someone would always propose solving the problem by jokingly suggesting that it should be put in the 'too difficult drawer'.

That's enough of the boring stuff so back to the better things in life. As I mentioned earlier, on the 2nd March 1974, Rosemary and I were married. Five years later, on the 7th October 1979 our son Andrew was born. Rosemary left her job in the brigade's control room after fourteen years' service and our way of life after both of us doing shift work for a number of years, changed for the better. We were extremely happy and content with the way our lives together had developed.

On the day Andrew was born I came home from a night shift with the intention of us both having a drive to Brighton with the intention of doing a spot of sea fishing. When I got home Rosemary was still resting in bed and complaining of a pain in her stomach. She suggested that I went fishing on my own while she rested. Her pregnancy still had four weeks to go for her full time, so she wasn't at all worried about the little pain. I decided to play safe and contacted the hospital. I was advised to take her in for observation, so after a token protest she got ready and we made our way to the local hospital maternity department.

Within a couple of hours the pain became more severe and I was informed that she was in labour. That was a bit of a shock to my system and relatively unexpected. I sat with her until at four o'clock in the afternoon when eventually Rosemary gave birth to Andrew. Being a premature baby he was rushed to the premature baby unit where he made good progress.

When Rosemary was working, our duties did not always coincide so she would pre-arrange or prepare meals for me to have when she wasn't at home. That worked very well but the surprise early birth of Andrew didn't allow any preparation and in any case, since Rosemary had left her job a few weeks earlier, that kind of preparation no longer applied. I took leave for the duration of Rosemary's confinement and didn't enjoy for one moment the experience of looking after the mundane tasks associated with running the domestic part of a household. However, I managed it and after a few days Rosemary and Andrew were allowed home where he certainly made his presence known.

The sleepless nights had begun. He wasn't very good at sleeping so any little sound would cause him to wake up. He had his own nursery room adjacent to ours and with the doors open we could hear every little sound that he made and of course every little sound had to be investigated.

The older Andrew got the more aware of his surroundings he became. After being put to bed he would lie in his cot refusing to close his eyes. He would keep them fixed on whoever was in his room and yell his head off if he was left on his own.

Like most people with a new baby Rosemary and I lost a lot of sleep in Andrew's early years but it gradually all came together and he settled down. He began to get a little anxious when he started in pre-school age classes, he had to fight back the tears because he didn't like to be left. Even when he started in the infants' school he hated it when he had to go into the school without one of us accompanying him. Thinking of the past makes me realise how fast the years went by. It seems that all of a sudden Andrew was grown up and the memories of his younger days seemed so long ago.

Time also influenced my attitude to my work situation. I realised that the part of fire fighting I missed the most in the rank of A.D.O. was the excitement of being the officer in charge of the first attendance at an incident. That was the part when the adrenaline really flowed and snap decisions had to be made. The nearest that I could get to that experience was when I was the duty A.D.O. and had to attend all incidents within the division where assistance was requested in the form of a 'make-up' and all incidents where persons were involved. That included fires, road traffic accidents, persons trapped in machinery etc, but the efficiency of the crews making up the first attendances often had the job successfully completed before I arrived, so all that was left to do was to praise the crews for work well done.

Sometimes a station officer in charge of the first attendance at an incident, would show visible signs of relief when a senior officer arrived on the job and be pleased to hand over command. Conversely, some others looked upon the arrival of a senior officer as their moment of glory being stolen from them and showed signs of resentment and disappointment at not being able to see the job through to the end under their own command. I must admit that I sometimes felt that way when I was a station officer. Nonetheless, if an incident comes within the remit of a senior officer, then that must be accepted and not thought of as questioning the ability of the junior officer, to handle the job.

Over the many years I had worked on both sides of the divide, I had long ago reached the conclusion that station officers should be given greater autonomy over their fire ground duties and senior officers should only take charge if the job was seen to be or suspected of going wrong. If there is no specific operational reason that warranted a senior officer to take command at a fire, for example its size or nature, then the job should remain the responsibility of and under the command of the station officer whose station's ground the fire was on.

Unfortunately, during my time in the job some 'high flyers' loved to hear their names being broadcast over the brigade's radio network so they seized every opportunity to have a message dispatched in their name by attending even small incidents where their presence was not required. The sad part about it all was that by the time most senior officers, myself included, arrived at an incident, it was usually more or less all over, or at the very least it would be under control except for large protracted incidents or the clearing up process. All of the difficult decisions and dangerous work had invariably been successfully completed by the first crews to arrive.

I knew which station officers whose judgement I could trust and those who were a bit suspect in their decision making. The speed and urgency that I responded to an incident was often determined by my knowledge of the ability of the officer in charge of the first attendance. I didn't see any sense in taking unnecessary risks by speeding to a job that was under control. Interpretation of the informative messages from incidents also gave a good indication about what was going on at the scene.

Driving to a fire one day along a fairly clear road, a woman walked in front of my fire car causing me to brake hard to avoid hitting her. Absolutely furious at her for ignoring my two-tone warning horns and my blue flashing light, I shouted at her telling her to keep her eyes open and look where she was going.

As I shouted at her to keep her eyes open I gesticulated by pointing at my eyes. Unfortunately, in my anger I poked my finger in my eye causing it to water so badly that I couldn't keep it open. I had to stop further along the road, out of the woman's view of course, because I couldn't see well enough to drive. I sent a radio message to brigade control stating that my car had broken down and that I couldn't proceed to the fire. Another officer was ordered to the incident while I, swearing and cursing, sat nursing my watery bloodshot eye at the side of the road. When I had calmed down I saw the funny side of it. Since then I have related the story once or twice causing a smile and the comment "Serves you right" – the poor woman might have been deaf.

My operational work, especially in the late evening and early morning, included many road traffic accidents and invariably the smell of alcohol was instantly recognisable. The majority of victims trapped in vehicles were held by their legs or feet, although I have come across many that have been trapped by their head and arms and even some that have been impaled by an object that had pierced their car. I was quite surprised at an incident when a man decided to drive straight across a roundabout and finished up with the car on its roof after first demolishing a road sign and rebounding off of a tree. He was suspended upside down in the car supported by his seat belt and trapped by his feet. With the aid of special hydraulic spreading equipment he was carefully released. It was thought at the time that he had broken at least one of his legs because he kept complaining that he couldn't feel his feet. He was lifted from the car and as he was being placed on a stretcher, he suddenly jumped up stamped his feet a couple of times then ran off down the road with the police in hot pursuit.

Being a practical hands-on type of person I often found it difficult to restrict myself to carrying out only the supervisory role at an incident by directing operations. Short duration jobs I could handle but when they became prolonged, the temptation to get 'stuck in' was often too powerful for me to control.

I became familiar with the capabilities of the crews that manned the emergency tender on my watch and knew the individuals that were confident and experienced enough to deal with difficult life and death situations.

The emergency tender fleet had been increased during the last reorganisation of the brigade and the additional E.T.s were strategically situated within the brigade's area. That had the desired advantage of getting specialist rescue equipment to an incident quicker, which was excellent.

More E.T.s meant more crews to share the work. Consequently it took longer for newly trained E.T. men to gain practical on-the-job experience. They had to rely more on training and exercises to use their equipment. Obviously, faking realism is nothing like the real thing, although it served its purpose of keeping crews familiar with the use, manipulation, scope and safety factors of their equipment. Unfortunately though it doesn't get them accustomed to working in the real life and death situations which inevitably involves handling screaming victims, blood and gore and medical teams working miracles with drips and pain-killing injections and sometimes amputations.

Another factor that affected the building up of practical on-the-job experience of new E.T. crews was the introduction of a limited selection of hydraulic tools stowed on some first line appliances for use at road traffic accidents. Although an E.T. was automatically ordered on to all road traffic accidents where persons were believed to be trapped, most victims were successfully released with local equipment before its arrival. Only the very serious or prolonged incidents that were still in progress or jobs that required specialist equipment that was only carried on E.T.s needed E.T. support. That was like throwing a weak swimmer in at the deep end and expecting him to carry out a rescue.

E.T.s were regularly being ordered by radio to return to their home station when they were not required at an incident. Therefore, without being given the opportunity to even observe the scene and aftermath of an incident or having the chance to discuss the rescue method with those at the scene, didn't exactly contribute much to inexperienced crew members.

When I was a young fireman at Lambeth, there were only two emergency tenders in the whole of the old London County Council Fire Brigade and the equipment carried then was primitive compared to what was carried later in my career. I remember being on parade, following a display that we had staged for a visiting V.I.P. when I heard Sir Frederick Delve, the Chief Fire Officer in post at the time, say as he walked along the line of firemen:

"These men are my Commandos."

He was pointing to a five-man E.T. crew, all of the older generation who possessed a wealth of experience between them. My generation had the privilege and opportunity of working with those Commandos for some time, learning a great deal from them.

Because of the advanced development in compressed air breathing apparatus, as opposed to pure oxygen breathing apparatus, plus the new health and safety rules, all modern fire-fighters are trained in the use and maintenance of compressed air sets which are available to them at all times. Some years ago breathing apparatus was only carried on pumps and at that time only three oxygen sets were available at a station. That is why E.T. crews during my service received additional training and were called upon to deal with difficult fires in basements and ships' holds etc. Modern E.T. crews attend less special service and breathing apparatus work because more specialist equipment is carried on first line appliances plus the availability of compressed air breathing apparatus sets to all firemen.

I believe that emergency tender crews as I knew them will one day become redundant.

The provision of compressed air breathing apparatus must have been the most useful and necessary purchase of fire fighting equipment for years. Before its introduction firemen took a great deal of punishment working without B.A. in heat and smoke, when fighting fires inside of buildings. The inhalation of the products of combustion is known to have long-term effects on a person's health, and of course it can kill in a very short time. Breathing apparatus allows work to be carried out in an atmosphere that would not maintain life.

When I joined the fire brigade, the older hands that I worked with liked to be known as smoke eaters. They took pride in being able to enter a building that was on fire, under the most adverse conditions and they probably paid for that with poor health in later years. One senior officer that I came across in not very friendly circumstances when I was a young fireman was known to, when he was not wearing breathing apparatus, walk past crews who were making their way into a smoke-logged building wearing breathing apparatus. Those old hands regularly risked their lives in their efforts to save life and property. Risk is certainly acceptable and often necessary to save a life but, in my opinion, property comes into a different category.

When you think about it, a sensible person has property adequately insured. If that property is subsequently damaged or destroyed by fire the insurance company foots the bill for repair or replacement. Therefore, fire brigades, by preventing the destruction of property and its contents are saving money for insurance companies. For example, if a building and contents worth one million pounds catches fire and the fire brigade successfully saves half of it by preventing the fire from spreading, then in theory, the fire brigade has saved the insurance company from paying out half a million pounds in compensation. Firemen, who are paid from the public purse, risk their lives for the benefit and profit of insurance companies, to the tune of probably billions of pounds every year but insurance companies do not contribute any more than any other business to the cost of running the service.

Other than operational responsibilities, an important part of my job was the welfare of station personnel. When a young recruit was discovered sitting outside a fire station in his car, after the start of duty on his first day following completion of his training, his officer in charge immediately contacted me. Puzzled by the story relayed to me I made my way to the station. The recruit was apparently frightened to go in.

The officer in charge had managed to persuade the young man to accompany him to the station office before I arrived. I spoke to him in a relaxed friendly way to try and gain his confidence. He explained to me that he was scared of meeting the others on the watch because they were all experienced firemen and he was only a recruit.

I discovered during the conversation that he was a very good football player and had already played for the fire brigade team while he was attached to the training centre. I couldn't understand how he could complete the brigade's training and play football in front of crowds, yet was not able to force himself to break the ice with new work mates. He explained that he was able to play football in front of other players and a crowd because he knew that he was a good football player. He didn't have any trouble in the training centre because he knew that all the other members of the squad were beginners too.

I instructed him to visit his doctor and sent him home. He was subsequently placed sick for three weeks suffering from 'acute inferiority complex'.

At the end of his three-week sick period, his mother contacted me suggesting that he was ready to return to duty and was determined to make a go of it. She told me that he had suffered from the problem since he was a child.

He failed once again to report for duty, so I telephoned his home. His mother told me that despite his best intentions he was unable to force himself to leave his home. Hoping to persuade him to give it a try, I went to his home. His mother, father and grandmother were all trying to reason with him and when I arrived it must have been the last straw. He ran into the kitchen and to everyone's horror, picked up a knife and began slashing at his wrist.

That man really did have a problem. To report for duty in front of experienced men remained an obstacle too large for him to overcome so he eventually lost his job. I felt sorry for him because his illness caused him so much suffering. That kind of illness is hard to imagine if it has not been witnessed.

As part of the progression of training for fire officers, command courses were held at the National Fire Services College at Dorking,

Surrey. They were residential courses spanning a period of nine weeks.

The courses were designed to prepare officers for further promotion and candidates attended from all over the U.K. I was fortunate enough to have been selected for one of the courses which I found to be very interesting and enlightening. It was particularly exciting when on a visit to Heathrow Airport I enjoyed the experience of sitting in the Captain's seat of a Concord Super Sonic Aircraft. I especially enjoyed the opportunity of meeting several fellow officers from other U.K. fire brigades. To be honest though I do not believe the content of the course was very beneficial to me in my present position but I suppose the idea was to assist in the advancement in one's career. However it was another qualification to add to my C.V. but privately I thought it was a waste of time; it did not make any significant changes to the way I carried out my duties, except perhaps the for the useful tips and proper way to conduct yourself when dealing with the 'dry lip' situation when confronted by a television interviewer asking difficult and sometimes sensitive questions, while his camera man is zooming in on you.

Mick French, my partner at the time, and I reported for duty one evening and were presented with the not unusual problem of a shortage of fire cars. Mick was the duty officer and as there was only one car, it meant that I was grounded. I was faced with the prospect of spending the fifteen-hour night duty in the A.D.O.'s quarters.

During the evening Mick was ordered to a road traffic accident involving a car and an ambulance carrying a patient. When he left our quarters I settled down to catch up on some paperwork. Within a few minutes I received a telephone call from brigade control informing me that Mick had himself, been involved in an accident.

Without transport I was snookered. Although it was against all the rules I felt morally obligated to use my own car to get to the scene and assist Mick. An officer from a neighbouring division had been ordered to cover Mick's original emergency call. The trouble was, I had used Rosemary's car for work that evening and that being a bright green 600cc Citroen 2CV6, was not much more than a pram with an engine. It was certainly not the type of car in which a fire officer would be expected to attend an incident.

Using the back streets I managed to park my pram in a side street without being seen. I walked the short distance to the scene of the accident with no one being aware of my mode of transport. Fortunately Mick was not injured, he was surprised to see me knowing that I was grounded for the night and even managed to chuckle when I told him how I got there.

Mick told me that as he was proceeding to the accident involving the ambulance, with his blue flashing warning light and his two-tone warning horns actuating, he was being overtaken by a speeding car. As the car drew level with Mick's fire car, another car some way ahead signalled to turn right. The overtaking car accelerated and tried to get through the gap between Mick's fire car and the one turning right. The result was a three-car pile-up. Mick was still a bit shaken so I noted all of the necessary particulars for completion of the accident report.

I spoke to a man who I thought was driving the speeding car which caused the accident and noted the smell of alcohol. He said that he was a passenger in the car and pointed to the driver standing by his wrecked car. He added to my surprise that they were police officers and the car was an unmarked police car. I immediately challenged the police car passenger by saying that he smelled of alcohol, and that I thought that it was reasonable to assume that his partner had also been drinking. He just shrugged his shoulders and walked away from me. I looked at the driver again and noticed that he was popping peppermints into his mouth and chewing them as fast as he could, obviously in an attempt disguise the smell of alcohol on his breath.

I reported my suspicions to a uniformed police officer who had arrived at the incident and was in the process of writing down the particulars of the accident. He appeared a little uneasy when I mentioned my suspicions but said he would look into it.

Having gathered all the necessary particulars for Mick's report, I stood on one side with him and discussed the situation. About fifteen minutes passed and the uniformed policeman had not even approached the plain-clothed police driver. I expressed my disapproval to the uniformed policeman who said that he did not have a breathalyser kit with him and that he had to wait for the accident investigation unit to arrive, which was attending an accident involving an ambulance, at least I knew that to be likely.

Eventually the accident investigation unit arrived and the uniformed policeman spoke for some time to the accident investigator. The first thing the accident investigator did was to make the plain-clothed police driver blow into a breathalyser. He then approached Mick. After explaining what had happened, Mick asked if the breathalyser test was positive. Understandably he didn't get a direct answer. As he walked away, the accident investigator nodded towards the police plain-clothed driver and said, "His troubles are just beginning."

We arranged for the damaged fire car to be towed away, squeezed into my petrol-powered pram, which was difficult for Mick because he stands about six foot three, and returned to our quarters to begin the search of the brigade for a spare fire car.

Mick was also the duty officer the evening we arrived on duty and were both ordered to relieve the off-going officers attending an aircraft crash at the Biggin Hill Air Show.

I had attended Biggin Hill Airfield on many occasions when light aircraft were suspected of having faulty landing gear but they had always landed safely.

I had been in the brigade for many years and had seen and dealt with most types of incident but not an aircraft crash.

An old wartime bomber had been flying at a display at Biggin Hill and had crashed at high speed off the airfield, at the side of a road in a valley, narrowly missing a bungalow. The scene was a heap of smouldering wreckage, partly in the road and partly in a crater that it made on impact at the edge of a field. No one was certain how many people were in the aircraft, so a thorough search of the twisted wreckage had to be made.

Up until that time, I could only imagine the effect on a human body of a high-speed crash, such as an aircraft diving straight into the ground. Pieces of flesh, some no larger than a fist and some as big as and resembling joints of meat displayed in a butcher's shop, were scattered over an area of about one acre or so. A complete spine, looking almost like a plastic model, without a scrap of flesh on it was lying about thirty yards from the point of impact, a seat with part of a leg and ragged overalls lay nearby. The scene seemed too horrific to be real. It appeared that the bodies scattered over the field had disintegrated on impact. The heavier pieces of flesh seemed to have ripped away from the bones and scattered in all directions. Those human remains were covered with anything that became available and left in position while operations were concentrated on getting into the main part of the wreckage, which had buried itself in the ground.

After a while the position of more bodies was located but it was clear that it wouldn't be easy to extricate them. We had no idea how many there were and the bloody mess that had been uncovered was unrecognisable as being human. The bodies had all burst open and had formed one large mass of flesh and intestines. To remove the grisly remains, crews had to judge the amount of the awesome mess that could be gathered on to a salvage sheet and carried by three or four men. Hand holds were made by rolling down the edges of the salvage sheet, to gather enough of it to get a firm grip.

Sometimes the entangled mass of bodies could not be separated and odd lengths of intestine had to be cut, to allow the firemen to carry the unstable load from the wreckage. Gripping the rolled edges of the salvage sheet as it sagged under the weight of its gruesome contents, they emptied the remains into eight tin coffins, making a sickening wet slopping sound as each one was filled. Although eight coffins were used, we learned later that there were only seven bodies.

Operational work was fine but lurking in the background was the unsettling question of maintaining confidence in the constant changes in senior management within the division, which gave rise to complacency that in turn caused an even more laid-back, almost couldn't care less attitude all round. Frustration had caused a lack of job satisfaction which seemed to get the better of me and I found that I was even thinking about when I could retire, although it was still a few years away I sometimes felt that it couldn't come soon enough.

The opportunity for a few more months of temporary promotion was offered to me. I accepted it on the understanding that I could ride from my home. I liked working alongside the residential officers because I could air my views about how easy the job was just pushing pieces of paper around the establishment and doing nothing constructive, it didn't make me very popular though.

One of the rare occasions that I attended a fire as a D.O. was at a school in Croydon, which was only about three miles away from my office. I monitored the messages over the radio listening post and heard the duty A.D.O., Bill Langworth, book in at the incident. Moments later an assistance message was dispatched from him, making pumps six and requesting two Hose Laying Lorries because of a water shortage.

Not being very busy at the time, I decided to poke my nose in, accepting of course that Bill was an experienced officer, more than capable of handling the job. I was met by Bill who was concerned about the water shortage. The school, which was in private grounds, was unbelievably hundreds of yards from the nearest street fire hydrant. It transpired that the school's private hydrants were not working. By the time that I arrived the fire had taken hold of most of the roof of the single-storey building and had spread to the large assembly hall roof supporting a clock tower. The assembly hall formed the main central part of the complex with the school classrooms accessible from corridors situated to the left and right from the rear of the hall.

After all of the water carried on the fire appliances was discharged onto the fire, hardly making an impression, I was told that the two hose-laying lorries, both capable of running out large three and a half inch diameter hose at a speed of twenty miles an hour, had laid out hose from separate street fire hydrants and had both run out of hose some distance from the fire.

To my knowledge, it was never discovered who ordered the hose layers to begin to run out the hose. The leading firemen in charge of each hose layer, not realising that the other was in attendance and probably working without the knowledge of the control unit or the officer in charge of the fire, to their disgrace began to lay out hose independent of each other. As if that wasn't bad enough they both decided to lay out twin lengths of hose, when a single length of three and a half inch diameter hose, from one lorry, would have covered twice the distance. Easily enough hose to reach the incident and would have initially supplied enough water capable of containing the fire or even extinguishing it.

I took charge and made pumps eight, ordering hose to be laid out by hand and an intermediate pump to be set in along the line of hose to boost the flow of water to the pumps feeding the jets.

Meanwhile, the assembly hall roof had become engulfed in fire and the clock tower, accompanied by a loud cracking sound, made a spectacular slow motion descent through the roof, among a massive shower of sparks and flying embers.

That embarrassing scene was witnessed by the divisional commander who had at that moment arrived on the scene. He was horrified to see the demise of the glorious clock tower disappearing before his eyes. He turned to me and said in a very serious voice that he was going to make pumps twelve. That prompted me, out of frustration, to respond with the sarcastic reply:

"You can make it one hundred and twelve if you like, Sir, it's not going out without water to put on it unless the bastard burns out."

After a lot of running about and exhausting work by the firemen, water eventually reached the fire, but not before the school was gutted and a wall collapsed, almost on top of a fire engine.

At the divisional Christmas dinner, arranged for officers and their partners, the divisional commander was delivering a speech and reflecting on the past year's work, when accompanied by much laughter, he described the school fire as the one that got away from Bob Franks. I thanked him for those few kind words.

I am centre of the middle row at the Fire Services College.

On our wedding day, 2nd March 1974.

Andrew about fourteen months old.

Chapter 11

As I mentioned earlier, the part of my job that I still enjoyed the most was the operational work which continued to be varied and interesting. To say that I enjoyed the work may seem strange when the work was inevitably created by someone's misfortune or disaster but enjoy it I did. I felt my mood change when I attended an incident. Being out of the office and away from the divisional headquarters was like taking an antidepressant pill, not that I have had any experience of that. It wasn't very uplifting to be among a management team that appeared to be satisfied with letting the division run itself day after day, with no specific or obvious strategy to inspire or motivate personnel but I have to point out that the comments and criticisms within these writings are based entirely on my own observations and opinions, of course not everyone felt that same way but that was the way I saw it.

I am not in any way suggesting that I had the answer or the expertise to solve the problems or could do any better than those in post or suggest that the task was easy. Thankfully that wasn't part of my job, I wasn't one of the selected potential God's gift to the fire brigade so the question or opportunity would never have arisen I am pleased to say. It was expected of those who were being groomed for higher office though, but it didn't appear to be working. Whilst I was in the division the officers seemed to be just jogging along waiting to be posted, promoted or retired.

I formed the opinion some time ago that conditions would not improve until a management team was left in position long enough to introduce a style of management that everyone could relate to. Along with a few others who carried on regardless I continued to perform my duties as well as I could, although some may question that. Even though my morale was at an all time low I did try to keep up to date and comply with the latest directives that were issued from time to time. Unfortunately in the "Lazy H" it was difficult to become enthusiastic about anything, other than operational work. I assumed that senior brigade management was aware of the state of morale and I presumed that the reorganisation that went on from time to time was their way of attempting to solve the problems.

During the years following the fireman's strike relationships between station personnel and senior officers had by a large extent improved. Probably the gradual change that took place had only been observed by those in charge of watches or who regularly visited fire stations, those officers being the same ones that had been in the firing line for a long time during and after the strike. I often made a point of inviting station personnel to air their views over a cup of tea around the mess table. It allowed them to let off steam and assisted in relieving bad feeling. It also gave me an idea of the true state of morale at shop floor level. I have a high regard for the rank of fireman, simply because without their skill, bravery and dedication to their work, small fires would become disasters and the number of fatalities occurring at fires and other incidents would be much higher, along with the associated massive financial losses to industry etc.

A side effect of regular face-to-face contact with station personnel was that they always seemed to be at ease and able to approach me to discuss a problem, be it brigade related or personal. Sometimes I was able to help and sometimes I was only able to offer advice and hope that I was able to help. However, it was satisfying to know that some of the personnel felt that they could confide in me.

Unexpected visits to stations, especially in the evenings, sometimes exposed some surprising activities. On a few occasions I have walked in on a party in full swing or discovered a fire engine parked in the drill yard and someone's private car parked in its place, or over the vehicle inspection pit in the appliance room with engine parts spread all over the floor. On many occasions I have found stations almost deserted, only to discover the television room crowded and a blue video being shown. Technology had advanced from the days of black and white 8mm films, to colour super 8mm films and then videos, which without the need for a film projector and screen were much more convenient to view. There always seemed to be a steady supply of pornographic videos being passed around the stations. Sometimes I was invited to join the audience but quite often I was too busy, or more than likely I had seen the video elsewhere.

On November 18th 1982 I was at a seminar organised by British Telecom in Croydon accompanying my divisional commander. I was asked to attend so I altered my plans for the day and went along. I had planned to visit Bromley Fire Station and following that I was going to make a brief visit to the nearby hospital where my father was a patient, he had been ill for some time.

The subject of the seminar was communications which I found interesting. During the meeting my pager was activated. I telephoned Croydon control and was given a message to telephone my younger brother Leonard. He gave me the sad news that our father had died.

That was obviously a shock and I immediately felt very annoyed that I had decided on the seminar and put off visiting my father, something that I regret to this day and always will. I immediately booked off duty and went with my brother to give support to our grieving mother. My other two brothers, Bert who lived in Leeds in the north of England and Peter who lived in Dapto New South Wales Australia, were informed of the sad loss to our family.

My mother insisted on arranging the funeral herself and at the crematorium many relations and friends attended to pay their last respects. It was obviously a very sad occasion which, after putting on a brave face, my mother finally succumbed and broke down in tears.

I am on the left with my brothers, Bert who lived in Leeds, Peter who lives in Australia and Leonard.

Following that sad family event I began to feel somewhat agitated with my working life, mainly because of some unnecessary extra demands that were being hoisted upon men of my rank by a few senior ranks shirking their responsibilities.

I didn't mind examining candidates for promotion, it was part of my job, but I did object to having to stand in at the last minute because of someone ducking out of their duties with some feeble excuse, when I had plenty of work of my own to complete. Admittedly it could be quite boring standing in the drill yard watching and marking those potential junior officers all day as they nervously worked their way through their set tasks. Some candidates clearly put a lot of work into their preparation and some plainly didn't bother. Nonetheless, most candidates managed to score a pass mark.

On reflection I suppose I felt somewhat dissatisfied with the conditions around the late nineteen-seventies and the early eighties but be assured, I did not stand alone in my feelings. Everyone with whom I discussed the situation with seemed to complain about variations of similar problems.

Some time ago a working party had been set up to examine ways in which the mountains of paperwork could be cut down. As a result, unnecessary duplication of work had become less, which was a welcomed move. Since then, due to empire-building by some officers, mounds of paperwork had again been created, that had the effect of bogging down the system and extending desk hours. No consideration seemed to be given to the time required to visit and monitor the running of stations or the interruption of having to attend emergency calls. It was always a good bet that when I was knee-deep in paperwork, I would get a shout.

Early one afternoon when I was the duty officer and taking advantage of a quiet period by ploughing through a mound of paperwork, I was ordered to a road traffic accident. Control informed me of the accident which had occurred on a fast stretch of road, on one of our outer London station's ground bordering Kent Fire Brigade's area.

I arrived fairly quickly, at about the same time as the emergency tender. The crew from the local station, with a sub-officer in charge, along with some policemen, were gathered around a car and a coach that had been in collision but there didn't appear to be much activity.

The sub-officer met me and briefed me on the situation. The car containing a young couple had collided head on with the coach, which was carrying a party of senior citizens. The front of the car had been rammed under the coach, forcing the engine and the two occupants, including most of the top of the car body, back into the boot area. It could be seen at a glance by the extent of their injuries, that the two young occupants were obviously dead.

The police requested that we did not extricate them before the attendance of the Police Doctor, who had to attend to certify the victims dead. That was the reason for everyone standing around doing nothing.

I closely examined the wreckage of the car and its occupants to determine the degree of difficulty which may be met when extricating them. It is always easier to remove a dead body from a wreck compared to a live person. It's not too bad if the person is unconscious but a conscious person in pain, who screams when you touch them, is always difficult because of the fear of causing more damage to their already serious injuries.

We were hanging around for what seemed like ages waiting for the doctor and I was becoming concerned because I had two fire engines and their crews plus an E.T. waiting at the incident, unavailable for other calls.

The police were dealing with the inevitable build-up of traffic passing the scene. The accident had caused a long tail-back of cars which were being slowly driven past the damaged vehicles. The expressions on the faces of the occupants in the vehicles passing the incident showed obvious concern in anticipation of what they might see, but it didn't prevent them from stretching their necks to see as much of the aftermath as possible. I suppose that could be accepted as human nature or morbid curiosity – or does that amount to the same thing?

A man called to me from a car, he said he was a doctor and could he be of any help. I was quick to take him up on his offer and asked him if he was prepared to certify someone dead. He agreed, so I sent a fireman to find the senior police officer present and made my way with the doctor to where the victims were still trapped in the wreckage, covered with a salvage sheet. In the presence of the senior police officer I threw back the salvage sheet to expose the two victims to the doctor. He swallowed hard, turned away and immediately declared the couple dead. I replaced the salvage sheet over the bodies and thanked the doctor. He told me that although he was no stranger to the sight of a dead body, he was shocked to see that couple still in the accident situation amongst the twisted and tangled wreckage of their car.

Immediately after the certification I ordered the crews to release the trapped bodies. On closer examination of them, I saw that they had received severe injuries by crushing to the body and that bleeding had occurred from their ears, eyes, nose and mouth. When we moved them I saw the full extent of their injuries, multiple compound fractures of their limbs and severe crushing and puncture wounds to their bodies. I had attended hundreds of road traffic accidents in my time and forgotten about most of them but I suppose that one must rate along with a few others as one of the more memorable.

When the job was almost completed I noticed that a television interview team was interviewing the senior police officer. I went closer to do a bit of rubbernecking of my own and heard the police officer say that the accident was one of the worst that his men had been called upon to deal with. I looked around and saw that the nearest policeman was directing the traffic more than thirty yards from where my crews had been dealing with the grim scene.

I wasn't really surprised at his statement because for years the media had always described the work at incidents, major or minor, as being done by 'police and rescue services'. Credit was rarely given directly to the work done by the fire brigade or the ambulance service, whose marvellous work I have witnessed many times. It has been my experience that the police contribution to the jobs that I have been on has been limited to investigation concerning the law, documentation of persons involved, liaison between all services, traffic and crowd control and follow-up investigations. All high profile and necessary work but not hands on, they always seem to receive credit for the rescue work carried out by fire brigade and ambulance personnel but in reality they were mostly spectators.

It was rare to get through a night duty without a shout of one kind or another but provided that they were before midnight, it was possible to get a fair night's rest. I remember going to bed one particular night and being awoken by a telephone call from Jock Anderson, the officer of the watch in the Croydon control room. It was early morning, about 0100 hours, when he informed me of a train crash that had occurred at East Croydon Railway Station.

In a very short time I was on my way to the incident, en route I heard a message from the officer in charge of the first attendance initiating major accident procedure. I was expecting many injured passengers at the incident because the receipt of that message indicates that there were at least fifty live casualties involved. After booking in attendance with control over the radio, I made my way to the platform adjacent to where the crash had occurred. My first reaction was that there seemed to be a fair amount of damage but an absence of casualties. I located the station officer in charge who with a guilty expression on his face, tried to justify why he upgraded the incident to a major accident.

Being aware that the police, ambulance service and hospitals would have been informed of the incident by our brigade control and their own predetermined major accident procedure put into operation, I had to act quickly. Immediately I dispatched a radio message cancelling major accident procedure, keeping my fingers crossed that not too much disturbance had been caused to the other services but knowing that there would be a few angry brigade officers on their way to East Croydon Railway Station.

The crash had occurred between a goods train and a mail train. I was informed that two people were involved – the driver who had been located was trapped in the wreckage and the guard, who couldn't be found. I organised a thorough search of the wreckage and the surrounding area and track, causing firemen to put themselves into dangerous situations by forcing access into the wreckage to locate the guard. I later learned that the guard had not been on the train, it appeared that he had unofficially taken the night off.

The train driver was trapped up to his neck in a tangled mass of steel, it was very surprising that he had survived the impact and was still breathing. Norbury's E.T. crew, with Sub-Officer Derek Troth in charge was beginning to make some progress in cutting away the debris around him and an ambulance crew began to organise the attendance of a medical team. It was clear to me that the rescue was going to be a prolonged operation.

Rescue efforts progressed, floodlights were erected illuminating the working area and the medical team arrived and set up their equipment to monitor the condition of the trapped train driver. A doctor positioned herself on the wreckage close to the victim regularly checking him for signs of deterioration as we cut away the debris that was entangled around his unconscious body, it was a difficult and slow job.

A divisional officer who had not held the rank very long and was promoted from a training reference arrived looking very anxious. He climbed on to the wreckage and I brought him up to date with the situation. He said that he was taking charge but told me to continue to direct the rescue operations. He was more concerned about the earlier cock-up, the initiation of major accident procedure and was worried about other senior officers attending. He began running around checking that all minor procedures had been attended to. Avoiding criticism was paramount in his eyes and the job had to be as near text book as possible before anyone senior to him arrived. He had absolutely no practical input to the rescue from the time that he arrived to the time that he left the incident.

The divisional commander arrived, that surprised me because he wasn't on duty; on reflection though, I shouldn't have been surprised. He didn't negotiate the wreck but shouted to me from the platform. I shouted back that the D.O. was in charge but he insisted on asking me whether asbestos or beryllium were involved. I wasn't at all impressed by him demonstrating his ability to recall what he had read on the subject of trains involved in fires or accidents, especially as he probably read up on it before coming to the incident. I ignored the question and concentrated on the job. Why I was asked was beyond me when other surplus officers and railway managers who could have supplied all of the technical information that he wanted were on the scene by that time. We continued to make progress and managed to free the driver's right leg but he was still well and truly trapped by his left leg, up to his hip. The doctor had set up a drip and had given him the necessary pain relieving drugs because he was showing signs of gaining consciousness.

At about 0300 hours the duty deputy assistant chief officer covering the brigade, arrived on the scene. He scrambled on to the wreckage to where I was working to satisfy himself on what was going on. He also told me to carry on, before scrambling off of the wreckage, nearly taking the floodlights with him.

Relief crews arrived and took over while tired crews returned to their stations. Steady progress continued in removing the remaining twisted steel wreckage from around the man's left leg but he had by then been trapped for more than three hours. The doctor was expressing some concern about the condition of the trapped driver and was reluctant to inject him anymore. At about 0500 hours I was still on the wreckage in charge of the rescue operations, more crew changes were made and as time passed, progress began to slow down.

I was deep in the wreckage working in an almost inverted position, trying to release the man's left foot, that being the only part of his body that was still trapped. It was a very difficult operation, railway workers had positioned heavy duty jacks, blocks and pulleys around the crews working on the wreck in an effort to make the area as safe as possible. Large capacity cranes had been manoeuvred into position and were taking the weight of the heavy sets of steel bogey wheels that were balancing precariously over and around our working position. For several hours the doctor was perched under the threat of a dangerously positioned set of train wheels as she tended to the injured driver. Firemen took turns in holding the intravenous drip container as ambulance crews and a nurse assisted the doctor.

Everyone was doing their utmost for the trapped man but the rescue seemed to come to a halt, as we found it increasingly difficult to work in the cramped restricted area in an inverted position around the man's leg. I had managed to reach down between the twisted steel and insert a knife down the back of the man's boot but I couldn't impart enough pressure and movement to the blade to cut the leather. I couldn't get the slightest movement from his foot despite a great deal of heaving, it was well and truly jammed more than an arm's length down among a mass of twisted heavy gauge steel.

At about 0600 hours the doctor became very concerned about the train driver's chances of survival. She suggested mobilising a surgical team to amputate the lower part of the limb and after a discussion it was agreed that it was the only way that he would have a chance of surviving, given the time that he had been trapped and his deteriorating condition. It was about 0630 hours as I remember, when I climbed down from the wreckage for the first time since I arrived on the scene at about 0100 hours. The surgical team took over and a short time after, at about 0700 hours, the train driver was released, minus his left foot.

As I came down from the wreckage I was immediately approached by a television crew. I was very tired but I agreed to be interviewed so I answered some questions put to me by an outside news broadcaster. As I walked away from that interview I was asked more questions by independent radio and newspaper reporters, who seemed to be trying to shove microphones and miniature tape recorders up my nose.

A few weeks later I had to appear at a public inquiry into the accident. I was questioned on the position of the driver in the wreckage and was asked some questions by the driver's trade union representative, in an effort to establish the cause of the crash.

During that train incident a disciplinary case was brought against a senior officer attached to the division. I had wondered why I was left alone to direct the rescue operations without much support. The reason became clear when I discovered that a demonstration of power had been made by the duty deputy assistant chief officer who was ultimately in charge of the incident, because of his presence. I was saddened but not surprised at the extent of ganging-up and victimisation, that took place against a fellow officer, over a dispute about the wearing of his fire fighting uniform.

Although the officer was very briefly present in the vicinity of the incident, he was not involved in the operation in any way. Because I was the only A.D.O. on duty in the division and was tied up with the rail accident, he was the only other officer available to attend any further incidents that may have occurred within the division. He had anticipated the possibility of fire or other incident occurring elsewhere or being ordered on to my job, so he had used his initiative and made his way to the incident as an observer but remained available for further calls.

He was noticed by the D.A.C.O. and ordered to rig in his fire gear but because he had not been officially ordered on to the job, he first checked with Croydon control to inform them of his whereabouts. He was told that no further assistance had been requested from the incident and as far as the control was concerned he was not required there, so he left the incident.

It was a demonstration of the lengths that some officers were prepared to go to remain in favour, and the priorities in their minds when they were told to witness and support the ridiculous and undeserving charge of disobedience to orders of a colleague.

A man was trapped and fighting for his life and a couple of officers lacked the guts to make a stand by stating the true facts against an unreasonably aggressive officer. They acted like puppets, by supporting him in trumping up a totally unwarranted disciplinary charge against one of their fellow officers, for fear of blotting their own copy book.

That indicated a complete about-turn on the thinking regarding disciplinary matters. But nearer the truth, in my opinion it was more to do with a long-standing personality clash and an opportunity to gain misguided personal satisfaction. Knowing both officers rather well I believe it could have been any one or even both of those reasons, but what transpired was certainly not in the interest of the brigade.

It was becoming increasingly clear though, that some senior officers considered that instigating disciplinary proceedings against some unsuspecting individual was a feather in their cap. Believing that it made them appear efficient in the eyes of the newly installed senior management at the brigade headquarters. The 'bully boy' era had arrived.

When the alleged charge was upheld and a disciplinary hearing was arranged, I was astounded. It emphasised the undesirable tactics that senior brigade management had adopted. By extracting statements from ambitious officers, for the purpose of exaggerating a trivial matter against a fellow officer was an uncomfortable experience for me to witness. Especially when a life and death operation was in progress and being ignored by them. That gave me a reason to form another adverse opinion. It was a bad feeling knowing that the officers concerned wouldn't dare to be seen as being contradictory, for fear of dropping out of favour. It appeared that officer bashing had become acceptable.

I admired the courage and strength of character of the victimised officer. Had he been made of lesser mettle, he may have crumpled under the stress that he was put under.

In my mind that diabolical episode marked another undesirable change in the brigade, it had the effect of boosting my desire to leave. Having to work in an atmosphere where one was continually looking over one's shoulder, for fear of being 'set up' by an ambitious colleague plus the officer promotion policies that I boringly wrote about in my previous paragraphs was not to my liking. Therefore, I wanted no part in it. To make matters worse the junior ranks were laughing at the pathetic examples that the officers were making of themselves. However, that undesirable behaviour developed into what one had to accept as part of the job.

The real job, the part that I had enjoyed for years, was attending the thousands of different types of incidents that occurred. Fires ranging from a waste paper bin alight, to thirty, forty and even a fifty pump fire in a Thames-side warehouse. Gas explosions, road traffic accidents, train crashes, persons under trains, persons trapped in machinery and lifts, persons impaled on railings, leakage of refrigerant, a terrorist bomb explosion, persons overcome, persons threatening to jump and those that had jumped, incidents involving aircraft, rescue of animals, minor incidents, major incidents, arson etc, all challenging and requiring a different method of approach. Obviously one encounters a lot of fatalities over the years, even so when something happens closer to home so to speak, it reminds you how vulnerable we all are.

Jock Pow, who was a station officer attached to a non-operational section at the division headquarters, collapsed while on duty and had subsequently died in hospital. Since he transferred back into the London Fire Brigade from Buckinghamshire Fire Brigade, in the rank of leading fireman, he had worked his way up to station officer rank. He had been in charge of a watch at Bromley Fire Station until ill health caused him to transfer into a non-operational job.

The Brigade Missionary Len Webb conducted the service at Jock's funeral, which was attended by a large number of his colleagues. Their soft low voices singing the hymn Amazing Grace was very moving and prompted one's thoughts. I am sure that there were many unsung heroes, in the midst of those mourners, with very large lumps in their throats.

I was talking to an old colleague, D.O. Alf Harris, at Jock's funeral. In April 1961 when I only had a couple of years in the job and Alf was a leading fireman, we took part in an Easter parade dressed as old-time firemen, riding a horse-drawn fire engine around London's Battersea Park. We talked about old times and about the sad affair that we had just witnessed. With a shrug of his shoulders, as we walked off to our cars Alf said:

"Makes you wonder who's next doesn't it?"

Early one morning while I was in the A.D.O.'s quarters resting, listening to a violent thunder storm rolling around the sky, I was informed by Brigade Control of an explosion in a house not far from my quarters. In my relaxed state I responded by saying that someone probably mistook the thunder for an explosion. I booked mobile and proceeded to the address. When I arrived I was surprised to see that a house had been completely demolished. It was probably me that mistook the explosion for a clap of thunder.

One other time when I was sleeping in my quarters I was dreaming that I was in the jungle and that I was surrounded by roaring lions. The next morning I could still hear the lions roaring. Puzzled? I looked out of the window and saw that a circus had arrived in the park opposite, in the early hours of the morning and was in the process of it being assembled.

Time marched onward, my partner for my last couple of years was Eric Shrimpton, a six footer with an appetite of four men. We shared a similar sense of humour and attitude towards our work and enjoyed the time that we worked together. I had first met Eric when he was a sub-officer instructor attached to the brigade training centre. When the green watch was created there was a shortage of firemen, the training centre became full of recruits and overflow squads were set up around the brigade, outside of the training centre. Eric used to bring his squad to Norbury Fire Station to train them, when I was in charge of a watch there. I also worked with him for a time when he was a temporary A.D.O. before he was made substantive and given his permanent posting in the division.

Another new divisional commander, once again this one left a lot to be desired for a man in charge of a division consisting of ten stations and about four-hundred and fifty men. It didn't take very long to form an opinion of him. He proved to be about as trustworthy as a hungry fox left to guard a fat chicken. I do not believe that I had ever met such an unprincipled person before or since.

Much to my surprise, when I was discussing an officer's association problem with him, he told me that his deputy, a D.O. (another new one) second in command of the division, was posted into the division to be taught man management. A bit late for that in the rank of divisional officer and I didn't believe he could learn a lot from him. Whether that was true or not I have no idea but it wasn't very professional of him to divulge that confidence, especially to me being junior in rank to both of them. It was absolutely typical of him and his character, just as many other people were to discover later. It highlighted once again the qualities and the type of men selected by the promotion boards for senior management.

He was an expert at giving the impression that his main aim in life was to help his subordinates. He would patronise anyone with a genuine problem or grievance by promising help by raising their problem at the next chief officer's meeting with divisional commanders. He would report back at a later date and repeat his favourite statement to describe his efforts. He would always say:

"I have pressed your case to the point of receiving personal threats and abuse, to no avail."

That had the desired effect on individuals, who would leave his office thanking him for his unsuccessful efforts.

Being the N.A.F.O. representative for the division for the last few years of my service, I had perhaps more opportunity than others, to discover his expert way of appeasing people. I was taken in by him a few times but after listening to his rhetoric over and over again, I began to take it as an insult to the little intelligence that I possessed, when he expected me to believe him. At times he showed his frustration by issuing idle threats when challenged but worst of all, he demonstrated his inability to exercise self-control.

Change of watch was the only time that the A.D.O.s met their opposite numbers on the other three watches. John Davis and I crossed paths again for the first time since we were interviewed along with Les Whyte, when we first applied to join the brigade. He was already a watch station officer in the division, attached to Addington Fire Station when I transferred to Norbury Fire Station. John had also been promoted to A.D.O. and our meetings at the change of watch often turned into a half hour or so of hilarity. John, Eric and I would regularly have a good laugh, normally at somebody else's expense, or when John was on form, by listening to his latest jokes which he delivered with the skill of a professional stand-up comedian.

A lot of jokes revolved around the rumours about recruiting women as fire-fighters. Everything pointed to that becoming a reality because the G.L.C. claimed to be an equal opportunities employer. Also, under the equal opportunities banner the brigade was trying to recruit more members from the ethnic minorities.

There were an extremely low percentage of men from ethnic backgrounds in the brigade for reasons unknown. Perhaps they didn't apply for the job, or it may be that they were blocked at the interview stage. In my opinion they were just as capable of becoming first-class firemen and fire officers as anyone else.

Many years ago the story was different, not necessarily for racial reasons, although that probably did exist. When all communications to stations from the brigade control were made by telephone, the accent of the early generations of immigrants, mainly from the West

Indies, made verbal messages very hard to understand. The risk of time wasting by misinterpreting messages was high and could have meant loss of life. Confusion had sometimes been caused by misunderstanding the many accents within the British Isles, especially some broad Scottish accents.

As an example – I remember when Jock Anderson, whose accent was bad enough, was working in the old London County Council Fire Brigade Control Room at Lambeth. He accepted a fire call via the three nines emergency system from a man with a West Indian accent stating that there was a fire in Diss Street. Jock, struggling with the man's accent thought he said there is a fire is this street, so he asked the man what the name of the street was. The man said again:

"Diss Street."

Jock explained again that he needed to know the name of the street before he could send a fire engine there and at the same time efforts were being made to trace the telephone call to get a location.

"It's Diss Street."

After a lot of questions the man finally spelt out the name of the street:

"It is D-I-S-S, Diss Street, understand?"

Sure enough the fire was in Diss Street, Bethnal Green.

That problem does not exist today due to the modern communications system the only verbal messages dispatched are those sent over the radio. Also, because of the second and third generations of immigrants adopting local accents, everyone more or less speaks the same language.

The decision to employ women as fire-fighters was hard to swallow. Fire-fighter is the phrase used in the modern fire brigade because the word fireman with emphasis on the 'man' is redundant. It is not politically correct. The employment of women for operational work in the fire brigade presented unique problems. Firstly the physical attributes required to be accepted as a recruit were lowered for women because of their obvious lesser body strength compared to men. Granted that the regular daily training had ceased to include the rescue of a colleague weighing at least one hundred and forty pounds, by carrying down a ladder from a third floor window of the drill tower. Nor does it include using such heavy equipment, like the rubber-lined hose with water absorbent hose jackets and the heavy wooden ladders that were around a few years ago. Nonetheless, the work on the fire ground and the strength and stamina required to tackle it, has not changed. In fact, the policy that all fire-fighters have to be trained to wear breathing apparatus at fires, calls for extra strength and stamina when it is worn, because of the substantial extra weight that has to be carried. I have been told by firemen that have worked alongside female fire-fighters that they are an added worry because they cannot help keeping a watchful eye on them.

Secondly, by thrusting females into a male dominated environment such as a fire station had its obvious risks attached to it, risks that the brigade's senior management and G.L.C. politicians had appeared to ignore. I say ignore because I do not believe they could be so naive, as not to realise the potential problems.

Whilst I am in full support for equality for women and have no personal feelings against them competing for any employment position or job. I do not believe that standards should be adjusted to suit them. They should not be accepted into an occupation just for the sheer hell of it or for political gain and publicity or for the appeasement of activists.

It is my opinion that a woman cannot perform the duties of an operational fire-fighter with a similar input of physical efficiency as a man, whatever her determination and intensity of her training. I do not believe that women are physically capable of carrying out the expected duties of a fire-fighter as efficiently as the average man employed by brigades. A man is expected to, and can normally maintain a degree of physical fitness that will enable him to reasonably perform the tasks required of a fire-fighter, until the pensionable age of fifty-five years. I doubt very much whether any female could maintain that level fitness until that age.

I am not suggesting that women should not be employed by fire brigades, they have been working in control rooms for many years, as I mentioned earlier my wife Rosemary worked in the London Fire Brigade Control Room. I am sure that there are many jobs that they could be employed to do even within the operational field, but not fire-fighting. Some non-operational jobs that have been accepted as being performed by men for years could easily be done by women as efficiently or even better, enabling the fit strong men to perform the work that they joined the fire brigade to do in the first place, fighting fires.

It was never foreseen that women would be employed on operational fire-fighting duties, so fire stations were not designed with accommodation suitable to house mixed personnel. Toilet and shower facilities were designed for a single male sex. Also the locker room usually doubles as a dormitory and that itself posed a problem. When my wife Rosemary was employed by the brigade, there was a rule that there had to be at least two females working in the control room at the same time on a night duty and that was a fully wakeful duty.

As suspected, it didn't take very long before the normally accepted horseplay that occasionally erupts between the inmates of a fire station, to degenerate into antics of a sexual nature. Inevitably the results of disciplinary action against firemen caused upset and anxiety. Not because firemen were sexually perverted or in any way different from other red-blooded males. It was in my opinion, the fault of a weak and inefficient management who bungled the introduction of female fire-fighters into a predominately male environment. The brigade was not suitably prepared to receive them and did not have the finances required for the initial, necessary and desirable facilities to accommodate them. It is my opinion that it was bungled just like the introduction of the watch related A.D.O.s many years earlier.

If the G.L.C. and the brigade management wanted that revolutionary change so badly, they should have made sure that the necessary requirements were in place to facilitate a smooth introduction. Essentially, before women were recruited, management should have educated personnel by spelling out the possible dangers and pitfalls to be avoided when having mixed sex personnel serving in such close proximity to each other, and by ensuring that all male employees clearly understood the consequences that could result from complaints of sexual harassment. The very least that should have been done was to closely monitor the situation and not take up their favourite posture of the proverbial ostrich and wait for the inevitable detonation of their self-primed time bomb.

Many impromptu discussions took place on the subject of women fire-fighters, even on the fire ground when neighbouring stations met up, especially when heavy work was being done, there would be the odd comment on the lines of, can you imagine a woman doing this?

Talking of the fire ground, I was in the divisional headquarters building at Croydon just after the change of watch one evening discussing a problem with Dave Perry one of the divisional staff sub-officers, when I was informed of a fire in Mayday Road, near Mayday Hospital, Croydon. I looked out from the staff office window in the direction of the hospital and could see a large column of smoke rising above the buildings. I booked mobile and made my way towards Mayday Road. The first appliances from Norbury booked in attendance over the radio, followed almost immediately by a priority assistance message from Station Officer Lindridge, making pumps six.

Being in close proximity to the fire Ken Lindridge seemed pleased to see me arrive so promptly. He updated me as much as he could, having only arrived a short time before me. I took command and quickly assessed the extent and potential spread of the fire. Ken and his crew rigged in breathing apparatus, laid out a jet and took it inside the building to fight the fire on the fourth floor.

The building was a modern block of offices, consisting of five floors with a frontage of about three hundred feet and about sixty feet in depth. The main entrance and staircase was in the centre of the building forming a firebreak between the two ends of the building. The two top floors to the right of the staircase were well alight.

Other fire engines arrived and I ordered more jets to be laid out and a water tower to be got to work from Croydon's Hydraulic Platform, that was the appliance that superseded the Turntable Ladder, which had been positioned in the middle of the road. I made pumps twelve and went inside the building to assess progress. I located Norbury's crew working well with their jet on the fourth floor and encouraged other crews who were laying out more hose to attack the fire from the staircase on the fifth floor.

I was pleased to see Eric Shrimpton arrive, he took charge of fire-fighting operations inside the building, leaving me free to concentrate on overall command. The crews did an excellent professional job, quickly bringing the blaze under control and preventing the fire from spreading horizontally past the natural firebreak of the central staircase. Salvage operations were carried out on the floors below the fire by covering all of the contents with waterproof salvage sheets preventing any unnecessary damage from water percolating through the floors.

By the time the main fire control unit arrived from brigade headquarters the fire was virtually out, thanks mainly to the courage and skill of the crews forming the first attendance from Norbury and Croydon Fire Stations, who were successful in their initial attack on the fire.

Divisional Officer Alf Harris was the duty D.O. in the division and he was ordered to the fire because the size of the fire required a D.O. to be in charge. He had a long drive from his home situated on the opposite side of the division to get to the fire, arriving at about the same time as the duty Divisional Commander Bill Butler. I met them both at the front of the building and brought them up to date with the fire situation and handed over command. Bill Butler told Alf Harris to use the hydraulic platform to survey the damaged floors from the outside and to check the state of the roof. He then told me to lead on and show him the extent of the damage inside the building. We had made a tour of the damaged area when we were informed that the duty Assistant Chief Officer had arrived at the scene. He caught up with us on the fifth floor so I left the two senior officers talking and went to check up on the clearing up operations, which were well under way.

As I walked down the staircase to the ground floor, there was a group of firemen and an ambulance attendant bending over somebody lying flat on the floor at the foot of the stairs. When I saw who it was I was shocked and very concerned. Alf Harris was laying on his back struggling for breath, I had no idea what had caused his collapse and for a couple of seconds I just stood there looking. No one seemed to be doing anything and that couple of seconds seemed ages, then Eric Shrimpton shouted:

"Get him on the stretcher!"

That seemed to spur everyone into action and Alf was quickly placed on a stretcher. With an oxygen mask fitted on him he was rushed straight into the casualty department of the adjacent Mayday Hospital, bypassing the ambulance.

I had known Alf for many years, since the days when I was a fireman at Lambeth and he was a leading fireman. I was extremely concerned at the sight of him struggling to breathe as we rushed him into the hospital.

The staff in the hospital immediately began giving Alf emergency treatment. I stood outside the curtained cubical with Eric and Dave Harn, who had arrived on the fire scene in the brigade control unit. Dave Harn was also a fireman at Lambeth around the same time as Alf and I were there. We could hear the efforts of the hospital staff trying to revive Alf, while we stood in silence willing Alf to pull through. We were stunned when a nurse appeared from the cubicle and told us that Alf had died.

Alf's death had a big impact on me and my attitude towards continued service in the brigade, after all, anyone of my rank and above was entitled to serve until the age of sixty, unlike the ranks below who had to retire at the age of fifty-five. I realised that the time would come when I had to make a decision. Alf had served two years over his full pensionable service of thirty years and could have been enjoying his retirement. His attitude to that was, as he told me a few months previous, that he would have to find a job to do rather than do nothing, so why not carry on with the job that he loved. An in-depth inquiry was set up within the brigade and of course an inquest was held.

Standing in silence at Alf's Funeral, feeling very sad, I began reflecting on the past and other funerals of brigade members that I had attended over the years. There were many.

When we were at Jock Pow's funeral I recalled reminiscing with Alf about our early days in the brigade and I remembered in particular Alf's comment as we went our separate ways when he said;

"Makes you wonder who's next."

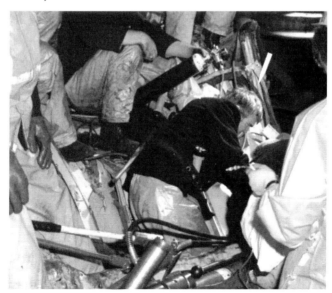

No 2.
I am in the centre working on the East Croydon rail crash

No 3.
Mayday Road Croydon. The fire where Alf Harris died.

Chapter 12

When possible I preferred to leave everything to do with my work behind me at the end of a duty period, including my uniform, I always travelled in civvies. Although I believe the fire brigade to be amongst the best occupations around, I couldn't eat, sleep and drink it like some people I knew. Home life was much too precious to allow the fire brigade to intrude. Work was necessary to exist and even though I enjoyed my work most of the time but in contrast I enjoyed my home life all of the time. To allow work to make demands on my private home life was something that I avoided as much as I possibly could, not always possible but I tried not to allow one to invade the other, that is what I considered right for my home life and my job.

Once again, rumours were in the air about yet another reorganisation. This time it appeared that the intention was at last to kill off the dreaded residential duty system. We didn't know for certain which system was going to replace it and we didn't know the conditions that would be attached to the new rota with regard to hours and pay. All of the brigade's officers were waiting in anticipation for the promulgation of the new system that would for a lot of them, seriously influence their future.

After a while the representative bodies circulated a few suggested rotas for which they had been negotiating with the employers. They also indicated that the A.D.O.s were to be taken off the forty-two hour watch-related duty system and were to be included in the new duty system, which was to be decided by a secret ballot.

It became common knowledge that the chosen duty system was linked with the chief officer's desire for all of his senior officers to live within the brigade's area, which would enable them when on night duty, to ride to incidents direct from their homes. Those officers, who lived outside the Greater London area, were to be billeted in brigade-provided accommodation whilst on duty, for which a rent chargeable on a nightly basis would be levied.

The new rota meant being on duty for a continuous period of about seventy-two hours during one part of it, averaging out over a six-week period to around seventy hours a week. Part of the new deal for senior officers was a ban on the use of station mess facilities. Senior officers were forbidden to eat in or belong to a station mess.

That ban was acceptable to those who lived within the divisions to which they were attached because they could plan their duties to include visits to their homes, just like the existing residential system, but it created a problem for others. It all seemed to fall into place as part of management's plan, to force all senior officers to live within the brigade's area. For the want of another name it appeared to almost be the rebirth of the residential duty system but to include the A.D.O.s once again. However, it did not include the perks of free rent fuel and light.

When the new system was to be introduced at the beginning of January 1985 which appeared to be in line with the chief officer's plans. I realised then that I had been integrated into a working system very similar to the one that I vowed I would never work. The pressure was on and I realised that there was only one remedy. Like many others who lived outside of the brigade's area it was likely that I would have to move to another division, that made me feel that it was really make my mind up time. I knew that I had to choose between the aggravation of working to the rules of the new duty system and leaving the fire brigade.

More rumours abounded about postings. To enable those officers who lived within the G.L.C. area to be on call from their homes whilst on night duty, they would be posted to divisions near their homes. That made sense when looking at it from management's point of view. Those officers who lived outside the G.L.C. area would be posted to the inner London divisions where house prices were exorbitant and not many fire officers lived.

Travel would more than likely have to be by public transport which I would not even consider as a regular part of my working pattern. Travelling to inner London by car from Sussex would be an even greater chore because as I mentioned earlier, it took at least two hours for me to travel to Old Kent Road. The inner London divisions were further on and travel by train into the heart of London was the only sensible alternative. It appeared to be a well thought out tactic to force officers to move home. Of course, living in West Sussex, I was a likely candidate for having my journey to work increased. There were at least six A.D.O.s that lived within my division who at that time were not serving there. That problem caused me great concern so I had to secure my position somehow.

Unknown to anyone I made my predicament known to a long-standing colleague, who carried a bit of weight in the right department at brigade headquarters. I was very grateful when the postings were published. It gave a lift to my sagging morale to discover that I was the only officer in the 'H' Division, who lived out of area to remain in post. I believe that puzzled my senior colleagues, especially my divisional commander, who tried to claim that he did me a personal favour by fighting to the point of receiving personal abuse and threats, to keep me in his division. That made me smile, yet again in his desire to impress and claim credit, he had to lie, but to disclose the way that I achieved it would have involved a third party and I wasn't prepared to do that, but I would have loved to have shot him down in flames.

1985 arrived and we began to work the new duty system. Once again the brigade management team appeared to fail in organising the change but I suppose that you can't please everyone all of the time. It seemed that some A.D.O.s got the booby prize as far as accommodation and office space was concerned. Those A.D.O.s who because of the location of their homes had to reside in provided rental accommodation while on night duty, of which I was one. On reflection that may have been a management ploy to achieve the eventual plan of having all officers residing within the divisions in which they worked.

The daily routine of office work continued under the new working conditions. Emergency calls came as a welcome relief to the monotony of the longer working hours, that part of the job remained more or less unchanged except for minor, so-called improved procedures.

An explosion occurred in a block of flats at Putney Hill, South West London, early one morning. A number of people were killed and some were trapped. The search for victims went on for a long time amongst the debris.

I was ordered on as a relief safety officer, sometime after the initial call. My duty was to watch for movement in loose masonry and other debris which was hanging precariously above the crews searching for victims amongst the debris of the collapsed building.

I noticed that while I was keeping a close watch on the dangerously suspended damaged structure, I was having difficulty seeing the cracks and the gaps clearly. The consequences of failing to notice a potentially fatal situation bothered me, so I was pleased when the search was called off and the crews withdrawn.

I had noticed for some time that I was having difficulty seeing clearly in low light conditions especially when I was driving, so I arranged to have my eyes examined. For about two years I had been using glasses for desk work, acceptable and not uncommon for someone approaching the wrong end of his forties.

As a result of my eye test I ordered a pair of glasses for use when driving. When I went to collect them the optician mentioned that my eyes were below the standard required for a heavy goods vehicle driver, so I should always wear them when driving, not just in low light conditions.

I pondered over the optician's words for a few days and gradually those words turned into sweet music. I wondered if I could be medically discharged because of poor eyesight. I felt comfortable at the thought of having an escape route. If things got so intolerable, because of the length of my service I could opt out without any penalties or anything less than a full pension.

Those glasses certainly made a big difference to the sharpness of my vision whilst driving. That was a great advantage but it also had a disadvantage. I had to drive more than twenty miles to work wearing them, and then change to my reading glasses for my desk work. When I booked mobile to an incident I would change back to my driving glasses until I arrived. Because firemen, sorry, I meant fire-fighters as they are now called, were at that time, not allowed to wear any type of aid to vision during operational work, I had to remove my glasses and work without them.

I discovered that after wearing glasses for some time and then having to manage without them, my eyes were completely out of focus. Working at a fire is a time when good vision is needed. I didn't mention it to anyone but I was concerned about the problem. Realising the consequences if I failed to notice a potentially disastrous situation on the fire ground bothered me.

After working the new rota system for a few weeks, I began to realise what it would be like in the long term. Sometimes I was leaving home carrying a small suitcase containing a change of shirts and underwear, plus a supply of food. Also, having to pay rent for night duty, even if I was out on an emergency all night, was in my opinion the last straw.

When I was on duty over a weekend, I sometimes arranged to meet Rosemary in a lay-by on the boundary of the G.L.C. area. She would hand me a freshly cooked meal which I took back to my quarters for my Sunday lunch. It really was unbelievable that some officers were forced to accept those working conditions.

During one lunch break at the divisional headquarters I was discussing the changes in the job with three other A.D.O.s plus the conditions that some of us were made to work under. We talked about officers' attitudes towards one and other, especially the fact that some of them seemed to be openly competing on a points scoring mission against each other. Ted, A.D.O. Ted Kinmonth, was among the small discussion group. I had known Ted since my days as a fireman at Lambeth when I used to drive the E.T. and he was the sub-officer in charge of it. With almost thirty years' service completed he could retire in a few months. Although the new conditions were not too bad for him because he lived within the division, he wasn't really happy with the new system. During that discussion I made a decision that I have never regretted. I put my glasses on that I used for driving and said that I was going to wear them all the time and hope that I would have to be medically discharged because of defective eyesight.

I could have predicted that it wouldn't take long for someone to spread the word about my new bespectacled image but the time that it actually took to reach my boss amazed me. Almost immediately following my decision to wear my glasses I was sent for by my boss the divisional commander. He told me that reluctantly, that was a laugh for a start, he had to report the fact that I found it necessary to permanently wear glasses to the brigade's medical adviser and that I may have to have my eyes examined by an eye specialist. He added that I would have to go on light duties immediately until the result of my eye examination was known.

I must say that the speed of events following my decision to wear my glasses was record breaking. My boss played right in to my hands and at once I began to cheer up. I began working day duties only and couldn't believe that I would not be doing any more shift work after almost twenty-seven years. The sad part of it all was coming to terms with not getting any more shouts because I knew that I would miss the operational side of the job. I consoled myself with the thought that I had attended and dealt with a hell of a lot of different incidents in my time. I had, as it is said, seen it, done it, worn the T-shirt, read the book and seen the film.

I tried to estimate the time it would take for me to be discharged, providing the eye specialist recommended it. A medical discharge meant that because I had served for more than twenty-six years and six months, I was entitled to a full thirty-year index-linked pension.

The date of my visit to the eye specialist eventually came and after a thorough examination of my eyes, the specialist asked me how I felt about leaving the brigade. I told him that I was prepared for that eventuality in the interest of safety for myself and others. That was a previously prepared reply to a question that I had anticipated and could only hope that I would be asked.

After a further four weeks the official confirmation for my retirement from the London Fire Brigade was sent to me. It was good news, my final good deed in the brigade would be to create a vacancy for yet another high flyer to bluff his way through the system on his way to the dizzy heights at the brigade's headquarters. My time had come and I was quite happy to retire.

There were six A.D.O.s due to retire from the 'H' Division around the same time; five of us, Dick Cheeseman, Bill Langworth, John Davis, Pete Tilling and myself were all transferred almost overnight to brigade headquarters for various desk duties. Not a popular move but understandable so that someone could act-up a rank for each of us to meet the essential operational officer cover within the division.

In agreement with the brigade's establishments section, my last day of service was determined. The 15th December 1985. By claiming the leave days that I had accumulated I made my last attendance about two weeks before that date. As I did at the end of any other working day I just walked out, the only difference was that I took with me my few personal items from my office and my feelings of great elation and satisfaction at not having to return.

A farewell social evening was arranged at the brigade's sports and social centre at Ewell in Surrey. It was a joint affair, organised for the six of us who had retired within a few weeks of each other. We were all presented with a very nice inscribed gift and our personal fireman's axes, mounted to display as an ornament or wall plaque.

Since leaving the brigade I have visited the sports centre as a guest at other retirement celebrations. In particular and one of the most memorable was Eric Shrimpton's retirement, my old partner from the watch-related duty system. He had a really enjoyable get-together. His presentation was made by our last divisional commander which didn't excite me one bit but surprisingly he delivered an excellent speech which at times greatly amused his audience. Even more surprising to me was the fact that he didn't claim any credit for anything.

As a civilian on the sidelines, I saw a side of him that I didn't know existed. Beneath his attitude of 'I will tread on anyone who gets in my way in my quest for promotion' it appeared that he was probably a nice person. We shook hands and were automatically pleasant to each other, he even referred jokingly to the misunderstandings we had during some heated N.A.F.O. meetings.

Unlike him, he began to express his own dissatisfaction with the brigade. Apparently, since I had retired, yet another reorganisation robbed him of command of his division. During our chat he seemed very serious, he uttered a sentence which echoed in my mind and fully described his dissatisfaction and change of attitude towards the brigade.

He said, "I am even taking all my leave days now."

It never ceases to amaze me how many so called 'dedicated officers' become disgruntled and disillusioned, when they finally woke up and returned to the real world.

Eric was medically discharged as I was but for a different reason, he also qualified by time in the job for a full pension, but sadly he wasn't able to enjoy his retirement for very long. In 1995 at the age of 57 Eric died after a short illness suffering from cancer. I was pleased that I had the opportunity to visit him when he was ill. We talked over old times and reminisced about some of the jobs that we had been on together and some of the characters that we knew, we had a bit of a laugh on that particular day. Only a couple of weeks after that visit, Eric passed away.

Although he was retired from the brigade, Eric was given a superb send-off. His coffin was transported to the crematorium on a fire engine. A guard of honour was formed by uniformed fire-fighters from the London Fire Brigade and the Kent Fire Brigade where Eric began his career, they lined the road to the entrance of the crematorium. He was keen on playing cricket and was well known among those involved in the game within the brigade and other opposing teams and organisations. His popularity could be measured by the dozens of mourners that attended.

During my years in the London Fire Brigade, I had the pleasure of meeting and working with some very nice genuine and interesting people, as well as some complete opposites. Some had been happy to continue their careers in the junior ranks and some decided to go for promotion and were successful in reaching senior positions. However, in my opinion they all achieved success and I'm sure that they all experienced from their work, the same degree of satisfaction that I did.

I have seen many changes take place over the years, fire engine bells replaced by two-tone horns and sirens, amber flashing lights mounted on the front of fire engines replaced by blue flashing lights situated on the top and visible through 360 degrees. Modern automatic fire engines and fire cars, fire calls received by teleprinter and automatically operated appliance room doors. New fire stations, drill towers and modern lightweight equipment. Development of compressed air breathing apparatus and chemical protection suits, along with up-to-date communications equipment. Changes in the design and colour of fire-fighters operational uniforms. The introduction of female fire-fighters. All of those changes and more, most of them for the better. I believe that the work of a fireman, or fire-fighter to be politically correct, is being recognised more and more as one of the most essential services necessary in the community. It is an organisation that is ready to respond to a call for help, 24 hours a day 365 days a year, it never closes. It provided me with secure employment, job satisfaction most of the time and a satisfactory standard of living for many years, culminating in an index-linked pension for the remainder of my life.

Chapter 13

During 1983 while I was still serving in the fire brigade I bought a small parcel of land. The purpose was to expand my hobbies and pastimes when I eventually left the fire brigade. At that time I had no idea that I would be retiring so soon. It was only four and a half acres of land but enough to keep me busy and give me some elbow room. Having been a keen bee-keeper since 1976 and have enjoyed growing various plants, my plan was to expand my apiary and hopefully produce enough honey for sale to cover my hobby costs, enjoying myself at the same time.

There were three large plastic tunnels on the land, the previous owner had intended to develop it into a nursery but had died before he had completed the project. One of the tunnels I heated with a propane gas heater, mainly for raising young plants from seed and also to use as a work area for potting on. The second tunnel I used for growing tomatoes and the third I used as a display area for bedding plants and young conifer trees. Rosemary and I really enjoyed spending our spare time working there and we did at one time, before I retired from the fire brigade, consider building it up to run as a business rather than just for a hobby.

Before finally deciding to spend money on building up a nursery business, I believed it to be essential to look at the possibilities of living on site, for security reasons amongst other things. That obviously meant applying for planning permission. As I soon discovered, in Mid-Sussex it is the next thing to impossible for any ordinary individual, with no backing, to obtain planning permission for a dwelling in the countryside, so that idea was dropped following three unsuccessful applications.

It was right not to embark on investing too much in nursery stock without the security of living on site because it wasn't very long before thieves found my hobby place and removed some of my stock, that was very disheartening.

Now retired and having much more time to spare, I decided that I needed some equipment to work on the land. An advertisement in a local paper caught my eye – it was for a small tractor, two pig arcs, a heavy roller, a hay trailer and a tipping trailer. A pig farmer was selling them so I went to view the items. I bought the lot and for good measure two young piglets as well.

That was when the fun started, I knew nothing about pigs. I didn't really want to keep them shut in a pig arc so I erected an enclosure out of stock wire which allowed them to root around. Early the next day I received a phone call from the land owner next to my few acres. She said that a couple of young pigs were running free on my land. I was very concerned because the frontage of my land was directly on the main A.23 London to Brighton trunk road. Two pigs running onto such a fast road could cause a serious accident. I immediately stopped what I was doing, jumped into my car and went on a piglet round-up. That was no easy task, after a couple of hours chasing them around my field I finally caught them by placing some tasty food in the middle of a loop that I tied with a slip knot, in a length of rope.

In turn they were tempted and when the first one ventured into the trap to sample the food I quickly pulled on the rope, tightening it around the pig's legs. Shutting the first one in the pig arc, I adopted the same procedure for the second one. That took a little longer because he was frightened by the squealing of the first pig. He seemed very nervous as he approached the food but the temptation was too much for him. With a tug on the rope I had him. The noise that he made was so loud that the woman from the farm next door came to investigate. I felt a bit of a fool but she put me at ease and showed me what I was doing wrong. Stock fencing on its own was not suitable for pigs, I had to reinforce it with strands of barbed wire especially low down. Those two little pigs grew up and one of them filled my freezer, the other was butchered and sold.

There wasn't much that I could do on my land without the injection of money and I had learned that it wasn't worth the risk of having things stolen. I had always been interested in country life and farming, probably since being evacuated to Devonshire for a short time during the war and had always enjoyed visiting the countryside, so when a young chap arrived at my nursery gate with a British Saanen goat on a lead, I became very interested in the animal. Her name was Harriet, I offered to buy her but the lad couldn't sell her because she belonged to his father. The following day the father of the young chap came to see me and we agreed a price for Harriet.

He went away and returned within a short time with the goat, we did the deal and he left.

I stood wondering what to do next with my newly acquired livestock on a rope lead, when suddenly I was jerked sideways. I looked at the goat and my attention was drawn to a beautiful red rose that she had plucked from a nearby bush, disappearing into her mouth. I pulled her clear of the rose bush before more damage could be done and began to wonder where I could safely house her. I decided to position my pig arc on some lush grass as a temporary measure for shelter from the weather. I tied Harriet to a tree, started my tractor and dragged a pig arc to a suitable position. Tethered to her new home, Harriet soon settled down to enjoy her new grazing area. Later I fenced in an area around the pig arc, which allowed her to roam and have access to some rough grazing and woodland.

With my life as a fire brigade officer behind me, I began to realise that my decision to leave the brigade was the right one. I felt comfortable with my intentions for the future, I could please myself what I wanted to do and when I wanted to do it. Motivation would not be a problem because getting enjoyment from my hobbies was the only motivation I needed.

I did find it to be a bit of a burden having to be available to open the place at weekends and bank holidays though. Because of the location in the Sussex countryside, sales could only be made to passing trade and people were only inclined to venture out during weekends and holidays and then only when the weather was fine.

In my search for knowledge about goats, I enrolled in a goat club. One of the members had a billy at stud and for a small fee I arranged to put Harriet to him. He accepted Harriet readily but she wasn't too fond of him. The owner of the billy became concerned because Harriet kept butting him, having rather large horns there was a risk of causing him some damage. Harriet's horns were useful for holding her so the billy's owner grasped them to restrain her so that the billy could eventually perform; when he did, it was over in a flash. The owner of the billy advised me to have Harriet's horns removed as a safety factor. I had realised the potential danger when she accidentally bruised Rosemary's leg and for some reason she didn't like Andrew very much. Every chance she had she would butt him square on his chest, knocking him flat on his back.

I arranged to take her to the vet recommended by the billy's owner. At that time I had a Volkswagen Campervan so I transported her in that. Parked on the forecourt of the surgery I went to find out where I should take her. The receptionist asked me to wait by my van. When the vet came out he was holding a plastic seed tray with a hacksaw and a syringe in it, I was a bit surprised to see such primitive equipment, to say the least.

As I held Harriet by her horns the vet injected her and within a very short time she collapsed unconscious. As I held her head up the vet began to hacksaw the first horn off, very close to her head. It began to bleed and when the horn fell off, blood began to spurt up in the air in time with her heartbeat. Feeling a bit disconcerted, I was about to say something to the vet when he slapped a wad of cotton wool over the wound and told me to hold it while he attacked the other horn.

With her head bound in bandages and still only half awake I took Harriet back to her pen at the nursery. She had graduated from the pig arc into a corrugated iron pen that I built for her. She was in such a sorry state that I couldn't leave her, so I took her home with me. After making some comfortable accommodation for her in a garden shed, I carried her from the van and propped her up in a kneeling position between two bales of hay. As the anaesthetic wore off she managed to stand but even after a couple of days she stood with her bandaged head hanging down, looking thoroughly unhappy and pathetic. Periodically I changed the dressing and the sight of two gaping holes in her scull made me wonder if I had done the right thing.

Eventually she began to look bit happier but the holes in her head didn't appear to show signs of closing. I returned her to her home at the nursery but I had to keep the wounds covered because of annoyance by flies. I suppose it took about twelve months for her head to completely heal.

As well as being visited by thieves the deciding factor, regarding the raising of nursery stock, was the great storm that ripped through the south of England in 1987. The wind tore down my plastic tunnels leaving only the bare steel structures. I decided against replacing the plastic covers and dropped the idea of a nursery business. Even though I didn't raise any nursery stock again, I still referred to my land as the nursery.

During the time of Harriet suffering the loss of her horns, she was also in kid. She grew rather large and I became a bit worried, in case of complications. The time for the birth was drawing near so I had to keep a close eye on her. One morning I went to open her pen and she began to bleat as soon as she heard me. Inside Harriet had just given birth to a little wet struggling bundle. I didn't quite know what to do at first, and then I remembered a little rhyme that used to be recited for a joke when I was in the fire brigade. "When in danger, when in doubt, run in circles, scream and shout." So I kept calm and moved the tiny sticky new born addition to my livestock nearer to Harriet's head. She began to lick the little kid and make soft muttering sounds that I hadn't heard before. She was obviously delighted with her new arrival.

I telephoned Rosemary with the good news; she was so excited that she immediately stopped what she was doing, got in her car and drove to the nursery to see the new born kid. When she arrived she found me playing midwife to a second kid, we were very excited about our new arrivals and very pleased with Harriet. We got a lot of pleasure watching the two kids learning to stand on their wobbly legs and searching for Harriet's teats to get their very important first feed of colostrum. In a couple of days the two kids were skipping around the field, they were growing fast and their long legs were getting stronger by the day. The unfortunate part of the idyllic scene was that one of the kids was a male and there was no demand for them. Billy goats were only good for breeding and eating. As I had no intention of breeding and had no appetite for goat meat, there was no future for my young billy.

I arranged for a vet to de-horn my young female kid, which Rosemary named Penny, I also took my young male kid, which we named Tuppence, with me to have it put down. Once an animal is given a name an attachment is made and it is difficult to make a decision to have it killed. We were stupid to have given the male kid a name knowing that we would not be keeping him. Some people castrate males and keep them for pets but I didn't want to do that.

At the vet's I met another goat keeper who was also having a youngster de-budded. De-horned isn't quite what it sounds like. Kids do not have horns, they have little buds which the horns grow from. They are de-budded by burning the small horn buds out so that the horns never grow. During conversation the goat keeper suggested that she took my young male goat home with her. I couldn't have been more pleased with that idea, greatly relieved I handed him over. The goat keeper immediately gave it a cuddle so I was satisfied that he was wanted.

I took young Penny into the vet's surgery. He knocked her out with an injection and proceeded to burn off the horn buds with a red-hot de-budding tool. It didn't take long before I was on my way back to Harriet with Penny, sporting two round singed patches on her head. Directly Harriet saw Penny she began calling her and Penny quickly responded by feeding.

Harriet didn't appear to miss Tuppence at all, she seemed quite content with having Penny around her heels as she grazed.

Time passed and I was looking for something extra to do at the nursery but before I could raise more animals I had to build more pens for them, so when I saw an advertisement for a row of nine concrete garages for sale, I made an offer. After about six weeks, when I had just about given up the chance of my offer being accepted, I received a telephone call asking if my offer was still good. I bought the garages which had to be dismantled and transported to my land about eight miles away.

Dave Perry, who was a staff officer at the 'H' Divisional Fire Brigade Headquarters at Croydon, lived only a few miles from my nursery and he had a passion for birds, the feathered kind of course. He kept a couple of peacocks and ornamental pheasants at the nursery. That was a good arrangement because while I was still in the brigade and on duty for sometimes seventy two hours at a time, Dave would keep an eye on Harriet and Penny, although Rosemary enjoyed going to the nursery to milk Harriett when I wasn't around.

Dave agreed to help me dismantle the nine garages, transport them on my trailer and re-erect them at the nursery. Together we put down the foundations and over a period of about three months we transported and erected the garages. It was hard work and we were pleased when the job was completed.

With the newly-erected animal pens available I began to ponder on what use to put them to. Harriet and Penny occupied one of them and a second one I used as a workshop, so I had seven more at hand.

I decided to try breeding pigs, so one of the garages I converted into a general sty. Connected to that I constructed a furrowing down pen, and next to that I made a weaner pen, hoping of course that I managed to breed some piglets.

Two young British Lop Eared Gilts were offered to me so I bought them and enthusiastically raised them to breeding age. By keeping a close watch on them I was able to determine when the first one was in season. When I was sure that the time was right I contacted a pig semen supplier and ordered sperm from a prize English White Boar.

The next day I prepared my artificial insemination equipment, which I had previously bought second hand, and was ready to perform the deed. The semen arrived promptly by post, in an insulated package containing two small plastic bottles which had to be mixed before use. I was a bit apprehensive but determined to put into practice all that I had read on the subject of artificial insemination of pigs. It was certainly a hell of a lot cheaper than keeping and feeding a boar and the pick of the best boars was only a telephone call away.

Andrew came with me in case I needed an extra pair of hands, not having performed such an operation before I didn't know exactly what to expect. The insemination applicator that I used was a rubber tube about forty centimetres long and one centimetre in diameter. It was threaded at one end and shaped to receive the nozzle of the semen bottle at the other end. The threaded end of the applicator had to be inserted into the pig's vagina and screwed in place until it locked into position inside her.

The first thing that I did was to sit on the gilt's back to find out if she was on standing heat and just as the book said, she stood still with her head down, she was ready. Not sure of the reaction of the pig, I slowly inserted the insemination tube into her vagina at the same time turning it to engage the thread and lock it in position, she didn't budge.

Andrew stood watching, holding the bottle of semen, waiting for my instructions. I am sure that at eight years old he was a bit confused to say the least. With the tube locked in position, I was ready to introduce the semen which I had mixed with the contents of the second bottle earlier. I bent the end of the insemination tube upwards and took the semen bottle from Andrew.

Inverting the bottle, I squeezed the contents into the tube, waited a short while then unscrewed the tube and removed it from the pig. Job completed. After more than twenty-one days the gilt did not appear to come into heat again so I assumed that she must be in pig. I then had to wait in anticipation of a good result.

Towards the end of her gestation period I prepared the furrowing down pen and put the pregnant mother to be into it, then waited for the expected litter.

On a very cold snowy morning I went to the nursery and was met by a very serious looking Dave Perry. He told me that there was a problem in the furrowing down pen. My heart sank and I immediately felt bitterly disappointed. A multitude of things that could have gone wrong flowed through my mind as I quickly walked towards the pen with Dave behind me.

Frowning heavily, feeling as though I had all the troubles in the world on my shoulders, I opened the door of the pen and went in. The sow was lying on her side making little grunting sounds of satisfaction and contentment and eleven hungry little pink piglets were jostling for the best position to suckle.

What a great surprise that was. David was smiling all over his face and I was shouting with delight. I switched on the infra-red heating lamp and one by one as the piglets had their fill, they settled down for a sleep under the warmth of the lamp, it was a very satisfying sight.

Insemination of my other gilt was also successful. I raised the piglets to about twenty weeks old before taking them to market. It wasn't a very profitable enterprise compared to the input of labour and cost of feed but I found it extremely interesting and satisfying. However, I decided to sell the sows and try another project.

Between all the fun and enjoyable events there were two serious situations developing. My mother's health was deteriorating and my aunt Else was complaining of problems with which her doctor did not appear to be able to control.

For certain, life ends in death. We all know that but do not like to think about it too much but it touches us all several times during our lifetime. I believe that the saddest experiences are when close family members die. That is when you question yourself about whether you could have done more for them, and when you wish that you could speak to them one more time. I know that when my father died, I regretted putting off visiting him in hospital simply to attend a meeting about fire brigade communications. Knowing that he had died while I was at that meeting made me feel particularly saddened, especially when I could have spoken to him that vital one more time.

My mother died on 21st May 1994. She suffered from Alzheimer's disease and had to live in a nursing home for the last few years of her life. To watch her health deteriorate was a painful experience. Before she went into the nursing home, she became a danger to herself and others because of her forgetfulness. Cooking pans left on the cooker, cigarettes left burning and telltale signs like burn marks on her clothing and on the carpet, plus uneaten meals left in the kitchen and many other things, all indicated that she could no longer look after herself.

The things that she said made me laugh and strangely she would also burst out laughing with me. As a regular thing when I visited her in the nursing home, I would stand at the door of the room where all of the patients who could get out of bed, would be sitting in armchairs. I would pick her out and watch her for a few seconds. Like most of the people in there she would look sad and uncomfortable, her thin frame sitting lopsided in her chair and her eyes just staring into space. I would walk towards her and as her eyes focused on me, her face would light up into a great big smile. She would, with great enthusiasm and pleasure, greet me with a loud and drawn out "Hello."

She obviously recognised me but every time I went to see her I would say the same thing to her. I used to tell her that she looked pleased to see me and then ask her if she knew who I was. She used to laugh out loud and say:

"I'm buggered if I know."

She knew that she knew me but didn't know who I was. When I visited her on the same day as one of my brothers, I would ask her if any other visitors had been to see her. She would always say with a frown:

"No, I never get any visitors, I haven't seen anyone for ages."

Unfortunately there wasn't a great deal that she could remember and in the end she slipped into a coma and died ten days later, just after midnight on her 80th birthday.

My aunt Else, a spinster who lived alone for most of her life, died a couple of years later. Again it was very sad and traumatic for her. Because she was so stubborn and independent, she could not be persuaded to give up her flat and go into a nursing home. She suffered from osteoporosis and Paget's disease of the bones. Obviously, the less mobile that she became, the less she could do for herself. Her flat was always kept spotless and when she couldn't do her housework, she used to get very upset. One day after a bad fall she was found by a neighbour and taken to hospital. She hated it and continually asked me to take her home. She began to deteriorate quite rapidly in the hospital and during her conscious moments she kept repeating: "Why doesn't he take me?"

Poor Aunt Else just wanted to die, she was in constant pain. Like my mother, she also drifted into a coma for a few days and quietly died aged 86 years.

The thoughts that run through one's mind, following the demise of loved ones in those circumstances usually include: Could I have done more to help them? Was I sympathetic enough? And so on. Perhaps that is a natural feeling of guilt, I don't know.

Even when death is expected it is always very upsetting. The worst part of those sad occasions is the job of clearing a close relative's home of their belongings. Items found in drawers and cupboards bring back memories of times past, it can be very emotional and disturbing. Even writing about those sad times is very emotional. Concerns about the health and wellbeing of close family members during the 1990s I found to be stressful and depressing while at the same time having to cope with ordinary everyday affairs but that situation has to be dealt with as best you can.

That's enough of the inevitable and the only certain thing about life, so back to some pleasant memories. Because Rosemary, Andrew and I were planning a trip to Australia for a few weeks, I decided not to rush into another project that I would not be able to leave for any length of time, even though Dave was always willing to keep an eye on things at the nursery.

Harriet and Penny had become a bit of a handful with regard to keeping them in their allotted area. Harriet, being a wise old goat, had even worked out how to get past the electric perimeter fence. Reluctantly I made the decision to give them to a breeder of Angora Goats. The breeder was mating his pure-bred Angora Goats, then flushing out the embryos and implanting them in surrogate goats of any breed. The method allowed the breeder to mate his Angoras several times a year, as opposed to just one mating. Apparently from one pair of Angoras, several valuable pure-bred Angora kids could be produced. After returning from our holiday in Australia I really missed Harriet and Penny and regretted getting rid of them.

Somebody told me that a local farmer had some orphaned lambs for sale so I went to see what he had. While I was there I saw a skinny little lamb looking like an empty sock, lying alone on some straw in the corner of a lambing pen. I picked it up and was told that it had been left to die because it was the runt of triplets and was too weak to feed from the ewe. What I was really being told was that no one had the time to raise it by hand.

I noticed that the lamb had not been castrated, so I thought that if I was able to raise him, it would be a cheap way of obtaining a ram for breeding. All the other older male lambs had been fitted with a tight rubber ring around their testicles, cutting off the blood supply, effectively causing their testicles to shrivel and eventually drop off. As castrated rams they would be raised as store lambs, for meat.

I put the pathetic little animal in a cardboard box and went to an animal feed store to buy some milk substitute for lambs. There was no way that I could leave him on his own at the nursery so I took him home. He wouldn't take a feed at first so I left him in the box next to a warm radiator for a while. As he warmed up he appeared to look a little livelier; he was trying to lift his head so I tried to feed him again. He swallowed about two teaspoons full of substitute sheep milk, which I considered to be progress. I continued to feed him very small amounts of milk at regular intervals, even getting up twice during the night for about a week. He became quite strong and lively, he grew quite rapidly but he was still too young to be left on his own at the nursery. We named him Rambo, and took him for walks on a lead, to the amusement of our neighbours.

When Rambo had grown large enough and was weaned off of milk, I took him to the nursery and let him loose. He skipped around and settled down to graze so I was happy to leave him. It was time for him to realise that he was a sheep.

Chickens for eggs and chickens for the table seemed to be a good idea so I bought about forty day-old White Sussex chicks. I raised them to the egg-laying stage and when they were about to become profitable, a small disaster happened. Rambo decided he wanted to make friends with them and pushed the door to their enclosure open. I discovered twenty-four of them mutilated by a fox and the remains of two more on the boundary of my land.

It was careless of me not to have the door more securely fastened because I had lost five ducks to a fox the year before. Discouraged but still keen to play at being a farmer, I made sure that it couldn't happen again and soldiered on. I eventually replaced my original stock with a few pure-bred Moran hens.

Rambo seemed to be a bit lonely so I responded to an advertisement and bought three ewes as company for him. His first response was to completely ignore them. He grazed at the opposite end of the field and only occasionally looked up to see where they were. Then he would find a lonely place to sit and chew the cud. After about two weeks he seemed to realise what the ewes were for and began to get more assertive. He followed them around holding his head up high, curling his top lip and tasting the air. He singled them out one by one and became quite aggressive, butting them in the side. I suppose he was demonstrating what a fine fellow he was.

At the end of February one of the ewes aborted, I didn't know the reason for it but I was told that a stray dog was seen running around the area, she could have been frightened by it which caused her to abort. Early in April the other two ewes had lambs, both female I'm please to say.

The following February, a neighbouring farmer asked me to look after his sheep for three weeks whilst he and his wife took a holiday. About forty-five of them were in-lamb ewes, with a mixture of about sixty castrated rams and young ewes from last year along with about six young intact rams he was raising for breeding, each batch grouped in separate fields. He assured me that his ewes that were in lamb were not due to start lambing until April.

Just a few days after his departure the weather changed for the worse, depositing about six inches of snow over my neighbour's eighty-seven acre farm. Trudging over the field through the snow one day, the previous year's lambs all began to walk towards me, as they always did in the hope of getting some extra feed. I noticed one sheep standing alone against the fence.

My first thoughts were that it had become caught up in the fencing wire. Then I saw what I thought was a small dog worrying her. As I got closer I couldn't believe my eyes, it was a newly born lamb. I had to work fast because of the weather. I picked up the lamb and managed to get the mother to follow me for about four hundred yards to a barn where I constructed a pen out of bales of straw and penned her in on a bed of nice clean fresh warm straw.

My farmer neighbour must have left last year's lambs together for too long, the uncut ram lambs that he wanted to keep for breeding must have been sexually mature before he separated them from the young castrated rams and ewes. That episode rang the warning bells and made me wonder how many more were likely to be carrying lambs.

By the time my neighbour returned, twelve lambs had been born. He couldn't believe his eyes either. In appreciation, he offered me the pick of the lambs. The lamb that was first born that I found by the fence had a dark patch on his back so I picked him because he was readily recognisable. I named him Patch and when he was capable of surviving without his mother, I took him and raised him with Rambo.

The following year I put Patch to Rambo's two daughters, one had twins and the other a single lamb. Rambo and his three ewes produced two sets of twins and a single lamb, making a nice little flock of fifteen sheep.

I kept sheep for a few years, sending most of them to market, and of course stocking my freezer. Unfortunately my land began to be visited more frequently by thieves. The first to go were my pure-bred Moran chickens, and then tools began to disappear. All together, I had eighteen padlocks broken off my gate and tool store. I began to worry that the thieves would leave my gate open allowing my sheep to get onto the road and possibly cause an accident on the main road, so I eventually decided that Rambo, Patch and their wives had to go to market.

All that I had left was my animal trailer and my little old tractor. I was desperate to try and keep them so I put the trailer in one of my concrete pens and backed the tractor right up against it. I then jacked the tractor off the ground and left it on blocks. That seemed to work but there were often signs that someone had been inside looking around. One day my heart sank when I saw that my tractor had been dragged away from the pen and my trailer had gone. There were some deep ruts in the ground where the thieves had used a lorry to drag the tractor out of the way before hitching up my trailer and driving off with it.

The problem facing me was that I needed to live on site and that was not possible because of the rules against building in the countryside. I appealed to the Minister for the Environment against the local Council's refusal to grant planning permission three times in all, to no avail. So I was left with four and one half acres of land and no confidence in using it.

I allowed someone to rent one acre, for growing Christmas trees. It appears that the thieves are not interested in Christmas trees because after five years they had not been touched and the first cut has been harvested for sale. Meanwhile, my little parcel of land remained unused except for bee hives but I still had my old tractor, which I used with a very old finger mower, to keep the grass from growing too long.

Because I was not using the nursery very much, just keeping the hedges trimmed and the grass cut, I needed something else to occupy my time. My other hobby which I have not yet mentioned is making pottery.

About twenty years ago I bought a second-hand treadle pottery wheel and a kiln. Mainly in the spring and summer months because my pottery is in the garden shed and it gets very cold in the winter, I throw pots but I don't do very much glazing. I mostly throw terracotta garden pots. I enjoy pottery and for that reason I don't make them for sale and I rarely accept orders. I feel that if I have a list of people waiting for pots it will become like a job. If I force myself to work in the pottery it may become boring and less enjoyable. I like to do it when I feel like it.

So, not doing much at the nursery and only occasionally throwing a few garden pots left me with time on my hands and time is money. I answered an advertisement in my local paper and became involved in the travel industry. Part-time work was what I wanted as opposed to full-time work. So that I could still enjoy plenty of leisure time I became a part-time tour operator's representative at London Gatwick Airport. I found it to be very interesting work, meeting stressed-out and disgruntled holidaymakers but that is, as they say, another story.

Whilst on holiday in Croatia in June 1998, Rosemary telephoned home to check on how our son Andrew was fending for himself. He said that he had received a telephone call from the occupier of the farm next to the nursery, telling him that my tractor had been stolen. She had passed my gate, which was wide open and was concerned because my car wasn't there, so she went in and noticed that my tractor was not where I usually kept it and marks on the ground indicated that it had recently been moved. I was extremely annoyed about it but there was nothing that I could do until I returned home.

Adding to my misery, as I discovered when I checked out the nursery on my return, my mower had also been stolen along with my tractor. My situation was then a helpless one, I couldn't even keep the grass under control to prevent the place becoming overgrown. So my little tractor and mower were gone. Without the security of living on site, replacing them would have been money down the drain. What a blow. All of my tools and machinery had been stolen from the nursery leaving me with the land and no tools to work it.

Being that the place was so vulnerable I made regular visits to the nursery to check and examine my beehives. While I was there I often walked the boundary on the roadway side, to check the fencing. Walking around one day I discovered what I thought was the end of a metal tube just visible above the ground. With a spade I levered it out of the soil and picked it up. I saw that the end of it was sealed so I cleaned some of the attached soil from it with my fingers and noticed what appeared to be a percussion cap in the centre.

Cleaning it a bit more I was surprised to notice that the cap was intact and had not been fired. Examining the other end which was corroded I realised that I was holding a live shell approximately eighteen inches long. It was obviously a relic from the Second World War. I had seen shells before so I knew immediately what it was and that it was live. I also knew that it was not a bomb. It certainly had not been dropped by an enemy aircraft. It was a large shell that had to be discharged from a large calibre gun.

Gently I placed the shell on the ground and stood gathering my thoughts on how best to deal with it. I asked the driver of a lorry who was parked outside of the nursery if he had a mobile phone, I told him what I had discovered and he informed the police.

I had my camera with me so I photographed the shell, first I placed my size ten boot at the side of it to get the dimensions of it in proportion. Two young police officers arrived, smiling and with a look of 'we don't believe a word of it' written all over their faces. I led them to the shell and watched the smiles disappear from their faces when they realised its potential danger. They radioed their control with as much detail as they could, who subsequently requested the army bomb disposal experts to attend from Aldershot.

A sergeant and a lance corporal arrived within an hour and a half, in a lorry containing a mass of bomb disposal equipment. I led them to the shell and straight away the sergeant told me that it was not a British shell. He explained that the brass casing was too long to be British.

Kneeling down beside it he scraped more grime from the percussion end and discovered the letters USA and the numbers 1943 – American made in 1943. Then he examined the corroded end; when he told me that he wasn't sure if it had a fuse in it or not I began to see it in a different perspective. He contacted his base by mobile phone and passed as much information as he could to them.

His base came back shortly informing him that it was indeed an American shell and could be one of three types:

1. A chemical weapon, in which case it would have to be transported, with a police escort to Porton Down by road, where specialists would be able to safely disarm it.

2. A white phosphorous shell which could be detonated locally but would render the land in the immediate area unusable for at least one year.

3. A high explosive shell, which could be detonated locally.

At the request of the army, all present were asked not to inform the press because if local radio reported it, inquisitive people would descend on the area to have a look and as far as the army was concerned and everyone else for that matter, safety was the prime factor.

After about two hours involving closer examination plus continuous communication with his control, the sergeant announced that it was not a chemical weapon. The choice was now white phosphorous or high explosive. He began to make plans for detonation and told me that he wanted to dig a one-metre deep hole in my field to detonate the shell and requested that the police arrange for the local council to deliver sixty bags of sand.

I was not happy with the idea of exploding the shell in a hole in the middle of my field especially if it contained white phosphorous. Every time that phosphorous dries out it spontaneously ignites and not being able to use the land for possibly more than a year, didn't please me very much.

I made my feelings known to the sergeant and suggested that if he had to carry the shell to where he dug the hole, he could carry it a little further to the natural hollow on my land, which was used as a slurry pit many years ago. I showed him where it was and he was more than pleased with its location. Being a hollow the naturally upward sloping sides would direct the blast safely into the air. While the sergeant continued to discuss the shell with his control, the corporal began to dig the hole in the old slurry pit.

Because there was not much happening and I had not been able to return home at the time I was expected, I decided to go and tell Rosemary what was happening and at the same time collect my video camera. I also made a flask of coffee for the soldiers. While I was away the soldiers X-rayed the shell to try to determine any other useful information about it.

A local council lorry arrived loaded with sixty bags of sand which were unloaded and placed at the edge of the pit. Police were instructed to inform the neighbouring farmers and to ask them to open all windows in their houses as a precautionary measure against any possible blast damage.

No further information was forthcoming so there was still a possibility of the shell being either phosphorous or high explosive. A few hours had gone by, the hole in the pit was ready and the sand was on site, so the sergeant began to assemble the detonating equipment. Meanwhile he requested the attendance of the fire brigade in case the shell contained phosphorous. Hose was laid out as a precautionary measure and seeing the crew do that took me back a few years.

The shell had then to be moved. The sergeant gently picked it up and carried it to the hole that had been dug in the old slurry pit and placed it at the bottom. Three plastic explosive charges were taped to the shell. One was placed over the percussion cap and one either side of the brass casing. At that stage I was asked to leave the area while the soldiers placed the sixty sand bags in the hole, filling it and making a large mound on the top.

Everyone except the sergeant retreated to a safe distance in the roadway and then we were given a twenty-second countdown to detonation. Even with the explosion occurring one metre underground, covered with sixty sand bags and directed upwards by the sides of the pit, the explosion still sounded quite loud. The sergeant gathered as much of the destroyed shell that could be found and only then did he disclose what it was. It was an armour piercing anti-tank shell. He explained what the two parts of the projectile that he found were – the first part was the part that made the hole in the tank and the second part was the part that entered that tank and killed the occupants.

When it was all over and the army was about to leave, the sergeant asked me not to release my video of the incident to the media because of the nature of his work. He did not want to be recognised by any terrorist organisations. I honoured that request.

On the following Monday I was telephoned by the neighbouring farmer who told me that water was running out of my nursery gateway. I thought that to be very strange because the water board

229

had cut the water off and removed the meter at my request, many months ago because of vandalism.

When I arrived at the nursery I discovered that someone had severed the incoming capped-off water pipe, and the meter pit outside was full and overflowing into the roadway. When I went into the nursery I was greeted by another very disheartening sight. The caravan that I used as a rest room had all of the windows shattered, my store shed also had all of the windows and door shattered. My greenhouse had all of the glass shattered and a number of young Christmas trees, which did not belong to me, had been ripped up. Some sick person must have had great fun doing such a thoughtless deed. The police duly made a note of the damage but as in previous thefts of my tools and equipment by vandals and trespassers, the crime was just another addition to the statistics and I heard nothing more.

The nursery was only used as an apiary after that and on occasions I have had a beehive knocked over. I can only hope that the bees managed to zap the person that did it before he made his escape.

Time seems to have flown by. I had owned the land at the nursery for the past twenty-five years at the time of writing this chapter. When I was a child the time seemed to go by very slowly. It took forever for birthdays and Christmases to arrive and it appeared that to reach the age of fifteen, school leaving age, would never happen.

Since those days I have had an interesting and sometimes eventful life. If I had to make a choice between which parts of it I enjoyed most I would have to say the latter part. I hated the time that I spent in the army and didn't like working in a factory. I enjoyed fire brigade work which was always varied and interesting. I would recommend it to any young adventurous person who wanted an exciting career. For satisfaction and pleasure I would have to favour working on the land in the countryside with farm animals. The country lifestyle beats rushing around in a town and putting up with the hustle and bustle amongst crowds and heavy traffic, which I had to put up with for many years.

Perhaps if I had to work for years to earn a living on the land in the countryside I would think differently, but my ideal way of life at this moment in time would be to spend my days on and around farms and farmland watching and tending animals and observing nature through the four seasons.

Harriet and her two new-born kids.

My two Lop Eared sows behaving like pigs.

Trying to keep young Rambo alive.

Rosemary and big boy Rambo. I think they were talking about me.

Some bits and pieces of my unfinished pottery.

Unexploded armour piercing anti tank shell,
measured against my size 10 rubber boot.

Swarm of honey bees.

The swarm walking into a new hive to start a new colony.

My bee hives.

A honey super with frames full of capped honey cells.

Me and Rosemary at Andrew and Jody's wedding.

Andrew and Jody on their wedding day.

Bonita's youngest daughter, Jessica, with Dylan and Jack.

My daughters, Bonita and Beverly, in their early twenties.

Me and Rosemary, with Andrew holding Jack next to Dylan and Jody.

Chapter 14

It always amazes me when coincidences occur. Out of the blue something seems to happen by chance in a surprising and unsuspecting way. Something happens that triggers a thought which is related to something that took place perhaps years ago in some instances. One such example astounded me when I discovered the outcome of an incident that I was involved in, when I was a young fireman attached to Lambeth Fire Station during the period of 1963–1964.

About mid-morning on a hot summer's day at the end of July 2001 I drove into the access road of my nursery and parked my car in my usual place. As I went to unlock my gate I glanced towards a man standing at the side of a car parked on the roadway just a few yards away. Our eyes met and he greeted me with a polite 'good morning'. I responded politely and, typically, I mentioned what a glorious day it was.

We began a casual conversation during which the man said that he often stopped at that spot because it was a quiet road. A new section of the A23 trunk road had been opened in 1993 which by-passed my land, leaving it in a remaining short secluded part of the old A23 London to Brighton road. He added that he often saw me arrive and leave and wondered what I used the land for. As we chatted he told me that he was originally from London but he had retired to Sussex where he and his wife enjoyed the countryside.

I told him that I was born in South London and asked what part of London he had come from. He said that he came from Lambeth and that he used to live in Lambeth Walk.

With a chuckle I said that I worked near there at Lambeth Fire Station for a few years. He laughed and said that he often watched the fire engines turn out and the firemen carrying out their drills on the station's drill tower. He then told me that his wife, who was sitting in his car watching us chat, used to work next door to the fire station, in the stationers W.H. Smith's warehouse. We both laughed at the coincidence.

To make conversation I went on to say that I attended an incident at W.H. Smith's warehouse many years ago when a young boy was trapped in the folding doors of the warehouse entrance. I saw his face change at what I had mentioned, purely as part of a mundane conversation, it seemed to ring a bell in his memory. His lips moved but no sound came out. After a quick intake of breath he said:

"That was young Jimmy Watts."

He stood looking at me with unblinking wide eyes and likewise I stood looking at him. It was then my turn to make involuntary lip movements with no accompanying sound. I was astounded. I told him that I never did find out if that youngster survived the ordeal. He told me that Jimmy Watts did survive and was now well into his forties, still living in Lambeth Walk.

He walked to his car to relate the story to his wife and she was just as amazed as we were. I laughed and casually asked if she knew old Kate. When she said that she did and that she used to live in the old flats in Whitgift Street, I was equally amazed again. She then went on to tell me that late one evening she lost the key to her flat and tried to climb over some railings on the first floor balcony and slipped causing a railing to go through her leg. You could have knocked me down with a feather. Two incidents that happened over many years ago, local to Lambeth Fire Station that I described in chapter five, were being recalled by a man named Bill Poole and his wife who I had never met before in my life. I thought that coincidence was truly amazing after such a long time and it answered the question that has been in the back of my mind for over forty years – young Jimmy Watts did not die.

That now leaves me wondering who the little boy was who sought the help of the local fire-fighters when his friend was in trouble. I believe that most young children would have run away or gone home to tell their mother or father. That particular lad showed a great deal of common sense at such a very young age by being so persistent and determined to get help for his friend. Undoubtedly Jimmy Watts owes his life to his friend. I wondered if he ever realised that and if they were still friends today.

In January 2008 history repeated itself. One pleasant sunny Sunday morning Rosemary and I decided to take a relaxing drive to Shoreham beach on the south coast. We took a slow stroll along the coastal footpath to blow the winter cobwebs away and to watch the swans elegantly gliding along the lagoon which separated the beach from the residential and holiday dwellings. We returned to my car after about an hour enjoying the mild weather for January. Intending to do a slight detour on our journey home to check on the nursery, we set of at a leisurely pace enjoying minimal amount of other traffic.

As we approached our land we noticed that there was some mud on the roadway outside and some large tyre imprints on the grass verge. Straight away we feared for the worst. Noticing that the padlock on the gate had been broken off our worst fears were realized. Deep wheel ruts in the soft ground coming from the direction where I parked my tractor was a depressing sight to say the least. My Ford 3000 tractor had been stolen. Some worthless individual had removed it. I made enquiries at the neighbouring farm and was told by the farmer's daughter that she saw it being driven at about 10 a.m. that morning by a person that she thought was me, with another person walking alongside. Normally on a Sunday morning I would have been there at that time and possibly prevented them from taking it. The police made local enquiries and checked the C.C.T.V. footage in the petrol station which was about 100 metres along the road but it didn't record much beyond its forecourt boundary.

That tractor was a vintage 1967 model and sought after by enthusiasts who renovate them and show them at country fairs, so it was probably stolen by someone who will break it up and sell it as spare parts.

My first tractor was stolen while I was on holiday in 1998 and now in January 2008 my Ford 3000 has gone too. I decided not to invest in another one because I have no facilities to keep it securely locked out of sight. That left me with a problem of cutting the grass and the hedgerows. The size of the area is too large to maintain it with hand-held tools or ordinary garden mowers.

At least setbacks like that only entail the loss of material things that can be replaced and doesn't compare to the loss of a family member or close friend. Last year my old friend Ron Brown who joined me at Old Kent Road Fire Station after he transferred from the Surrey Fire Brigade in the rank of sub-officer, died after a short illness. We had kept in touch during our retirement. He was a local magistrate, well known and liked by a lot of people. His funeral was attended by many retired and still serving members of the London Fire and Rescue Service, among them the Commissioner of the

London Fire and Rescue Service, Sir Kenneth Knight, who passed through the Surrey Fire Brigade Training Centre as a recruit while Ron was an instructor there.

Earlier in these memoirs I mentioned my older brother Bert, he worked until he passed the age of seventy and after he retired decided to sell-up and move to a small village named Herepian in the Languedoc region in the south of France. What I haven't mentioned before is that Bert is married to Rosemary's older sister Margaret. Therefore, we have a double reason to visit them, so two or three times a year we pack our bags and fly off to the south of France for a few days to enjoy the fine weather and the wine.

During the past couple of years since Bert and Margaret have been living in France they have made friends with other English couples and socialise regularly with them. The first time we met one couple, Jennifer and Keith, it came up in conversation that I was a retired fire-fighter. Jennifer said that she knew someone who was in the London Fire Brigade and asked me if I knew a man named Norman Rose.

There I was lounging under a large multi-coloured sunshade casually chatting and sipping wine in the company of people that I was meeting for the first time, when that word coincidence came up again. I had been retired twenty years and I had not for one second expected to meet someone who was a close friend of Norman Rose's family, especially in the south of France. You may remember that I mentioned Sub-Officer Norman Rose when I was in the brigade's training school and again when he was a divisional officer when I nearly missed my slot for my sub-officer's promotion interview. Then following my success at passing my station officer's examination during the time that he was in command of the division that I was serving in, he gave me the opportunity to be in charge of a watch at Dockhead Fire Station, in the rank of temporary station officer, which preceded my promotion to substantive station officer rank. You couldn't make it up if you tried. He had reached the rank of assistant chief officer prior to his retirement. Since we had both retired from the brigade we had met a few times at the London Fire Brigade Retired Members Association annual reunion and on a very sad occasion, the funeral of Ron Brown.

Since my tractor was stolen I became concerned about my small mechanical digger which I kept at the nursery. I had bought the digger a couple of years ago, it was a bit ancient but I installed a new engine and repaired the hydraulics where necessary. It was ideal for digging out some old tree stumps that were in the way and levelling off some uneven ground. The thieves that stole my tractor obviously knew it was there so I decided to sell it and cut my losses before I lost it altogether. I sold it within a day of advertising it, to a man who had bought an old barn in France and needed it to dig trenches for his water supply and drainage pipes. So I hope the thieves were disappointed when they returned to steal it, as I am sure they did.

During 1993 the Highways Agency opened part of a new three-lane London to Brighton dual carriageway. The existing two-lane trunk road which was built in 1936 was replaced but parts of it remained and were adopted by the West Sussex County Council as local roads. The new road bypassed my land leaving it on a short section of the old road. That section of the old road formed an off-slip from the new dual carriageway which serviced a local country lane and a petrol filling station before passing my land and terminating in an on-slip back to the new dual carriageway.

Regrettably that caused my land to become secluded and isolated and worst of all the lay-by fronting it, which was originally a deceleration lane from the old dual carriageway to my entrance, had been extended. The ease and convenience of leaving the fast trunk road and the straightforwardness of rejoining it presented drivers with an ideal place to rest, which over the years has become a very popular rest area for commercial vehicles.

Because of the popularity of the area by drivers and bearing in mind the law restricting the continuous driving hours of heavy goods vehicle drivers, it occurred to me that my land would be an ideal place to develop a Truck Stop. The cost of such a development would be prohibitive for an individual so I had to embark on some research to assess the viability of such a project.

The West Sussex County Council Highways Department was keen for such a project and the Government Highways Agency recognised the need for the facility but in both cases it was the financing that caused both organisations to be non-committal about the project and in any case, like most government departments, the wheels turn very slowly. I was told that the only way forward was private enterprise but letters to various organizations drew a negative response or mostly no response at all. The present day economic situation was always used as an excuse for the lack of interest but I believe the real reason was that it was thought not to be profitable enough for the amount of investment required. It seems that the stock excuse of the present day economic situation never goes away. Nonetheless, I hope that someday we may reap a little profit from the sale, if not I am sure Andrew will enjoy the proceeds.

I am now getting on in years and lately following one or two niggling aches and pains plus emergency visits to my dentist, I am recognizing the fact that I am physically slowing down. I suppose that is something that I should have acknowledged and not ignored when I found that working on my land and around the house and garden caused me to tire more rapidly than a few years ago when doing similar work. I suppose in short it is called getting old. Diabetes and high blood pressure obviously do not help but I consider that doing some regular physically taxing work, even if it is a mundane task like digging over a flower bed or sweeping the garden pathway or mowing the lawn, is achieving something and is better than sitting around doing nothing. In my opinion it is better and more satisfying when you can see the results of your time and spent energy, rather than working out in a gym when all you get at the end is wasted time and feeling knackered.

Having mentioned diabetes, unfortunately during late 2001 following my sixty-fifth birthday I began to feel unwell. In hindsight I realise that some time ago I had become short-tempered, moody, tired, couldn't sleep and couldn't satisfy my raging thirst. Finally my eyesight deteriorated and I submitted to Rosemary's demands that I should make an appointment to visit my doctor.

I explained my symptoms to my G.P. who tested my urine. The result of the urine test alarmed my G.P. to the extent that he immediately telephoned the East Surrey Hospital in Redhill to have me admitted for more tests and treatment for diabetes.

Apparently I was suffering from Diabetic Ketoacidosis, D.K.A. for short. D.K.A. occurs when the body has no insulin. That leaves the muscles, fat and liver cells unable to use glucose in the blood as fuel. The consequences of that causes fat to breakdown within the cells into glucose and fatty acids. The fatty acids are converted to ketones resulting in the body literally consuming muscle, fat and liver cells for fuel.

I was shocked when my doctor said that I must not drive home and that I should phone Rosemary to come and get me. He told me to go home and collect the necessary personal items and go directly to hospital.

At the hospital, blood was taken and a valve was inserted in my wrist ready to receive a drip. After some time passed I was taken to a ward where a drip was fitted to the valve in my wrist along with an automatically introduced insulin measure from a preset electrical dispenser.

I was now a prisoner attached to a drip, plugged into an electrical socket and confined to bed. It then occurred to me that my biggest dread was that I may have to use a bed pan, something that I was determined to do my utmost to resist. The ward that I was taken to was a mixed sex ward with six beds in it. I settled in as best as I could feeling rather depressed because I had never been ill enough to be hospitalised before. There was a rather loud-mouthed Canadian woman in the bed opposite mine, who seemed to have a mental problem. Next to her was a rather unfortunate man who seemed to have an I.Q. of a six-year-old. And the other bed was occupied by a woman who slept all of the time. To my left was a man who refused to remove his clothing and was in bed with all of them on, including a leather jacket. Every time he moved his blankets a disgusting body odour smell wafted towards me, so I reached out and pulled the curtain around that side of my bed. On the other side of me was a young lady who I later discovered suffered rather severely from epilepsy, she also kept her curtain extended which allowed me to lie there with a degree of privacy but I thought it strange that I was in a mixed ward and I wasn't very comfortable with that thought.

Every hour a nurse arrived at my bedside to test my sugar level by pricking my finger and placing a small deposit of blood on a meter. That routine went on right through the night. Unable to get any sleep I felt really tired the following morning. Rosemary came in to see me later and thoughtful as she always is, brought me some food from home because she knew that there was no way that I was going to eat hospital food. While Rosemary was with me we heard a thump from behind the curtain on my right. When I looked on the floor the young lady from the next bed had appeared on my side of the curtain and was lying there having a fit. Rosemary went for assistance, leaving me attached to my drip mechanism and feeling quite helpless. Nurses attended that poor girl on the floor beside my bed for about one and a half hours before they put her back to bed.

That evening I was feeling really shattered so I thought I would be able to drop off to sleep between finger-pricking blood tests. I couldn't have been more wrong. The Canadian woman seemed to come to life around midnight. She walked about the ward continually reciting the Lord's Prayer at the top of her voice. After about an hour or so of that noise I was just about ready to explode. I managed to get the attention of a nurse and asked her to stop the woman shouting. The nurse apologised and said that she had refused to take her medication and there was not a lot that she could do. What with the foul smell periodically wafting over me from my left, the nurse continually pricking my finger and a mad woman shouting aloud the Lord's Prayer combined with having had no sleep for two days, I was just about at the end of my tether.

The curtain around my bed moved and thinking it was the finger-pricking nurse I sat up, only to be confronted by the mad woman who immediately started shouting the Lord's Prayer. Angrily raising my voice I shouted at her to go away. She fell silent for a moment and then said, "Shall I?"

In a stern voice I replied, "Yes clear off!"

"Shall I go right away?" she asked.

"Yes!" I said, showing my displeasure. "Go right away."

Then she quietly left my bed space.

At last it was quiet so I was able to relax and try to get some sleep. I was disturbed by the finger-pricking nurse once again and while that was taking place I heard a bit of a commotion going on. Through the gap in the curtains around my bed from which the finger-pricking nurse had emerged, I saw two male nurses pushing a woman in a wheelchair. The woman was shouting and appeared to be soaking wet. I couldn't see her very well but I soon recognised her voice when she began chanting the Lord's Prayer. Apparently she had taken me literally when I told her to go away. She was found wandering in the street in the pouring rain, wearing only her nightdress.

When the day staff arrived on duty I demanded to be moved to another ward or I would disconnect the drip mechanism and go home. Rosemary arrived and while we were talking a nursing sister came and told us that I would be moved. The sister checked my drip while she was there and cried out, "Oh my God! Who the hell put this on here?"

She immediately removed the drip bag and said, "This is glucose and it should be saline."

Rosemary and I looked at each other in surprise and concern as the correct drip was put in place.

"What else is going to happen in this place?" I remarked angrily.

It appeared that I was being fed glucose directly into my blood stream along with an automatic dose of insulin designed to combat the glucose that had already built up in my body.

A little later I was moved a short distance to another ward opposite, which was a mirror image of the one I was leaving but was an all-male ward. I felt more comfortable there. Soon after that I was taken off the drip and given a tablet to take. The patient in the opposite bed spoke to me and asked what was wrong with me. I told him that I had apparently become diabetic. He nonchalantly remarked, "That's nothing to worry about, I have been diabetic since I was fourteen – about thirty years."

That cheered me up a bit until he told me that he had to have dialysis because of kidney failure and he was in hospital because he had a stroke and was waiting for test results.

At least it was a bit more acceptable with someone to talk to and that I was not on the drip so I did not have to use a bottle to urinate in. It was now Saturday, the start of the weekend. I visited the nearby toilet and the sight that greeted me was absolutely diabolical. The floor was soaking wet and it seemed that everyone that went in there put a load of paper towels on the floor in an attempt to have a dry place to put their feet. Consequently the floor was covered in a thick mass of urine-soaked paper towels.

I reported it but nothing was done, so it got gradually worse over the weekend. The amount of tablets that I was given did not alter the glucose reading of my blood so I asked for an increase. I was told that the doctor would be informed and he may alter the dose. My new friend opposite became more concerned because he was having more difficulty in standing and walking so he also asked to see the doctor.

Both of us requested the doctor many times during the weekend but no doctor arrived. Monday morning arrived and the ward was prepared for the doctor to do his rounds. When finally a doctor arrived at the foot of my bed he cheerfully said good morning and looked at my chart. I asked him if he had enjoyed his weekend and when he replied in the positive, to his amazement I let him know that I hadn't and went on to tell him exactly how I felt about the treatment I was getting. Then my new-found friend in the opposite bed joined in. That poor doctor appeared very embarrassed but within a few minutes other doctors arrived and seemed to show some concern over the stroke victim's condition.

The diabetes nurse was asked to come and see me and when I described my feelings about the treatment that I had experienced at that hospital and my concern that my blood test showed a reading of twenty when I arrived at the hospital four days earlier and now it was twenty-nine, she said that she wasn't surprised. She told me that I shouldn't be lying around in bed, I should be at home walking about getting plenty of exercise helping to burn off the excess sugar in the form of energy. I looked at her with raised eyebrows and asked her if she was saying that I could go home. She said that she would speak to the doctor. I saw them having a chat along with a bit of arm-waiving and pointing in my direction, then the doctor came and asked me if I was happy about the diabetes nurse's suggestion. What a silly question!

I telephoned Rosemary and changed from my pyjamas into my outdoor clothing which I had stored in my locker. When she arrived I was ready to depart, and after saying goodbye to my friend opposite and wishing him good luck I was out of there, picking up a large packet of tablets from the dispensary on the way.

Even being more mobile and taking the prescribed amount of tablets my sugar count still did not lower satisfactorily. I contacted the diabetes nurse by telephone at my local hospital and she increased the amount of tablets that I had to take.

A couple of weeks passed and still my sugar count had not lowered so I again made an appointment to see the diabetes nurse at my local Crawley Hospital. With no hesitation she produced an applicator incorporating a phial of insulin with a vicious-looking needle protruding from the end. She demonstrated how to adjust the dosage and how to apply the needle when injecting my stomach.

Feeling a little apprehensive I grasped the applicator as instructed and held it against my stomach. Showing no emotion on my face but feeling a bit nervous about pushing the needle in, I tensed up a bit and froze for a couple of seconds. Here goes, I thought, and pushed the needle in. Surprisingly it seemed to go in quite easily without much feeling. With my thumb placed over the end of the applicator, I pressed the plunger to inject my first dose of insulin.

My instructions were to inject eight units of insulin in the morning and eight units in the evening. What a difference that made; my sugar count lowered to a satisfactory level which I have been able to maintain ever since by occasionally adjusting the amount of insulin that I needed, which at the present time is a minimum of 50 units a day, and with a great deal of help and support from Rosemary via her great cooking skills and wise shopping. So ten years on I am an established type 2 diabetic, fully dependant on insulin.

Hopefully if nothing drastic happens to me I will be able to soldier on for some time to come and enjoy the rest of my retirement along with Rosemary, the love of my life, to whom I will be forever grateful for the love and support that she has given me throughout our marriage. I feel proud, privileged and grateful to have married Rosemary who gave birth to our now grown-up loving son Andrew.

My most memorable family occasion was that on the 20th August 2005 Andrew married his fiancée Jody. A wonderful family event that I was very pleased to be part of, even though I can only remember the beginning of the reception due to the affects of excessive intake of alcohol and jumping around like an idiot trying to dance. I could only hope that I will be around when they decide to have a family of their own. It would be wonderful to see their children but if that is not to be, then in years to come this book may be of interest to them.

Thanks to my first wife Maureen, I was fortunate to have had two loving daughters, Beverly and Bonita. To date, I have three grandchildren, Hayley and Daniel White and Jessica Manwaring plus three great-grandchildren, Jacob, Evan and Toby Hatch. Who knows, it may not stop there.

I began to write these memoirs in 1986, to date that was 26 years ago. Obviously I put my manuscript away for some long periods and added my post fire brigade activities to it from time to time.

Once again I had reason to put my manuscript away for a short time to await the outcome of some brilliant news. Andrew and Jody visited me and Rosemary unexpectedly one day and appeared unable to contain their excitement, they told us that Jody was pregnant. Rosemary couldn't believe the very exciting and welcome news, her face was a picture of delight as she embraced them both while trying to hold back tears of joy. I stood back enjoying Rosemary's reaction thinking what a wonderful sight that I was witnessing, she was absolutely elated with the news. I had a great feeling of relief and for some reason satisfaction because I often wondered as time went by whether or not I would be around to see Rosemary's greatest wish come true, it was truly a moving moment. Andrew and Jody told us that it had been confirmed that Jody was three months' pregnant. I was very pleased for them both but most of all I was especially pleased for Rosemary because I knew how badly she wanted a grandchild of her own. She was ecstatic and gave way to the tearful emotions of joyfulness as she digested the wonderful news. Although she enjoyed my grandchildren and always treated them as her own, I knew that in her heart she longed for Andrew to provide us with a grandchild. After four years of marriage and at the age of almost thirty years, he and Jody provided us with a gorgeous grandson Dylan James William Franks. He entered the world at 10.21 pm on Sunday the 19th July 2009 weighing 6lbs 14oz.

As I approach the final parts of my ramblings I feel compelled to include my memories of Winifred Browne, a wonderful lady that I had the pleasure of knowing for only a few years. Rosemary's mother died suddenly at the age of fifty-two, when Rosemary was only twenty-one years old. She was a very inoffensive gentle family-orientated lady whose departure was a terrible shock to everyone. Some years later I discovered that before she was married to Rosemary's father Richard Browne, during the 1939–1945 Second World War she was an Auxiliary Fire Brigade Control Officer. It transpired that her devotion to duty during an air raid earned her an expression of commendation from His Majesty King George VI. Her brave conduct was recognised by the presentation of a certificate by Sir Winston Churchill, the Prime Minister and First Lord of the Treasury at that time.

When I think about the past, the years seemed to have raced by. I often recall my mother's words when I said to her that I wished I was fifteen years old so that I could leave school, she told me not to wish my life away because life was too short – how right she was. I also often wondered whether or not I would ever finish putting my ramblings on paper, so I decided therefore to make a concerted effort to reach a final full stop. However, with the best of intentions that plan was soon scuppered.

Once again Andrew and Jody told us the wonderful news that there was another little Franks on the way. On the 11th July 2012 Jack Reid James Franks was born weighing in at 5lbs 5oz. Another grandson who generated just as much excitement as Dylan who reached the grand old age of three on 19th July 2012.

Well here I am again winding up my memoirs. Now at seventy-six years old life still goes on but this is the end of my ramblings. I will not be adding anything more to my life story. This is my final paragraph describing my journey through life to date. It is my way of telling anyone in the future who may be interested in reading these memoirs, that I existed. I now stop looking back on my journey and look only to the future however long that may be. Today is Tuesday 28th August 2012 and I am celebrating my seventy-sixth birthday.

So there you have it, end of ramblings.

Rosemary's mother Winifred Browne, her single name Winifred Bolch.
Commended by King George VI for brave conduct whist on duty in the
Auxiliary Fire Service in London during the 1939–1945 Second World War.

By the KING'S Order the name of
Winifred Frances Bolch,
Auxiliary,
London Women's Aux. Fire Service.
was published in the London Gazette on
28 March. 1941.
as commended for brave conduct in
Civil Defence.
I am charged to record His Majesty's
high appreciation of the service rendered.

Prime Minister and First Lord
of the Treasury

Rosemary's mother and father, Richard and Winifred Browne

Appendix

As I approached the end of my memoirs I realised that I had overlooked something. The purpose of writing about my life was for future generations to know that I existed but there is nothing other than mentioning my parents and grandparents to include earlier family history. So far I haven't included anything about my more distant ancestors. The reason for that is that my parents, if they had any knowledge at all to pass on to me, were not very forthcoming. Therefore, neither myself nor my brothers have any knowledge that goes further back on our father's side than our paternal grandparents.

Curiosity inspired me to do some research and what transpired on my paternal side was inconclusive, leaving me somewhat disappointed and in limbo. I could not trace back any further than my paternal grandfather Albert Edward Franks who was born around 1875 and died in 1956. He married my grandmother Caroline Elizabeth Dawson in December 1899 and raised seven children. On the other hand I have traced my maternal Whitehead name way back to 1791.

In an attempt to probe further into the past, despite a lot of help from my second cousin Susan Kavenagh, the result of a search for my paternal great grandfather did not reveal very much at all, other than bewilderment. A document from 1895 in the form of a sworn oath by my grandfather when he enlisted in the Royal Scots Regiment, which was probably required because he was unable to produce a birth certificate, only added more confusion. Again with a lot of help from Susan when investigating my great paternal grandmother, our research became even more baffling. Her name was Louisa Martha Corne and she was born in 1859 and married Frederick Watts in 1880. According to the 1881 census she was aged 22 years and Frederick Watts was aged 20. The census also stated that a child named Albert Watts aged 6 years was living with them.

Louisa gave birth to my grandfather Albert in 1875 when it appears she was about 16 years old. Because I could not locate a birth certificate for my grandfather I found that the dates were somewhat unreliable along with their names which left some doubt in my mind as to whether or not I was researching the correct people.

Again thanks to research by Susan it appears that my grandfather Albert Franks was illegitimate. Referring to the sworn oath document from when he joined the Royal Scots Regiment in 1895, in which he stated that from a young age he believed that his name was Albert Edward Watts. In the 1891 census at the age of 16 years he was still recorded as Albert Watts. In the sworn statement it was recorded that he was told by his mother that she was a spinster named Louisa Martha Franks at the time of his birth and that he was illegitimate. For unknown reasons it seems that she lied about her own maiden name when she told him that his real name was Albert Edward Franks. In all probability my great-grandmother Louisa Martha Corne, when pressured, decided to pass on the name of the father of her illegitimate son but not to identify him.

The mystery of the origin of the name Franks in my family is deemed not to be solved. It seems that during the eighteen hundreds and earlier, different names were used for a variety of reasons. For instance, my grandparents Albert and Caroline's marriage certificate dated 1899 states that the name of Albert's father was Frederick Franks. It appears that Frederick Watts became Frederick Franks for the day. However, it now seems that I have to accept that the family's age-old secret established many years ago will remain a secret forever but I intend to do further research in the hope of solving the puzzle.

Further research by my cousin Susan solved another mystery. I was confused by the information seen on the military documents discovered by Susan that my grandfather had two army numbers. Susan's research revealed that my grandfather enlisted in the Royal Scots Regiment during 1895 under the name of Albert Edward Watts, which led to him having to state on oath that his true surname, as stated by his mother, was Franks.

He re-enlisted in the 1914–1918 First World War, in the Queens Royal West Surrey Regiment on the 28th May 1915 at the age of 44 years, being the father of four children. In all he had six children, all carrying the name Franks. I now conclude that the true origin of the family name Franks may never be discovered. But who knows what further research may discover.

The following is a copy of the original Oath sworn by my grandfather in 1895. Because of the poor print and the damage caused during storage I have included a transcription of the legible parts.

........private in His Majesty's Army do
......and sincerely declare as follows:-

I enlisted in the Royal Scots Regiment on the eleventh day of April One thousand eight hundred and ninety-five in the name of Albert Edward Watts and obtained my certificate of discharge from the Royal Scots Regiment on the Third day of April One thousand eight hundred and ninety-six.

2. My mother's maiden name was Louisa Martha Franks and when I was quite a child my mother married a man named Frederick Watts.

3. I was brought up by my mother and the said Frederick Watts and was always of the opinion that Frederick Watts was my lawful father and that my name was Albert Edward Watts.

4. After having enlisted in the Royal Scots Regiment I was subsequently informed by my mother that I was born before her marriage and that I was an illegitimate child of my mother who at the time of my birth was a spinster and whose name was Louisa Martha Franks.

5. I enlisted in the Queens Royal West Surrey Regiment at Upper Norwood on the Twenty-eighth day of May One thousand nine hundred and fifteen in the name of Albert Edward Franks.

6. My proper name is Albert Edward Franks and I am the illegitimate child of Louisa Martha Franks I having been born before the said Louisa Martha Franks married the above named Frederick Watts.

AND I make this declaration conscientiously believing the same to be true and by virtue of the provisions of the Statutory Decla...... One thousand eight hundred......

(-----------------private in His Majesty's Army do------and sincerely declare as follows:-

1. I enlisted in the Royal Scots Regiment on the eleventh day of April One thousand eight hundred and ninety-five in the name of Albert Edward Watts and obtained my certificate of discharge from the Royal Scots Regiment on the Third day of April One thousand eight hundred and ninety-six.

2. My mother's maiden name was Louisa Martha Franks and when I was quite a child my mother married a man named Frederick Watts.

3. I was brought up by my mother and the said Frederick Watts and was always of the opinion Frederick Watts was my lawful father and my name was Albert Edward Watts.

4. After having enlisted in the Royal Scots Regiment I was subsequently informed by my mother that I was born before her marriage and that I was the illegitimate child of my mother who at the time of my birth was a spinster and whose name was Louisa Martha Franks.

5. I enlisted in the Queens Royal West Surrey Regiment at Upper Norwood on the Twenty-eighth day of May One thousand nine hundred and fifteen in the name of Albert Edward Franks.

6. My proper name is Albert Edward Franks and I am the illegitimate child of Louisa Martha Franks I having been born before the said Louisa Martha Franks married the above named Frederick Watts.

7. AND I make this declaration conscientiously believing the name to be true and by virtue of the provisions of the Statutory Decla------ --------- One thousand eight --ndred --------.)

Overleaf is a copy of a document recording the marriage between Louisa Martha Corne and Frederick Watts on the 5th July 1880. My grandfather Albert Edward Franks was then about five years old. On the 1881 Census when he was six years old he is shown as living with Louisa and Frederick Watts and again on the 1891 Census when he was 16 years old, still believing his name was Albert Edward Watts.

FAMILYSEARCH
England Marriages, 1538-1973

Groom's Name	Frederick Watts
Groom's Birth Date	
Groom's Birthplace	
Groom's Age	
Bride's Name	**Louisa Martha Corne**
Bride's Birth Date	
Bride's Birthplace	
Bride's Age	
Marriage Date	05 Jul 1880
Marriage Place	St. Martin In The Fields, Westminster, Middlesex, England
Groom's Father's Name	Richard Watts
Groom's Mother's Name	
Bride's Father's Name	William Corne
Bride's Mother's Name	
Groom's Race	
Groom's Marital Status	Single
Groom's Previous Wife's Name	
Bride's Race	
Bride's Marital Status	**Single**
Bride's Previous Husband's Name	
Indexing Project (Batch) Number	M01361-0
System Origin	England-EASy
Source Film Number	1701793
Reference Number	v 98 p 187